Christ and Freedom
A Christocentric Analysis
Of
Suicidal Behavior

By
Constantino Vincent Riccardi

Illustrations by
H. Travers Newton, Jr.

WIPF & STOCK · Eugene, Oregon

Wipf and Stock Publishers
199 W 8th Ave, Suite 3
Eugene, OR 97401

Christ & Freedom
A Christocentric Analysis of Suicidal Behavior
By Riccardi, Constantino Vincent
Copyright©1972 by Riccardi, Constantino Vincent
ISBN 13: 978-1-60899-709-1
Publication date 5/24/2010

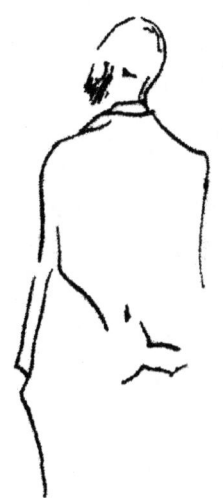

*In memory
Of
Richard Bard*

He was someone who truly loved Dostoyevsky. He was also someone who lived his life in accord with Christ's teaching: "To whom much is given, much is required." (Luke 12:48)

Thirty Years Ago

Thirty years ago I had a friend named John. He was nineteen. One Saturday afternoon we watched *Moby Dick* on television. John became very thoughtful when Captain Ahab addressed his ship's crew and told them their purpose was to hunt and kill a great white whale, Moby Dick. Ahab had lost a leg to this whale and the captain's rage was volcanic. His words were these:

> "The whale took my leg . . . but he did more than that. He took my broken body and burned my soul into it until I became dark spirit . . . But the whale is but the pasteboard mask, the symbol of A DEEPER THING . . . THE THING that has mauled and mutilated our race since time began . . . not killing us outright . . . but making us live on and on with half a heart and half a lung. . . . The whale tasks me. . . . He heaps up hate within me . . . and I'll hunt him around perdition's flames and through the Northern Maelstrom! I'll not give him up!!! I'll not rest until I see the white whale roll out flat dead, and I see his black blood flow!!! Are you whaling men? Will you throw a harpoon down the devil's throat and leap in after? Aye, I think you do look proud! Certainly such proud whaling men will not shy away from the greatest hunt of all. MAY GOD HAUNT US ALL IF WE DO NOT HUNT MOBY DICK TO HIS DEATH!!! DEATH TO MOBY DICK!!!"

After this ode to vengeance is delivered, the crew falls into a type of frenzy, brandishing harpoons and vowing "Death to Moby Dick!"

As the movie progresses, later that evening Starbuck, Ahab's first mate visits the captain in his cabin. Ahab has been obsessed for years in finding the great white whale. He has designed marvelous charts which map the movements of whales in different oceans at different times of the year. Moby Dick has become an inward idol to Captain Ahab, an idol that will give him no peace. Starbuck sees the whale maps and is overjoyed. Starbuck tells the captain with such maps the crew could go home in record time with great profits. Captain Ahab is really only interested in killing the white whale.

Starbuck, a man of duty and stewardship, says to him:

> "Captain Ahab, it is our task to hunt whales so that we can provide for our wives and children. You have made wondrous maps charting the movements of whale herds. The maps are marvelous! Why, with them we could fill our oil barrels and be home in half the time! We would prosper. Captain, think of the ship's owner and the orphans and widows of our former shipmates who have drowned at sea! The orphans and widows share in this ship's profits. Certainly we have a grave obligation to them. If we are stewards of God's gifts and do our duty, then our acts are pleasing to God. But to chase a captain's vengeance, to chase a brute animal because it has harmed you . . . to jeopardize a crew and the money for orphans and widows . . . why, that is blasphemy!"

Captain Ahab (scowling and raging):

> "Money is not the measure of a man! Don't speak to me of blasphemy! I'D STRIKE THE SUN IF IT INSULTED ME!!! (With a clenched

right fist, his thumb extended, he points to his own heart.) It will give me satisfaction here."

Starbuck (understanding that nothing will remove Ahab from his inward idol of the white whale):

> "My captain, I tell thee calmly I am against thee. But you need not fear Starbuck. Let Ahab fear Ahab."

Ahab scoffs at Starbuck's confidential reasoning. Starbuck now understands that he and the crew are under the authority of a madman.

The movie ends with the crew and the whale being destroyed with only one sailor surviving to tell the tale.

At the end of *Moby Dick* John looked at me with a very strange smile and said, "I understand Captain Ahab."

I told John that I understood that Captain Ahab was a very sick man. John simply repeated, with a type of quiet peace, that he understood Captain Ahab.

That was on Saturday. On Monday I was listening to a lecture on God and suffering at a theological seminary I was attending. My goal at that time was to become a professor of the humanities and world religions. I was given a note during the lecture. Two people wanted to see me. Walking out of the class I saw John's mother and sister. They told me that John had killed himself the night before.

He had closed the garage door, turned on the car engine, and died.

For thirty years I have been watching *Moby Dick* with students. Sometimes I talk about John. Sometimes I do not. I have tried to discover the inward, tormented path that lead to his death.

Because I show the movie in a world religions class I have attempted to relate self-destruction to the universal warnings against illusions, idols, and/or obsessions found in all major religions.

To help the students along, I often quote Calvin Klein. Mr. Klein in one of his commercials has a very attractive young woman and a very attractive young man romping at the beach. The commercial ends with the line: "If obsession is a sin, let me be guilty." Hmmm . . . harmless enough. Obsessions can fun.

But obsessions might not always be fun. Prior to John's suicide, he had stabbed himself twice in his left side under his heart. John had been in love with a young woman who had rejected him. When I asked him why he had stabbed himself under the heart his answer was: "Because she lives there. I can't get rid of her."

In trying to understand and explain the development of illusion, the idol, or the obsession beyond Calvin Klein, I have found a profound helper in Stendhal (1783-1842). Stendhal was a staff officer under Napoleon Bonaparte. He was also a novelist and a psychologist. He had numerous affairs, basically remained a playboy until the end of his life, and was fascinated by the happiness of pursuit. He developed a "crystallization" theory of love.

The theory explains the process of idol formation. Take a log and throw it into a salt mine; leave it there for six months. Go back and try to find the log. What will you find? You will find a log with crystals attached to the wood. Further these crystals will have bred other crystals until most of the log appears to be a mass of crystals. It may even be difficult to discover if there had ever been a log.

Stendhal's theory can best be illustrated by the attitude of my lifelong friend, "Guido the Gigolo." Guido, an attractive man of fifty, has engaged in predatory pursuits for the past thirty-five years in the Santa Monica/Malibu area of California. Often he has recounted his conquests to me. A typical scenario is that Guido sees a new woman, The Vision, at a trendy bar restaurant on the ocean. Eyes lock, he looks away, again eyes meet. Both are alone. There is the pounding surf. Hot winds are blowing. They are falling in love.

Phone numbers are exchanged. By the time Guido and The Vision each get to his and her car both are absolutely sure that this <u>is</u> "the right one."

What does each person know of the beloved? They really know nothing. Guido or The Vision could be axe-murderers with a dead body in each car trunk. But who cares? They are falling "in love."

What has occurred? Guido and The Vision are each beginning to write an inward script. Projections or "crystals" are being formed which portray an ideal world of romance and passion. Guido and The Vision each begin to wonder what their children would look like, where they might live, what sort of dog would be appropriate.

Illusion feeds illusion. Crystals form on crystals. Give the crystals a week to breed. What will happen this weekend when Guido and The Vision meet again?

The weekend arrives. Guido and The Vision meet again at the same oceanfront bar/restaurant. After a few drinks it is time to walk on the beach. Strange stirrings envelope the souls of the two crystallizers. Guido remembers the lines from the movie *Elmer Gantry*. *Elmer Gantry* is the story of an evangelist preacher who always told his congregation about the devil and hell, but Elmer never told them about his whiskey and his women. Elmer's pick up/seduction line had been mastered by Guido in both English and Italian. Guido recites Elmer's words to The Vision:

"Is not love all powerful? And what is love?
Love is the Morning and the Evening Star.
Love is the rocking of a cradle. Love is the

soft, sweet moonlight in the eyes of a loved one. . . . And what makes the philosopher write his philosophy and the poet his poem? Why, it's love. And what makes the great composer sit down in awe and rapture and listen to his own creation? Why, it's love. For what is music but the voice of love. I am speaking of the divine love, not the carnal love."

The Vision smiles and then . . . amidst the moonlight, hot winds, and crashing surf asks, "By the way, what is your net worth?"

("What is your net worth?" Is this "love"? If this is love can Guido afford it? Perhaps love is just the imagination working overtime, oftentimes, without pay. Perhaps love is just a four-letter word.)

An immediate sensation of crystal-breaking, illusion deflation is inwardly experienced. The Vision is after Guido's money. Of course Guido has no money. In fact he owes approximately $100,000 on credit cards. But Guido does not want to lose The Vision just yet.

He replies that his net worth is only $100,000 less than that of Mahatma Gandhi when he died. Love is born. The Vision thinks that as mysterious a fellow as Gandhi must have had a great fortune. Gandhi, in her mind, must have been an Arabian oil sheik. Thus love is born.

Guido and The Vision live together for six weeks. After six weeks The Vision learns how to spell "Gandhi." The Vision discovers that Gandhi at his death was worth $2.00. In fury, she kicks Guido out of her Santa Monica condo. Guido is indifferent. He got what he wanted. She began to bore him by asking such demanding questions as "Where are you going?" Besides, Guido has met another Vision who has a house in Malibu.

In analyzing crystallization within the context of

John's suicide and Guido's cavorting it becomes obvious that obsessions can become self-destructive or part of a playboy's pastime. Youth with its hypersensitivity is far different than manipulative sexual exploits. One can lead to self-destruction. The other simply leads to a rather empty, animalistic type of self-gratification.

In the history of world religions there are some remarkable instances of crystallization and profound reflection. The beach city of Santa Monica, California (near Malibu) was named for St. Monica, the mother of St. Augustine. Augustine in his youth was a wild playboy. His prayer to God was: "Almighty God, save me but not right away." Augustine wanted to meet a few more women before he "got saved." His philosophy is profound. Basically he says that all is good because God made it. But our love is disordered. We expect from the finite . . . the infinite. We can love things, self, others, and God. Our problem is that our crystals make of finite things . . . divine things. We want our crystals to justify our lives. But often our crystals lead to emptiness and self-destruction.

The problem of illusion, crystallization, or idol-formation does not stop with a sensitive young man suffering from the intolerable pain of unrequited love. Nor does it stop with the emptiness of the playboy-predator. I have often put on the documentary *Mein Kampf* after showing *Moby Dick*. *Mein Kampf* is a documentary on the rise and fall of Hitler. The documentary estimates that 60 million people died during Hitler's reign of terror from 1933-45. Many students have remarked that Ahab is but a fictional representation of Hitler. Their comments have merit.

It has merit because of T. M. Parker's statement in The New Cambridge Modern History.

"Indeed, as experience of our own century shows, ideologies and political calculation form a psychological amalgam which is difficult, if not vain, for the historian to try to analyze."¹

Perhaps Stendhal's theory of crystallization can help us understand this "psychological amalgam." Just as a lonely person can leap to the inward idol of the beloved, so can a frightened and/or furious nation leap to the inward idol of an ideology, political calculation, and/or a dictator. Certainly Germany after the Treaty of Versailles leaped to Hitler. Hitler, of course, worshipped <u>his view</u> of the German nation.

In Hitler's own words:

> "What is life? Life is the Nation. The individual must die anyway. Beyond the life of the individual is the Nation. But how can anyone be afraid of this moment of death, with which he can free himself from this misery, if his duty doesn't chain him to this Vale of Tears. No!"²

The context of this statement is Hitler's fury that one of his generals had surrendered with 91,000 German soldiers taken captive at the Battle of Stalingrad in the winter of 1943-44. Hitler expected a suicidal stand in which the general and the men would have been killed. Then the general could have gone "into eternity and national immortality."³

Ahab took himself and his crew to destruction. Hitler took himself and 60 million people to destruction.

Does this not tell us something about illusion, crystallization, obsession, and our inward idols? Sure, there are playful obsessions which come and go. But when the

---

¹ Parker, T. M. *The Papacy, Catholic Reform, and Christian Missions* in <u>The New Cambridge Modern History</u>, ed. By R. B. Wernham, vol. 3, chap. 3, p. 63. Cambridge: Cambridge University Press. 1968.

² Shirer, William. <u>The Rise and Fall of the Third Reich</u>. New York: Fawcett World Library, p. 1218.

³ Ibid., p. 1219.

obsession becomes adamantine, hard, cold, and vicious; then destruction and self-destruction can result.

Our analysis can help us understand the words of Mahatma Gandhi: "The only devils we have to fear are those running around in our own hearts. That is where all our battles should be fought."

What are these devils but crystallized and hardened idols?

If John Calvin (1509-1564) (a different sort of Calvin than Calvin Klein) is correct in saying that "The human heart is a perpetual factory of idols," then it would behoove us to be vigilant over our inward crystals, projections, and obsessions. These inward crystals can be a lover, family, money, country, social position, and/or religious tradition.

Western religions maintain that the Lord God is not to have false gods before him. Eastern religions maintain that illusions keep us from Ultimate Reality. Both Western and Eastern religions would agree with the Buddha that reaching spiritual freedom and enlightenment is similar to "an elephant climbing out of the mud."

To find help in climbing out of the mud, thirty years ago I studied classical formations of Christology. Who was Jesus? What were his claims? What is his message? How will his message free us from idol worship and lead us to freedom from self-destruction? That is the discussion which follows.

General References:
Those interested in Stendhal should see his On Love and his novel The Red and the Black. With respect to Augustine and disordered love see Stumpf's Socrates to Sartre, 5th ed., chap. 6, McGraw-Hill, 1993. See also Augustine's Confessions. For Calvin and idolatry see Riccardi, Light in the Labyrinth, (Redlands, CA, 2000).

Movies: *Moby Dick* (1956)
Mein Kampf (1960)
Elmer Gantry (1960)
Gandhi (1982)

CONTENTS

PART ONE
Freedom as a Benefit of Jesus Christ within the Context of Suicidal Behavior
Introduction. 1
Chapter I 8
    The Biblical Witness 8
    1.   The Two Commandments............................8
    2.   The Person of Jesus Christ...........................9
    Intermission 10
    3.   The Work of Jesus Christ............................13
    4.   The Death and Resurrection of Jesus Christ 23
Chapter II 30
Reflections upon Christ's Freedom and the
Problem of Suicide in the Thought of Justin
Martyr, Athanasius, Augustine, The Council
of Chalcedon, and Thomas Aquinas 30
    A.   Justin Martyr 30
    B.   Athanasius..36
    C.   Augustine..42
D.   The Council of Chalcedon..48
E.   Thomas Aquinas and the Roman Catholic Church's Proclamation on Suicide 51
Chapter III 56
Luther's Denunciation of "The accusing christ" and Calvin's Denunciation of "The Vested Wonders"...............................56
    A.   Martin Luther...56
    B.   John Calvin...64
Chapter IV 68
    Suicide in the Thought of Kierkegaard,
    Dostoevsky, Schopenhauer, Nietzsche,
    and Camus 68
    A.   Soren Kierkegaard..68
    B.   Fyodor Dostoevsky..73
    C.   Schopenhauer, Nietzsche, and Camus..........91
        a.   Arthur Schopenhauer 91
        b.   Friedrich Nietzsche..........................94
        c.   Albert Camus 97

Chapter V 103
Three Notes on General Culture
    and Suicidal Behavior 103
    Footnotes 115
    Selected Bibliography 131
    Acknowledgements 151

PART TWO 157
    Introduction 159
    Saul 163
    Judas Iscariot 191
    Paul Sanctus 205
    John Sanctus 223
    Luke Sanctus 245

PART I

Freedom as a Benefit of Jesus Christ within the Context of Suicidal Behavior.

**Against the
darkest night**

CHRIST AND FREEDOM

INTRODUCTION

As can be seen from the title of this essay, the reality of suicide determines the context of discussion. In order to refrain from theorizing about suicide, I have selected six incidents which either describe or pertain to suicidal behavior. These incidents are not termed "clinical case studies," because I have never spoken with "cases." I have moved cases, unwrapped cases, and packed cases. But I have never really spoken with a "case." Consequently I have chosen the word "incident" simply to describe what occurs within the context of suicidal behavior.

I am not a psychiatrist and I am not a clergyman. I once had the opportunity of listening to suicidal patients at a hospital in the San Francisco area. Which hospital it was, how the opportunity presented itself that I should work there, who the psychiatrist was with whom I worked, how the thermostat in the building worked, how long I worked, what the nurses looked like, etc., are all of course interesting questions. But for varied reasons, some of which will become obvious, such information ought actually to be ignored.

When I say that I had the opportunity of listening to suicidal patients I must, of course, include that I also listened to myself. I say this because anyone who thinks that he or she is not in any way suicidal, or could never become suicidal, is simply a vigorous liar. Too often this is overlooked and suicidal patients are placed "out there" as some type of strange phenomena of another world. Such an attitude only increases the isolation of individuals preoccupied with suicidal behavior. It also increases the probability of actual self-destruction.

Thus I am not scientifically, theologically, or philosophically hovering above anyone. Nor am I trying to be "with it" as another "involved" writer who went slumming in order to fill some pages with little black letters. I am going to describe what I am going to describe simply because I feel like describing it.

Incident One

A young man, age 20, stands overlooking the gnarling currents combating each other beneath the Golden Gate Bridge. To his right the varied grays and whites of San Francisco's buildings stand forth in a shadowy tomb-like relief against a darkened sky. To his left the natural beauty of Marin county's hills, lakes, and mountains are hidden by the thick fog which will soon engulf the bridge on which he stands.

As he stands gripping the orange-colored railing, his mind races from hidden emotions to known thoughts. His mind whirls, his stomach tenses, inner dissonance wishes to hurl him below to where his false brothers -- the combative waves -- wage war with one another.

In this spinning, turning, gnarling hell; in this dungeon of the clenched stomach and reeling mind; can he establish any inner clarity concerning himself? Or, does it take another to establish a harmony? That is, does it take another to enact a harrowing of this hell, to bring him into his right mind and to give him lasting and viable truth about himself?

Incident Two

It is 9:30 in the morning. A psychiatrist enters his office. His mail has been placed on his desk. Among his letters of correspondence are contained circulars advertising new drugs for the therapeutic care of suicidal patients. There are also a few circulars informing him of new organizations, both religious and secular, which are involved in the prevention of suicide.

Next to his mail are the appointments, problems, and difficulties which will occupy him throughout the day. His desk and office are scattered with articles and books concerned with suicidal behavior and its treatment.

People and rooms like this can be found in most of the major cities of the world. How do they come to exist in this combination? What philosophy lies behind this many faceted concern for human life?

Incident Three

A man, age 35, says that he has been suffering from suicidal preoccupations for a period of years and has recently attempted to kill himself. In speaking about himself he casually announces that he has raped and murdered a four-year-old girl. He also mentions that he has had sexual relations with animals, but he really prefers children. Women and/or men are also possible subjects for his wild advances but they only rank third after children and animals.

After this description of his appetitive tastes, the patient boasts that he has used every drug known to man. Authoritatively he speaks of their effects when combined with alcohol. With bravado he announces that drugs, alcohol and the molesting of children, when and if they can be combined, are the highest forms of pleasure. (Pleasure is for him the highest good.)

Towards the end of this interview when the boasting and bravado had partially subsided, the patient inquired of the interviewer, "Why am I suicidal?" Before the interviewer can answer, the patient begins to tell him that he was solely conditioned by the world for this type of behavior. That is, he was absolutely controlled by fate to act as he did. When the interviewer asked him whether his statement that he was determined, was also determined, the patient quite pontifically announces that of course not -- he was a free man and he would bite to death anyone who thought otherwise.

His view of freedom was pursued. Freedom's ugly concomitant responsibility (an old-fashioned middle-class word no longer necessary for the "free" man), was also pursued. The patient finally concluded that "maybe" he had "something" to do with being in a suicide ward.

The interviewer in this incident was not a moralist. He did not jump up from his chair and to the tune of "Onward Christian Soldiers" proclaim "There, you stinking sinner, repent." The interviewer only wondered by what criterion one is to judge himself responsible and to what extent this sort of judgment is to be rehabilitating for anyone. In this incident passing down general verdicts based upon the abstract view of humanity that "You are guilty" will only increase an individual's wrath and further isolate him. Obviously the patient feels at least partially responsible but in relation to what or in relation to whom?

Incident Four

A young girl, age 14, quite indifferently announces that she no longer wishes to live. It is the second time she has been admitted to the suicide ward. Her mother died when the young girl was born. Her mother had never been married and had no living relatives. After six years in an orphanage the patient passed through four foster homes. In the first foster home the patient had been mistreated and laughed at by other children of the household. She ran away and was again placed in an orphanage. In the second foster home, the patient (now eight years old) was molested by the lady of the house's lover. The patient ran away and was again placed in an orphanage. In the third foster home the patient (now eleven years old) was expected to be the perpetual babysitter for three younger children. When one of the children got a bloody nose, the patient was beaten and kicked by her foster father. When she was returned to the orphanage, she was told by the authorities that if she did not adapt to the next foster home, she would be placed in juvenile hall. In the fourth foster home the man and woman were trying to get together a singing act. They thought the patient would be a definite asset to their group. The foster mother tried to teach her to play ukulele. Further the patient was forced to wear Hawaiian dresses which the patient despised. Her fourth foster father and mother also introduced the girl to LSD. Under the influence of LSD the patient tried to jump out of the "family" car while it was still moving. She was admitted to the suicide ward. After a two-week period (the girl was at this time twelve years old), she was released. However her foster parents no longer wanted her. Since she failed in the fourth foster home, she was placed in juvenile hall. It was in juvenile hall that she used a razor blade to slit her wrists. She was rescued in time and brought to the suicide ward.

At the age fourteen the girl is simply numb. She does not want to get better, mistrusts everyone, and simply awaits the next opportunity when she will have the possibility of killing herself.

Incident Five

An exhausted looking man, age 45, has been complaining of suicidal thoughts. He has been a heavy drinker experiencing the less heightening effects of alcohol such as the shakings of the body and blackouts. In describing his past life, he said, "I have never had a single happy day in my life." His father had been a coal miner in Pennsylvania. His father was sixty years old at the time of the patient's birth. His mother was fifty years old. The patient said that he had always admired the hardworking honesty of his parents and their devotion toward each other. However his father often came home so exhausted (he continued working until he was seventy) that he barely had the strength to pour himself a glass of whiskey. When his father reached the age of sixty-five his devotion toward his mother did not cease, rather it increased. But his father became susceptible to strange fits of raging. This sudden raging was not understood by the patient as a small boy. His father had previously been exhaustedly quiet. But now his father began to complain of the black depths of the mine, began to wonder if he was only born to dig his own grave, began to shout obscenities against his life which seemed to him always bound to the small openings of a mine shaft lit with artificial light. About this time, the boy's mother would begin sobbing. His father would try to console her. When she could be consoled all three were happy. When she could not be consoled, his father drank whiskey.

The patient could not remember a full day of happiness. This father died at the age of seventy. His mother died a year after her husband's death. The boy, age eleven, traveled an isolated path from relative to relative. When there were no more relatives (four of his parents' relatives with whom he stayed died before the patient was sixteen), he began to wander through cities, pick up odd jobs and drink alone. The patient said he had always been afraid of the violence of men. He also said that he had too high of an estimation of women to ever touch one if he could not marry and support her. He never felt that this would be a possibility for him. Thus he spent the time from the age of sixteen to forty-five alone with his memories and alcohol.

The patient was presently out of work, without money, and suffering from both alcoholism and suicidal preoccupations. He said he wanted to continue living simply because he wanted to think about one memory -- the times when his mother could be consoled. This was only a memory. The length time of happiness even when his mother had been consoled had not lasted for the continuity of single day. But he wanted to live just for that memory and nothing more.

Incident Six

A woman, age 65, enters a group therapy session in the depression-suicide section of the suicide ward. There are five other patients and the psychiatrist. The woman suffers from suicidal preoccupations and inconsolable grief. Her only son used to punch tickets on the trolley cars. He was an alcoholic whose disease had caused him to gain weight. At the time of his death he weighed close to three-hundred pounds.

But his death.

Her only son, age 39, died of alcoholism. He died choking on his own blood from internal hemorrhaging. His mother, the woman in the suicide ward, tried to stop his choking to death by sucking the blood out of his throat. Her son died gasping in her arms.

As she sits in the suicide ward, she only cries. The other five patients snarl, yell, scream and talk; but she only weeps. When the session is over she goes home picking up discarded tickets from the trolley car stops.

Is this the last thing one can say about this woman? Is she really only an unfortunate statistic and a pitiful creature who suffered way beyond a breaking point? She cannot be reached by any therapeutic method. If she continues to live, her life will only be a numb, black night darkened by the punched paper scraps of nightmarish memory. Is this to be the final word on her behalf?

CHAPTER ONE

The Biblical Witness

1. The Two Commandments

Scripture (the Old and New Testaments of the Bible) is a vast and cloudy sea. It contains <u>logical</u> contradictions, verbal ambiguities, mental absurdities and redundant statements. Regardless of this, some clarity is to be found among its ambiguities, contradictions, and absurdities. In fact it appears that the whole of scripture can be summarized in two commandments. The summation is found in the sentences

> You shall love the Lord your God with all your heart, and with all your soul, and with all your mind. This is the great and first commandment. And a second is like it, you shall love your neighbor as yourself. On these two commandments depend all the law and prophets.[1]

Apparently these two commandments really are a summation and completion of the Old and New Testaments. The reason for this is that scripture simply says that "there is no other commandment greater than these."[2]

"Well, so much for that. Everything is solved, scripture is mastered, and it is time to read something else." Actually this is completely true. Scripture states that there are no other general rules of life which are more important than these two commandments.[3] Further, the substance of the Old and New Testaments are contained in these two commandments.[4] Of course there may be a few difficulties which remain somewhat unclear. Questions could occur in the mind of the reader such as "So what?" "Why bother with scripture anyway?" "What right does any book have to legislate general rules about me?" "Who is this God we are supposed to love?" "Why does he deserve anyone's love?" "Love your neighbor as yourself? What if you're trying to kill yourself?" "More rules, more guilt; who needs either one?" "Who's the Big Mouth with all the advice?" "What's the Big Mouth getting out of the deal?"

Apparently then, although the two commandments summarize scripture, they do not fully explain it. How is one to find a fuller, more definite explanation of these two commandments? Perhaps an investigation of the speaker's identity (previously referred to as "the Big Mouth") will offer some answers to our questions.

2.   The Person of Jesus Christ

In attempting to describe the person of Jesus Christ, scripture gives us a definite focus in our search by telling us that Jesus Christ is "God with us."[5] Further scripture describes Jesus Christ as "the Word"[6] through whom "all things were made."[7] Christ also speaks of himself as the only teacher.[8] For our purposes these descriptions may perhaps indicate something concerning the proclaimer of the two commandments. Jesus Christ is truly and completely God. He created all that there ever was, is, or will be. Jesus Christ is also truly and completely a human person. What this means is simply that, since Jesus Christ is fully God and fully a human person, He is the only one who could possibly claim to teach anyone about God and what it means to live as a human person. If He were not God He would be an interesting sage with plenty of worldly wisdom. This wisdom would just be another man's opinion and that is all it would be. However, Jesus Christ is completely and fully God who created everything. If Jesus Christ were simply God, or something in between God and the human race, then He would have no right to speak to the human race. Why should anyone listen to a god who does not know what it means to be human? If a god sat back on his divine posterior and theorized to himself about man, man's problems, the height of the moon, the depth of the sea, etc., why should he be taken seriously? Such a god would not have become man. He would not know what it is to run the gauntlet of human wretchedness, bear the burdens of this world's pain, or die the death of isolation. A god who has not become truly and completely human should simply be mocked, spit upon, and forgotten. However Jesus Christ became a complete and full human being, that is, He who created the universe needed a diaper change just like any other little "critter."

The consequences of Jesus Christ being completely and truly God and completely and truly a human person are that Christ Himself is the only one who really knows who God is and who human beings are. This is the real basis of his statement that He is the only teacher. As was partially seen, Christ did not teach from sublime heights with pedagogical prowess. On the contrary, he became a human being. He ate, drank, belched, went to the bathroom, suffered, laughed, and experienced death. He also enacted a specific series of works. But before I describe the activity surrounding and working in Christ, I should declare a brief intermission in order to answer some unanswered questions. I know that there is no aesthetic or scholarly precedent for such an intermission; but then, this essay is not written just for aesthetes and scholars.

Intermission

Thus far there has been an attempt to describe the person of Jesus Christ in order to have some definite focus concerning the meaning of the two commandments. It seems that perhaps enough has been learned. After all, this whole discussion should terminate itself so everyone can get on with the more important things of life such as making money, babies, and trouble. "But what if you're trying to get rid of living?" "What if there is little chance of your making money or babies?" "What if you're already in too much trouble, especially with respect to yourself?" "What if you would like to put an end to this trouble without destroying yourself?" "What if you're unable to distinguish whether you are in trouble or not?" Now one must be fair. The author of this discussion is not the Teacher he is discussing. Further the author does not wish to annoy anyone who already finds this discussion "too basic," "superfluous," or otherwise. However I shall leave the choice up to the individual whether to continue reading this or not.

Thus far an attempt has been made to understand two commandments which profess to answer a rather old-fashioned and unsophisticated question. The old-fashioned and unsophisticated question is "Why are we born?" Now it is obvious that this question seldom appears on the front page of the newspaper. Further if someone (very hypothetical) did discover why he was born, there is some doubt as to the possibility of this discovery being printed in the morning or evening news. After all, given what the world is, with a growing scarcity of pulp for newspapers, the new discoveries in the halls of higher learning, and the "miraculous" changes brought forth in the era of the hydrogen bomb; there is little chance that the words "Oscar W. Nobody Found Out Why He Was Born at 11:30 P.M. in Joe's Bar and Grill" will appear on the front page. However in the back pages of the morning or evening news (usually close to the obituary section unless, of course, we are speaking of celebrities) there can be found a few lines about someone's suicide.

Actually about 26,000 people in the United States kill themselves each year.[9]

> Suicide is the eleventh most common cause of death among all ages in the United States. Between the ages of 20 and 45 among Caucasians, suicide is the fourth most common cause of death exceeded only by accidents, heart disease and cancer.[10]

"Among the student population, suicide is the second most frequent cause of death."[11] The topic of suicide is not one surrounded by the garlands and plumes of human achievement. Few people wish to discuss the subject. After all, it is not a reality which confirms the thesis that America (or any other country) is a "land of opportunity." Nor does the subject of suicide concur well with dinner conversation, coffee breaks, or making money. Thus those stricken with suicidal behavior are always isolated, caged in the cell of social indifference, and emotionally poked with sticks of "the busy people" who have "arrived." (Where "the busy people" arrived or what they did when they got there is never mentioned by "the busy people.")

Fine; the statistics are in and the public attitude has been announced. For the individual preoccupied with his suicidal behavior the statistics are a matter of indifference and the public attitude is a source of continuing guilt. The suicidal person in America's "land of opportunity" with its "manifest destiny" finds he has no opportunity but he does have a definite destiny. His destiny is to be shut off alone, cornered in himself. Now if a rat is cornered he goes for the assailant's throat. But if a human being is cornered in himself, his energy, his spirit, and his imagination become so mangled and confused that he becomes his own assailant. This is a law of suicidal behavior, applicable at any time, in any place, for anyone. Against this law I have thus far asserted two other laws or commandments which profess to be applicable at any time, in any place, for anyone. The aim and character of these two laws assert that it is God's will (and God is Love) to refute and condemn the law of suicidal behavior <u>without</u> (!) in any way condemning the person who is tortured by the law of suicidal behavior. It is not Christ's two laws in themselves which denounce the law of suicidal behavior. It is the <u>Activity</u> surrounding and in conjunction with Christ's two laws or commandments which denounce and overcome the law of suicidal behavior.

Consequently, two commandments have been discussed, and the person or annunciator of the two commandments has been described. The source of this information has come from an old book which has been a best seller for years. Unfortunately (or fortunately) in every age this book has not always had the sensational coverage which it deserved. By this I only mean that the book, The Bible, has not qualified to be front page material any more than have the reports of suicidal deaths. Perhaps they have something else in common. To discover who or what this is, it would be worthwhile to return to the subject of scripture, who is Jesus Christ.

3. The Work of Jesus Christ

Jesus Christ has been described as being completely and fully God and completely and fully a human being. This was established through the assertion of His creative activity in forming the universe and in becoming a particular individual. Now this occurrence did not remain divided but brought forth a particular activity which can only be described by the word "love." If the unity of God and humanity is called love, this love must be of a particular type. This would also imply that the love operative in the unity of Jesus Christ's divine and human natures would have a particular aim or goal. But before this goal can be fully established it will be necessary to discuss the work of Jesus Christ.

One of the first things said about Jesus Christ's work is announced by John the Baptist. John the Baptist states that Jesus Christ will baptize with the Holy Spirit and with fire.[12] (John the Baptist himself baptizes others with water, but makes it plainly understood that Christ's act of baptizing will be far greater than his own.)[13] In this context the Greek word "baptizo" means to consecrate[14] someone to God by removing[15] from him or her that which stands against God. "What?" "What's going on?" "Who's this Holy Spirit?" "Who needs any more fire?" "What's wrong with water?"

According to the Bible the Holy Spirit is that reality which seeks, proclaims, and makes definite the deepest things of the Divine Activity.[16] The Holy Spirit seeks, proclaims, and makes definite the deepest things of the Divine Activity because it seeks every individual human person in order to proclaim that God (who is Jesus Christ) is actively and constantly with us. That is, the Holy Spirit energetically denounces all gods above us, all gods beyond us, all gods to the side of us, all gods below us, all gods that we have made, all gods that we make, and all gods that we will make. The possible combinations contained within any human being's capacity to make gods is astounding but not infinite. What is infinite is the lasting power of the Holy Spirit to distinguish and overcome such gods. The way in which the Holy Spirit has accomplished this prior to John the Baptist's proclamation has already been summarized in Christ's two commandments. That is the Holy Spirit (in conjunction with the Word's free decision) proclaimed to the prophets of the Old Testament the Divine Will manifested in the two commandments.

The Holy Spirit is also active in Christ's becoming a human person.[17] That is, the Holy Spirit works in conjunction with Christ's (also referred to as "the Word") free decision to become a human person and is thus always tightly bound to the Divine Human Love operative in Jesus Christ.

But this Divine—Human Love (who is Jesus Christ) created the entire universe and everyone therein. The Holy Spirit is tightly bound to this activity. Therefore the Holy Spirit participates in the creation of all things. Since the Holy Spirit participates in the creation of all things, the Holy Spirit cannot be a thing or a creature of any type. Since the Spirit is not a creature it must be creator simply because it remains so tightly bound with the creative activity of Christ. Therefore the Holy Spirit is also God. Thus the Holy Spirit is an active Divine Power in the Divine Activity not only because it seeks, proclaims, and makes definite to each individual the deepest things of God all of which are determined by the Divine-Human Love of Jesus Christ; but also because the same Spirit seeks and makes manifest the deepest things of Christ in the actual creation of the universe.

Now that the Holy Spirit has been described, perhaps some sense will be made of John the Baptist's statement that Jesus Christ will baptize with fire and the Holy Spirit.[18] What Jesus Christ is offering to everyone is a life with Him. Now life with Him (or a life of "God with us") means the purging of all false gods, world-constructs of false gods, and all mammoth projections of false gods. They are "burned out" not by the will of nature or man[19] but by God's own Will. God's Will for this particular work is accomplished through and with the Holy Spirit. Thus the Holy Spirit baptizes or consecrates us to a new life with Christ. This is the baptism of the Holy Spirit. The purgation accomplished by the Holy Spirit is a real "burning out" of all that is not "God with us." This is the baptism of fire. This is <u>not</u> (!!!) a human work which anyone can arbitrarily inflict upon himself, but is gently and wisely accomplished through the Will of God (Who is Love) and God's Will is that every individual shall live with Him in Love.

Now a new set of words has been brought forth. This set of words is "God's Will." Whatever one can say about God's Will is that it must first begin with Jesus Christ, completely God and completely man, who conjoins Himself with the activity of the Holy Spirit. The Holy Spirit seeks, proclaims, and makes definite this Jesus Christ (who is God with us). However in speaking of Jesus Christ's work a problem occurs because Jesus Christ quite specifically states that it is His Will to do the Father's Will.[20] Thus Christ's Will and The Father's Will are One Will.[21] Now this Father is Jesus Christ's Father and apart from Jesus Christ there is (of course) nothing known about Jesus Christ's Father. Some people might speculate that apart from Jesus Christ there is indeed a god or divine activity of some sort. But it has already been shown from scripture that there is no other god apart from Jesus Christ. The Holy Spirit forbids any other divine activity which does not proclaim Jesus Christ as the God of Love who is with us. The Holy Spirit is God and any other spirit which proclaims someone or something other than Jesus Christ as a god is not the Holy Spirit. Since this is so, all that can ever be known about the Will of Jesus Christ's Father must proceed from the words and works of Jesus Christ.

But perhaps this is confusing. "Does not nature manifest the essential goodness of the created universe?" This is not true. Any single individual who has been born <u>and</u> has been forced to face either an external or internal typhoon will agree with me. "Are not most fathers good?" "Most" is a difficult word to talk about. If one father is not "good" his child is incapable of knowing about what "most" fathers are or are not. The patients in the suicide ward are in many incidents such children. Thus such a question is too general and vapid even to be answered within this discussion.

Quite definitely Jesus Christ's Father is simply Jesus Christ's Father. This Father, through His Son's activity joined with the Holy Spirit's proclamation, wills to become everyone's Father.[22] But Christ, who is our only Teacher,[23] makes it extremely clear that we have only one Father.[24] This Father is not the "general father," the "confused father, " or "the good and bad father." Neither is Christ's Father the "father of modern psychology." Quite definitely Jesus Christ's Father is simply Jesus Christ's Father and can only be known, contemplated, apprehended and believed in and through Jesus Christ's activity in conjunction with the Holy Spirit.

In coming to know the Father of Jesus Christ it is best to examine John's symbolic baptism of Jesus. This baptism merely indicated that the full Spiritual baptism of Jesus Christ was now to be everyone's concern.[25] This is the first time in the known history of this world that the fullness of the activity of the Triune God (Jesus Christ, the Holy Spirit, and Christ's Father) distinctly manifests Itself. The Father publicly reveals Jesus Christ to be His Son. The Holy Spirit manifests Itself as that guiding Spirit which is ever present in the activity of God.[26] Now a sophisticated man could automatically draw back and say that this is a mystical occurrence and an empirically non-verifiable statement. Such a sophisticate or sophist possesses the full mental acuity of the solid empirical observer. I agree totally with his observation, thank him for his comment, and ask him to further realize that every statement which I have made is of such a nature. But due to the <u>fact</u> that much of what is known about suicidal behavior is not strictly empirically verifiable by human criteria, due to the <u>fact</u> that twisted views of whom or what god is plague everyone sometimes to the point of self-destruction, and due to the fact that empirical verification does not determine the Love of God (indeed, empirical verification need love no one); I will continue my rather "unsophisticated" analysis (hoping to answer "unsophisticatedly") the "unsophisticated" question "Why are we born?"

After the disclosure of the Triune God,

> Jesus was led up by the Spirit into the wilderness to be tempted by the devil. And he fasted forty days and forty nights, and afterward he was hungry.[27]

It is to be understood that Jesus Christ was led into isolation solely by the activity of the Holy Spirit for a particular purpose. He was led to be actually tempted "by the devil." In the New Testament the devil is characterized as that power which desires to mutilate,[28] confuse,[29] or harm[30] the universe created through Jesus Christ's activity. The devil is not any individually created human person as an individually created human person. In this instance the Holy Spirit leads Jesus to the wilderness for the specific purpose of temptation. Divinely seen the Holy Spirit is acting as a fight promoter. The universe and everyone within it belongs to Christ since it is His creation. That power, the power of destruction, known as the devil, wishes to disturb Christ's creation. In preparation for the battle Christ has fasted for forty days and nights specifically to make it known to us that even the weakest of human beings can do battle with destruction if he is empowered with the Holy Spirit. Thus although the Holy Spirit promotes this fight, this same Spirit is completely active throughout the battle. That is, the Spirit does not buy a ringside seat, eat popcorn, and drink beer.

The devil approaches. He asks Christ to do three things; 1) to change the stones into bread, 2) to cast Himself from a tower, 3) and offers Him the Kingdoms of the world if He will worship the devil.[31] Well, Christ is not one bit happy with these demonic requests. The devil is asking Christ to commit Spiritual and physical suicide. The Spirit has led Christ into the wilderness. In conjunction with the Spirit Christ has decided to act in order to fulfill the Will of the Father. No power is allowed to disturb this free relationship of God's self-communication within Himself. When Christ responds to the devil's first request that "Man shall not live by bread alone, but by every word that proceeds from the mouth of God,"[32] He means that man really lives by and through that free Activity of God which has created him and wills to fulfill him. The devil is simply attempting to pervert the close connection between God and His creation. There is nothing intrinsically wrong with eating bread. Bread is also a part of God's creation and thus very good.[33] But man cannot really live simply by created good. Man is far too complex for that and needs sure and definite reasons concerning his birth and destiny. Such knowledge and life is contained in the person of Jesus Christ or the Word "which proceeds from the mouth of God" who at this time is speaking His own words. To deny this basis for human life would be to deny that very Spirit which testifies to man that man is truly alive when God is with him. This Christ will not do.

The devil's second request that Christ throw Himself down from a tower might sound absurd since Christ is actually in the desert. One could call it an hallucination by which the devil tempts Christ to forget His identity, His created body, and the Spirit's actual intentions for the human body. Every individual person's body is not simply so much waste material valued chemically at ninety-seven cents. Nor is it simply a "thing" housing certain psychological phenomena. Each and every human body is created within the plan of the Divine Activity of Jesus Christ, the Holy Spirit, and the Father. Any hallucination, whim, or mad impulse which threatens the peace, stability, and survival of the human body is acting against the Divine Activity. This is by no means an abstract moral judgment. It simply wishes to describe the close relationship of Love operating between the Divine Activity and the human body. When Christ says to the devil "You shall not tempt the Lord your God,"[34] He makes it clear that God refuses in any way to be turned aside from His purpose to maintain and strengthen the intimate bond which exists between Him and His Creation.

In the last temptation scene the devil offers Christ all the kingdoms of the earth if He will fall down and worship him. Christ with disgust simply says to the devil "Begone Satan . . . you shall worship the Lord your God and Him only shall you serve."[35] At this point the real difference between the devil (or the power of destruction) and the human person is established. The devil is dismissed by Christ. Each human person is approached by Christ because of the very fact of Christ's becoming a human being. The devil is commanded to worship and serve God. Each human person is, through the power of Jesus Christ, invited to love God.

"What, then, is the devil's function?" As was seen at the beginning of the temptation scene, the Holy Spirit acting as a divine fight promoter led Jesus into the desert for the expressed purpose of His being tempted by the devil. This is for Jesus also part of the Father's work which He must accomplish. Thus the Divine Activity is completely active. The Divine Activity, operating in this instance through Christ's temptations, manifests 1) the correct order of creation, 2) the actuality and limitation of evil, 3) the place of evil in the universe. The correct order of creation has already been shown. Briefly it means that everyone's real physical and spiritual identity rests with the activity of Love as it manifests itself in Jesus Christ's creative purposes for the world. Through Christ everything was created. Evil was therefore not a necessity in creation. However evil does occur. Its exact origin is always in debate. "How did a good God make anything evil?" is always a question which no one has ever answered properly. Regardless, to deny that there is evil is simply a lie. This is verified by Christ's own combat with the devil. What Christ's combat simply shows is that evil is not absolute. It is well under His control. As creator of the universe, He and He alone really knows of its origin and what specific role it plays in every occurrence. <u>But whatever is to be learned about evil must be learned from Christ.</u>

He alone is able to circumscribe and define its exact power. In the three temptation requests the devil tempts Jesus to both physical and spiritual suicide. People are tempted to kill themselves at every moment of every day. It is not the temptation that is in anyway unusual. What is unusual is the putting of temptation in its place once and for all by telling it to be gone. This was not the last time Christ was tempted in His life. However it was the last time in the Bible that evil attempts to argue for its own infinite power. That is, evil always wishes to appear to be a power that should be obeyed and worshiped. It wishes to take the place of God. It even requests that the Son of God worship it. Unfortunately for evil, as soon as it wishes to attempt this final assault on Christ, it is quite bluntly dismissed. Evil loses all absolute pretentions completely because its own limitations are once and for all circumscribed. Further evil, against evil's will, has established Christ's sovereignty over it by the very act of temptation. If the Spirit had not led Jesus Christ to the desert for the expressed purpose of being tempted, the definiteness and relativity of evil would never have been known. Evil against evil's will has been beaten by the eternal slyness of the Holy Spirit.

"So the Holy Spirit won? So big deal." According to the major thesis of scripture, the Holy Spirit, Jesus Christ, and Christ's Father really have nothing to win in the sense that there is an entity or power standing outside of the Divine Activity's control. In this sense nothing was really won. However, in another sense, everything was won. The conquerors who really share the plunder are all those who wish to believe in that Power which overcomes evil. The Holy Spirit has not ordered the first beer, Christ has not taken a shower, the Father does not sleep. What occurred in the desert occurs in everyone of us. Jesus Christ is really and truly a human being. Further, the Divine Activity has willed to strengthen and affirm every individual by showing us an example and granting us the power of overcoming evil.

To further describe the Divine Activity in relation to the human person and evil it is only right that Jesus Christ should be seen in His work among people. Although Jesus spends a brief period of his life in the desert, He does not remain in the desert. Soon after His denunciation of the devil, or the power of destruction, Christ is found among men, women, and children. To summarize this activity among men, women and children it is best to analyze the use of the word "temple" as it is found in the Bible. First of all it applies to Christ's human body[36] and anyone else's human body. There is absolutely nothing different from Christ's human body and anyone else's human body who has ever lived, is, or ever will live. That is, Christ's body was subject to heat, cold, eating, drinking, digestion, excretion, muscular and neurological pain, and all other bodily functions, growths, pains, and pleasures. This body is referred to as a temple. The human body of every individual is also biblically referred to as a temple.[37] It is exactly the same (which means that it is in no way different) from the body of Jesus Christ. Thus the first meaning of the word temple is this -- it is the human body.

The second meaning of the word "temple" refers to a rather famous public and religious building located at Jerusalem, Israel, at the time (First Century, A.D.) when Jesus Christ began to work and preach.

Now both the temple of the human body and the external temple in Jerusalem were created, preserved, and given their significance through the activity of the Triune God. Through the activity of the Triune God various prophesies and laws (all of which are summarized in Christ's two commandments) were revealed to certain individuals of the Hebrew race known as prophets. (The Hebrew race was merely an ethnic designation of language, custom, and geographical location no better and no worse than any other people with language, custom and geographical location.) These same Hebraic individuals who prophesized and devoted themselves to the activity of the Triune God had been executed or denounced by the "busy" religious people of their times. That is, the religious people involved with the deaths of the prophets were simply those who had placed human traditions, human laws, and human authority before the Triune God's two commandments and the Divine Activity.[38]

The external temple at Jerusalem had also been the scene for the execution of those prophets who had attempted to proclaim the truth of the Divine Activity.[39] Christ is not one bit pleased about their having been executed, According to Christ the external temple at Jerusalem was His Father's house.[40] Thus it was supposed to be a place which manifested God's love to every human individual. Instead the external temple had been the scene of death for those who really wished to manifest God's love. Further the clergymen of the time (known as Scribes, Pharisees, and Sadducees) had burdened the bodies, souls, and minds of the common people with a vast number of guilt-forming, insipid and harmful regulations which had nothing to do with the Will of God. In Christ's words these clergymen

> bind heavy burdens, hard to bear, and lay them on men's shoulders; but they will not move them with their fingers.[41]

Jesus refers to such people as descendents of the devil.[42] It is true that they are human beings and are created by the Divine Activity. However they have attempted to tear Christ's creation away from Him by absolutizing their human laws and traditions. In this sense they are no different than the devil who tried to get Christ to destroy Himself in the desert.

These same clergymen had also turned the external temple into a bandit palace which did homage to the god-dollar instead of the Living God. Psychologically and materially the simple people of the time were being bludgeoned to death by a group of "religious" thugs. The simple people were being psychologically destroyed because the Truth concerning the Living God's Love had been totally mutilated by the false, guilt-forming traditions of men. These people were not only shut off from Love, they were also forced to support a bandit culture which was really indifferent concerning their welfare. Thus both the external temple in Jerusalem and the individual temple of each human person's body were approaching destruction.

"Well, why doesn't God do something?" As has been previously seen it is Christ's Will to do the Will of the Father. The external temple is the Father's house and the temple of the human body is also the Father's house (since it is part of creation). What and/or who is evil is anything or anyone who wishes to destructively disturb or destroy that relationship between God the Father and his own temple or house. Jesus Christ, or the Word who speaks and acts on the Father's behalf, wills to do the Father's Will. He wills to consecrate (baptizo) the human body completely and fully as God's temple. This same Will is active for any external temple and for all creation. So what does Christ do? Reaching for the whip of the Holy Spirit (that Spirit which testifies that "God is with us") He enters all temples -- the human body, the external temple, and all of creation. To evil and evil's evil he says, "You have made my Father's house a den of thieves."[43] Against evil and evil's evil He rages in Love and Power to claim what is His, His Father's, and the Spirit's. The whip cracks across evil's face and drives out. "Drives out?" The Spirited whip drives out death and death's power -- despair, the broken will, the anxious mind, the diseased imagination, the twisted one's scream. "Drives out?" The Spirited whip drives out physical pain -- the leper's sores, the racked body, the flowing hemorrhage, the widow's lament. "Drives out?" The Spirited whip drives out the butcher-bandits -- human authority, human traditions, human religions, and all human laws which attempt to obstruct Christ's, the Spirit's and the Father's Will. "How shall such a thing be comprehended?" Simply by seeking the Activity surrounding the scriptural statement "perfect Love drives out fear."[44]

4.   The Death and Resurrection of Jesus Christ

In reclaiming the Father's house, Jesus Christ acted in a physical manner using the whip of the Holy Spirit. This means that Christ's particular human body is of vast significance in accomplishing the Will of the Triune God. In the Bible the most decisive utterance which Christ makes about His particular body or temple is that He will "Destroy this temple and in three days I will raise it up."[45] "Is Jesus

Christ going to kill Himself?" "How can He who wills the health of every individual's body destroy His own?" It should be remembered that Jesus Christ and only Jesus Christ is completely and fully God and is also completely and fully a human being. In conjunction with the Holy Spirit it is His Will to do the Father's Will. Being fully God, Christ foresees and predicts His own death.[46] He also foresees and predicts that this death will occur on a cross[47] at a definite time.[48] With respect to His own life he says "No one takes it from me, but I lay it down of my own accord. I have power to lay it down, and I have power to take it again; this charge I have received from my Father. "[49] That is, Jesus Christ does not act on impulse, wild whims, twisted passions and grotesque thoughts. Rather He acts to correct suicidal impulses, wild whims, twisted passions, and grotesque thoughts. He does this by making it quite clear to every individual that it is not anyone's particular faults which force Him to die. He does what He does because He has freely decided to do it.[50] He has received a charge from His Father and he has freely consented to fulfill that charge. No one really has to howl, beat their breasts, and bellow to the skies about Christ's blood, the heaviness of the cross, the length of the nails, and all the other pagan vitalistic cult activities which usually surround Christ's death. He does what He does simply because He has freely decided to do it.[51]

"Nonsense, He wants to kill Himself because of the 'general father' within Him." If Christ wanted to kill Himself or be killed, because of suicidal preoccupations based on a general Oedipal complex (or any other complex or syndrome), He had two opportunities[52] to be killed by a mob of thugs in Jerusalem. Instead He chooses to remove Himself from the mob. Now if He were really suicidal in the modern sense why would He let such "choice opportunities" pass Him by?

"Well, maybe He was ambivalent and finally decided at a later time to call it quits." If His divine-human person alone is not convincing, if Christ's work of overcoming destructive behavior is not convincing, if His assertion that what He is going to do is a completely free and unique act, is not convincing, if His twice denying Himself the opportunity of killing Himself is not convincing; then perhaps one of the final scenes in Christ's life will be convincing. Directly proceeding Jesus Christ's trial and execution, Jesus is at the Mount of Olives. He is praying to His Father (who is not the general father). His words are "Father, if thou art willing, remove this cup from me; nevertheless not my will but Thine, be done."[53] These are not the words of a person who is ambivalently faced with the alternatives of natural life or death. On the contrary Christ's human nature does not <u>in any way</u> desire death. But Jesus Christ <u>and only Jesus Christ</u> is fully and completely God and is fully and completely a human person. The human fear of death is not to jeopardize His work which is to do the Will of the Father. His Will is to do the Father's Will, and such a Will is not one broken by suicidal behavior.

Now one can argue, twist scripture, rant, rave, weep and bellow that Jesus Christ was another high-minded fellow who gave up his life for "deeply human" impulses, ideas, ideals, etc. Like the name of the local hero or "Christ figure" at any given time or place, Jesus Christ's name is used to speak about what is "highest" in "MAN." Such statements as "Jesus was one of the few who 'truly loved'" or "Jesus was a two-fisted fighter who died in pursuit of the 'brightest star'!! (?)!" permeate general culture, church lore and spring lawn parties. All such statements are vastly edifying. They are vastly edifying <u>for a few seconds</u> until the topic turns to sports, the length of women's skirts, the width of men's neckties, and all else that aids in building the rising tower of social chatter. Unfortunately it is never made clear that He who participated in the creation of the universe died in complete and absolute freedom on a man-made cross. Unfortunately it is never made clear that Christ was not suffering from idealistic delusions. Unfortunately for the phantasms of general culture, church lore, and lawn parties -- Christ says that He will destroy His body <u>and</u> raise it in three days. Further His life led in conjunction with the Holy Spirit for the purpose of doing the Father's Will does not permit the possibility of His being in any way a person controlled by suicidal impulses, idealistic, demonic or otherwise.

"All right Christ died like no one else ever died before. What's all this noise about His Father's purpose and Will?" When Jesus Christ says that He will freely destroy His body and raise it in three days, He proclaims that He and He alone will fully and completely conquer death once and for all. "Impossible, absolutely impossible, how can that be?" It is to be remembered that Jesus Christ is the Creator of the human body. What He creates, He wills to sustain and preserve. It is also to be remembered that apart from the activity of Jesus Christ absolutely nothing else is known about the meaning of the word "God." Jesus Christ manifests the sustaining and preserving power of Creator in conquering death. Prior to this occurrence accomplished in this way the world knew nothing of its Creator nor of the Creator's actual purpose for this world. Scripture in testifying about Jesus Christ that Jesus Christ's <u>body</u> (not just a soul but Christ's individual body which had been dead for three days) is resurrected by the Power of the Triune God, testifies to the complete death-conquering Power which is Christ's Father's Will.

This fulness of Power contained within the occurrence of Christ's resurrected body manifests the decisive decision on God's part for this world. What has been created in the form of the human body is to be preserved and sustained in the form of a spiritual, indestructible body[54] formed and moulded by the activity of the Triune God. Such a spiritual body is to be the final end of everyone.[55] It is the real promise and basis for the reality of "eternal life"[56] in this life. That is, the promises of God as manifested throughout the life and teachings of Jesus Christ do not bow to death. On the contrary, death is to be overcome entirely. The hope of death's destruction through Jesus Christ is the basis for all activity in this life. Such an activity based in hope is known as eternal life. Eternal life construed in this way for this life manifests itself as a life of peace and free spontaneous giving. There is peace because the anxieties concerning death and loss are overcome. There is spontaneous giving because the activity of the Triune God remains immediately present and wills to aid each individual in the overcoming of all and any authority which does not manifest Divine Love.

Thus eternal life in this life does not end but, through its Author and Controller (who is Jesus Christ) continues, grows, and indicates the final state of life for everyone. This final state of life is not a cloud race among harp players trying to pass away the boring afternoon with some "heavenly" amusements. Nor is the final state of life a big gang of "good" people sneering at and condemning "bad" people. Jesus Christ in the fulness of His Activity (which is God's Activity) is the only real meaning of the word "good."[57] The final state of everyone is this -- it is the complete fulfillment of every individual's life. "Well what does that mean?" It means that a child born dead is just as complete a creature of God as any and all famous figures of world history.[58] It means that a child who dies a tenth of a second after birth is just as brilliant to Christ as the brightest scientist or writer.[59] It means in the final state of life with Christ the most vicious tyrant (i.e., a tyrant against others or against himself) will be equal with the most tormented victim (i.e., one who is either a victim of others or of himself).[60]

"Well that's just fine for the first two instances. I've got nothing against children: I'm indifferent to famous people; and I hate to read. But the last bit about tyrant and victim just isn't fair." It is to be remembered that this chapter did not begin with any general code of justice and retribution. Rather it began with two commandments or laws. It was seen that these laws were so general and ambiguous as to confuse and even be harmful to some individuals. In the hope of overcoming the ambiguities and possible harmful nature of these two laws, it was necessary to describe the person, work, death, and resurrection of Jesus Christ. From this description the close bond of the Triune God with His creation became apparent. It was also seen that anything of a destructive nature (i.e., despair, anxiety, death, etc.) which threatened Christ's creation was driven away from His creation through His Activity. Christ Himself also says that out of the heart of man comes "evil thoughts, murder, adultery, fornication, theft, false witness, slander."[61] However for Christ no one's identity is defined such that he or she is <u>ultimately</u> to be a murderer, adulterer, thief, liar, etc., towards others or towards oneself. Just as no one is finally despair's, anxiety's or death's, so no one is murder's, theft's, or adultery's. First, last, and always the Bible says this: "You are Christ's,"[62] That is, Jesus Christ is the basis for everyone's identity forever. This is also the meaning of the word "Gospel" or good news. Everyone belongs to the God of Love who is only completely manifested in Jesus Christ. This means that a tyrant is ultimately not tyranny's. This also means that a victim is ultimately not death's.

With respect to the title of this essay it also means that anyone who is to himself or herself <u>both</u> tyrant and victim is ultimately not suicidal behavior's. Of course at the time when one attacks oneself, verbally or physically mutilates oneself, it is believed that one is totally controlled by suicidal behavior. However, the final word whether one lives or dies is not the destructive word. The final Word is Christ and His activity of Indestructible Love despite any and all adversities which a person confronts.

That everyone is Christ's means that everyone shall be loved actively and eternally. I did not imagine this thought. How could I? Practically everything in the world says "NO" to such a thought. However, I am not the Teacher and neither is the wretchedness of this world. The Teacher is Jesus Christ. He says "YES" to this life and everyone in it. He simply won't accept destruction's or death's "NO." Being the most stubborn Teacher He has proven His thesis through His death and resurrection. What am I to say? How can one fail in such a classroom? The fight is fixed for us. Christ has died for all to show death's limitations over all. There is no need for anyone's sacrifice. Christ does not desire sacrifice but mercy.[63] This means that He who is God desires everyone to be merciful with themselves as well as others. It also means that Christ's, the Holy Spirit's, and the Father's Will is ever active to give the Power and Love to make this mercy towards oneself a reality. This must be so for Christ definitely desires everyone to keep the two commandments of love. He desires that everyone love God but He certainly also desires that everyone love themselves in order to love others. It must, therefore, be in properly understanding the first commandment of loving God that we will be aided in the correct type of self-love and love of neighbor. It was already seen that God is God with us acting through and with the Holy Spirit to accomplish the Father's Will. This entire Activity is an Activity of indestructible Freedom, a Freedom which is only obtainable in its ripe fullness through Jesus Christ's active giving of Himself to everyone. Christ's giving of Himself to everyone is the real, persevering, and immediate Freedom which is a completely gratuitous benefit for everyone. In the following pages this benefit of freedom will be further described and analyzed.

N. B. It is of course to be remembered that there is but one Teacher who is also our benefit of freedom. He is also our only God. No one else is our Teacher and no one else is our God. This simply means that the following individuals who have written about our Teacher are human beings. They are not giants, wizards, or fathers of anything. (We have but one Teacher -- Christ. We have but one Father -- Christ's Father. We have but one true Spirit -- the Holy Spirit.) What is to be said about the following individuals is simply a curious inquiry with respect to their sentiments about Christ's Freedom. Since an attempt is being made to carry out this discussion with as much freedom as possible, no one is bound either in conscience or by any human authority to take the following individuals seriously. For that matter nothing in this essay binds anyone's conscience. It is simply a descriptive attempt to discover Christ's Freedom in relation to suicidal behavior.

CHAPTER II

Reflections upon Christ's Freedom and the Problem of Suicide in the Thought of Justin Martyr, Athanasius, Augustine, The Council of Chalcedon, and Thomas Aquinas

In this chapter a brief description of varied aspects concerning Christ's Freedom in relation to suicidal behavior will be portrayed. That is, the discussion of personal truth and identity will be historically set forth through the lives and thoughts of a few individuals who sought to apprehend and analyze Christ's Freedom. Their thoughts and apprehensions bind no one. What they have to say is what they have to say, and nothing more.

A. Justin Martyr (c. 114-c. 165 A.D.)[1]

Justin Martyr's life is the finest defense for the freedom of investigation which is contained in the search for Christ's Freedom. Justin attempted throughout his life to seek and find wisdom. This is confirmed by his <u>Dialogue with Trypo, a Jew</u> (c. 137),[2] his <u>First Apology,</u> (c. 150),[3] and his <u>Second Apology</u> (c. 155).[4] During his search he investigated the Stoic,[5] Peripatetic,[6] Pythagorean,[7] and Middle Platonist[8] schools of thought. Following upon his studies in Middle Platonism he became converted to Christ's Freedom. Justin realized that individuals who had lived before the manifestation of the Divine Will in Jesus Christ such as Socrates, Heraclitus, and the Hebrew prophets, had discovered elements or fragments of the Divine Will. That is, a Power had always been active in the universe other than natural processes,[9] human reason,[10] and destruction.[11] Justin, writing in Greek, calls this Power the <u>logos spermatikos</u>.[12] A modern translation of these Greek words with reference to our present discussion would be "the seeds of Full Creative Power." For Justin Martyr this Full Creative Power, active before and at the beginning of the universe, took definite shape and form in Jesus Christ.[13] This Creative Power draws men, women, and children away from confused thinking, twisted emotions, and mythological phantasms. This same Power overcomes death and the fear of death.[14] Justin can actually say to the persecutors of the Christians "you can kill, but not hurt us."[15] He says this in defending and strengthening other Christians. Because of the Source and Fulness of the <u>logos spermatikos</u> Justin believes in and has knowledge of a life indestructible in relation to the murderous designs of men. "Well, why don't Justin and the other Christians simply kill themselves, join the indestructible life, and be done with it?" In answering why Christians do not commit suicide Justin says:

> "We have been taught that God did not make the world aimlessly, but for the sake of the human race; and we have before stated that He takes pleasure in those who imitate His properties and is displeased with those that embrace what is worthless either in word or deed. If, then, we all kill ourselves, we shall become the cause, as far as in us lies, why no one should be born, or instructed in the divine doctrine, or even why the human race should not exist; and we shall, if we so act be ourselves acting in opposition to the will of God."[16]

It should be noted that during Justin's lifetime the Bible as we know it today was non-existent.[17] What he knew of Jesus Christ must be attributed to his own search and the scattered writings which were extant at that time.[18] Thus there is no possibility of deifying a particular book or rigid human tradition based on such a book. On the contrary, what Justin Martyr discovered to be Indestructible Life was far from being the fanatical exuberance often found in fundamentalist Bible worship. He has been trained in rigorous philosophical disciplines. He has found such disciplines to be wanting. But he has not condemned the philosophies as so many abstract father figures. On the contrary, he has found one underlying thesis "the seeds of Full Creative Power" to be active in the teachers of such disciplines. But the fullness of such power is contained in the person, activity, death and resurrection of Jesus Christ.[19] When Justin says he has been taught that the world possesses a particular order "for the human race" he is not repeating an abstract, philosophical world-view. He vehemently denounces repetitions.[20] Nor is he making a fat salary spouting would-be truths.[21] Justin is simply bearing witness to his belief in Jesus Christ. The modern word "martyr" is derived from the Greek words "martus" and "marturion" which mean "a witness"[22] and "that which serves as testimony or proof."[23] Thus the Greek verb "martureo" means to "bear witness" by proclaiming one's belief in his or her beliefs.[24] One does not technically have to die a violent death in order to "bear witness" to one's beliefs. However a person who does die for his beliefs also bears witness to those beliefs which he holds to be true. In Justin's opinion the death of those who bear witness to Christ's Freedom do not in any way add to Christ's Freedom. Christ has died once and for all.[25] His Freedom is active in its own right and depends on no one. Those who do die bearing witness to His Truth and Freedom are examples used for strengthening the faith of others.[26]

Justin Martyr actually became such an example himself. He was beheaded during the reign of Marcus Aurelius.[27] The actual date of his execution is placed between the years 163 and 167 A.D.[28] There are a number of reasons for his execution. Justin had proven the ignorance of a certain Cynic philosopher named Crescens in the <u>Second Apology</u> (c.155).[29] For Justin, it is impossible for a Cynic philosopher "who makes indifference his end, to know any good but indifference."[30] Crescens was indifferent about many things but he was not indifferent about being proven ignorant. This same Cynic philosopher had strong connections with Marcus Aurelius and persuaded him to condemn Justin Martyr.[31]

This combined with the facts that Justin refused to stop defending Christians,[32] that he did not in any way deny God's plan for the created world,[33] that he refused to deny Christ's Freedom,[34] and that he would not sacrifice to Roman gods,[35] contributed to his actual execution.

Now historical testimonies and the writings of certain individuals are only what they are. Justin says that he as a Christian would not commit suicide because he would then be "acting in opposition to the Will of God."[36] Justin Martyr cannot be put on a couch surrounded by psychoanalytic degrees. Nothing is known about the size of his mother's breasts, how he fared during the anal stage, or whether he got a red chariot (bicycles being non-existent) at the age of thirteen. His head was not available for electric shock treatment. It was only available for Marcus Aurelius's axe. Therefore psychological projections concerning Justin's motivation cannot be really considered valid apart from his belief in Christ's Freedom.

In further analyzing Justin's view of Christ's Freedom it is necessary to elucidate his statement made in connection with suicide which asserts that "God did not make the world aimlessly, but for the sake of the human race."[37] A contemporary and adversary of Justin Martyr's, the gnostic Marcion, represented another view of creation.[38] According to Marcion there is not one but two gods. One god is just; the other god is good.[39] The just god or god of "the law" has supervised the creation of this world. His creation is characterized by disgusting pettiness.[40] Because of his poor job as supervisor of the world's formation he can be known and his actions can be predicted[41] as being just as paltry as his creation. This same "god of pettiness" is also paltry in his view of morality. He demands "formal, narrow, retributive, and vindictive ('an eye for an eye, a tooth for a tooth') justice"[42] and "this justice, not outright evilness, is the cardinal property of the creator god."[43]

Different from the god of justice is the "good god." For Marcion this good "god' is the father of Jesus Christ.[44] This god is "unknown, alien, and good."[45] His goodness is unknown because his petty world cannot in any way manifest his presence.[46] Further:

> Being not the author of the world, including man, he is also the alien. That is no natural bond, no pre-existing relationship, connects him with the creatures of this world, and there is no obligation on his part to care for the destiny of man.[47]

Further, the good god does not concern himself with the governing of the physical world.[48] The only thing this good god really does is to send his son into the world to save people from the petty creation of the just god.[49] In this scheme of things Christ's death functions to cancel the creator's claim to his property.[50] Everyone's duty is to shun all the things of this world in order to mock and overcome the creator god.[51] This means abstaining from food, sexual intercourse, and marriage. Again, the purpose for this is to mock and destroy the power of the paltry god and created pettiness.

The difference between Justin Martyr's view of God and Marcion's two gods is astounding. First of all for Justin Martyr, the <u>logos spermatikos,</u> or "seeds of Full Creative Power" have their source and full embodiment in Jesus Christ. Jesus Christ together with the Spirit and Father have created this world. Therefore the world is essentially good and has a definite purpose. For Marcion the world is a paltry dump made by a petty and legalistic god. There is no purpose for this world other than getting out of it through <u>Marcion's</u> son of god and self-denial. For Justin Martyr we are born to realize the inward seeds of Creative Power in us which are in turn fully manifested in Jesus Christ who is in us.[52] This is not a general creative power. On the contrary this very Creative Power struggles and fights against the power of destruction referred to in the first chapter of this essay as the devil. Marcion, on the other hand, fails to distinguish the power of pettiness which makes the world appear evil from the world itself. No one denies that the world can appear petty and evil. But to say that at <u>all</u> times and in <u>all</u> places the world is <u>completely</u> petty and evil would be to foresee possible future possibilities in life. The future for Justin Martyr is a time reserved for the increased disclosure of Christ Himself in us in this life.[53]

Redemption (or the process by which evil is overcome) is for Marcion accomplished by a "good" god who wants nothing to do with the physical world. For Marcion Jesus Christ never becomes truly and completely human.[54] Nor does the physical world ever participate in the overcoming of evil. The logical consequences of such thinking would be immediate suicide. If the body is petty, why keep it? For Marcion there is only the continuance of the soul into another life.[55] Thus there is no real fulfillment of bodily existence. If a "good" god will not tolerate or continue in the existence of the body, why should anyone else?

However, for Justin Martyr, there is real purpose among and with the physical entities of this life because the world is created by a God who loves and wills to redeem His creation. Further, Jesus Christ becomes completely and fully a human being with a human, physical, material body. This same body is of decisive importance in manifesting the Divine Will. Far from being shunned, Christ's human body is actually effective in procuring eternal life through Christ's teaching, work, death and resurrection. Every human being is also invited to seek and find Christ who, for Justin, is in every created person. Everyone is invited to a new life which occurs in this life through the logos, Word, or Jesus Christ. Justin describes this new life in this life as follows:

> And thus do we also, since our persuasion by the Word, stand aloof from them (i.e., the demons), and follow the only unbegotten God through His Son -- we who formerly delighted in fornication, but now embrace chastity alone; we who formerly used magical arts, dedicate ourselves to the good and unbegotten God; we who valued above all things the acquisition of wealth and possessions now bring what we have into a common stock, and

communicate to everyone in need; we who hated and destroyed one another, and on account of their different manners would not live with men of a different tribe, now, since the coming of Christ, live familiarly with them, and pray for our enemies, and endeavor to persuade those who hate us unjustly to live comformably to the good precepts of Christ, to the end that they may become partakers with us of the same joyful hope of a reward from God the ruler of all.[56]

Many other facets of Justin's thought could be of interest. However for the purpose at hand, let us briefly summarize what has been said. Justin Martyr freely seeks the truth. He accepts no human traditions but only what appears to be true to him. This truth, although being active in many wise men, is really fulfilled and completed in the teachings, person, work, life, death and resurrection of Jesus Christ. This same truth is in everyone and everyone can find it. This same truth distinguishes itself from gnostic world-denying teachings as found in Marcion. Further this truth is of such a quality as to announce the <u>essential</u> goodness of being alive and attempts to lead everyone to a new life of Freedom in <u>this</u> life.

B.   Athanasius (295-373 A.D.)[57]

In Athanasius, bishop of Alexandria, there is found the same robust and tenacious battle for Christ's Freedom as was found in Justin Martyr. However with Athanasius the theater of war is not located among the variety of philosophical schools but in the struggle of the early church to establish doctrine congruent with the liberating activity of Christ's Person. This same struggle was to be fought by Athanasius concerning the liberating activity of the Holy Spirit whose activity is of course (cf. chap. I) never to be isolated from the activity of Christ's Person. Athanasius was actually exiled five times for defending and fiercely holding fast to his beliefs.[58]

"Well so what? Ancient history is pretty far removed from the suicide ward. What is needed is RELEVANCE, ReLeVaNcE, relevance; here and now, man -- Here and Now!!!" Precisely, and what was integral to Athanasius' battle is completely relevant here and now. His whole doctrine and life are concisely established in the concluding words of his small work, The Incarnation of the Word of God (c. 318).[59] These concluding words referring to Jesus Christ (or the Word of God) are: "He, indeed, assumed humanity that we might become God."[60] What is therefore relevant is that any person "here and now," "there and then," or "in the future," is invited to become God by Jesus Christ.

For Athanasius the possibility of becoming God is made available to everyone through the Power and Love of Jesus Christ. And, the Power and Love of Jesus Christ is fully and completely the Power and Love of God. This is the central teaching of Athanasius. This same teaching caused him to be exiled five times by his adversaries, the Arians. The two basic principles of Arianism (which also claimed at that time to be true Christianity) are (1) "the son is not eternal"[61] and (2) "He (i.e., the son of god) is created out of nothing."[62] This means that Jesus Christ was created out of time, before the world and time;[63] and that "god" remains in himself rigid abstract being[64]. For Arianism Christ is not of the same essence of the father.[65] Although Christ occupies a middle and unique position between "god" and the world[66] and creates the world[67] the extremely lofty "god" of Arianism does not allow for any communication between himself and human beings.[68] The consequences of Arianism are devastating and can still be found in the proclamations of local churches of all denominations. The substance of these proclamations is that Jesus Christ is someone or something "special" in between god and man. Like some type of Galilean bat, he hovers aimlessly over the world loving the world with a love neither human nor divine. He is an "ideal" one half of which has been projected from the human side, the other half rather loosely documented by Biblical quotations. The consequences of this are that each individual winds up communicating with his ideal Jesus. In the end this means that the individual remains locked up inside of himself. Thus "god," an abstract, quiet, completely hidden blur remains amorphously removed from every human decision. Thus "god" remains living and doing something (just exactly what this "something" is, no one, not even Jesus, knows) in noble inaccessible heights. Thus "god" really forgets about his creation, passes the blueprints over to "Big Jesus" (some type of transcendental, second in command gang leader) and goes off to enjoy a rather isolated divine snooze.

Against this type of thinking, against this type of human construct, against this type of "god"; Athanasius vehemently and decisively rebels. To fully understand the fullness of Athanasius' rebellion it will be necessary not only to take into account his <u>The Incarnation of the Word of God</u> and his <u>Three Orations Against the Arians</u> (c. 335 or 356 A.D.),[69] but also his <u>Letters to Bishop Serapion</u> (358—362 A.D.)[70] concerning the divinity of the Holy Spirit. This is entirely necessary because if any activity is to be attributed to God it is to be attributed to the

> Triad, holy and complete, confessed to be God in Father, Son and Holy Spirit, having nothing foreign or external mixed with it, not composed of one that creates and one that is originated, but all creative; and it is consistent and in nature indivisible, and its activity is one.[71]

The same Arians, who had wished to claim Jesus Christ only as a creature and not completely divine,[72] had also contended that the Holy Spirit was a creature and not completely divine.[73] For Athanasius the Holy Spirit is not another created ministering spirit, such as an angel (angels were part of the world-view prominent in Athanasius' time).[74] Nor was the Holy Spirit "the spirit of democracy," "the spirit of socialism," or "the spirit of self-destruction" all of which are prominent in our own time. For Athanasius the Holy Spirit is that Spirit which desires to re-create each individual anew as a child of God.[75] That is, the Holy Spirit desires to <u>adopt</u> each created human person into that familial relationship which already exists in the Divine Activity between Jesus Christ and His Father. For Athanasius Jesus Christ is totally and fully the Father's Son from eternity.[76] Christ was not created by "god" but rather existed in and with the Father.[77] He had, has, and will have the exact same substance as the Father.[78] Athanasius describes the Father's relation to the Son as one of "begetting."[79] However this "begetting" has no human equal or model.[80] For our purposes it will be sufficient to say that the word "begetting" is used to describe the inner communication and activity of the Triune God. Only that which is of the same nature (the Father and Son have the same nature) can be said to beget its equal. The activity of begetting done among those of equal nature is different from the act of creation[81] which describes a distinction between the natures of the Creator and the creature. For Athanasius every human person is created through the Word or Son of God in conjunction with the full activity of the Triune God.

At this point a few statements must be reviewed. The satirical statements made in this section concerning the Arian "christ" who is only a creature was seen to be a man-made god which really was able to do very little but lock up the human person in himself or herself. This is what the general ideal always does to the individual. An individual projects and controls for a time the perfect man, the perfect relationship, or the perfect way of life. The individual is thus the originator of the projection. Further he feels guilty when he does not fulfill the ideal man's (i.e., the ideal man that the individual has himself projected) way of life. The individual also feels guilty when he does not himself fulfill the ideal relationship which he has himself projected. The individual then begins to accuse himself of his failings. According to his own human projected laws, he sins. In some forms of pathological behavior the guilt increases to staggering proportions. The individual becomes so confused that he cannot always remember the real source of his ideal projections. He becomes judge, jury, and periodically -- executioner. Of course the individual is not a solitary organism but is somehow connected with a family, a society, a nation, a particular religious tradition, etc. And of course each society, nation, and particular religious tradition has its own guilt-provoking ideals. It not only has its ideals but it has sin scales which weigh and evaluate who or what is "good," "bad," or "indifferent." Into this, vortex of would-be ideals and gods everyone is thrown. Upon the sin scales of human projections everyone is weighed. And, at last, after fighting for some pure air in the center of the vortex where the individual had become overweight because of <u>human</u> sin scales, what occurs? Why what occurs is something designed for everyone -- six feet of turf in the local cemetery. Or, if it has been <u>humanely willed</u> with a probate lawyer, one may receive a marble slab in an edifying mausoleum. There are of course other <u>human</u> alternatives obtainable through the probate lawyer. One could have the choice of burial at sea (where many sharks do not make their home) or one may choose the crematorium. As far as the eye sees, the mind deduces, and all <u>human</u> teachers can tell us, the earth is becoming a gigantic cemetery or one of its above-mentioned equivalents. Whatever good moments occur last a few seconds and die unless there is a Power which <u>Wills</u> otherwise.

    In analyzing this Power it should be remembered that the basis of this Power is the Activity of Jesus Christ, the Holy Spirit, and Christ's Father which are unified in one activity of Love.[82] The potency of this Love is, according to Athanasius, capable of refuting the law of death.[83] "Capable of refuting?" More so, this powerful Love destroys death, destroys the power of human projections that desire death as an escape from human laws. The powerful Love twists the twisting vortex to establish calm seas. It overcomes that worldly power which says "You are death's." Christ, the Father's Son and fully God, activates the Spirited whip. Those protected by the Spirited whip inquire of death "O death, where is thy victory? O death, where is thy sting?"[84] Against what the eye or mind can conceive, against the marked grave, and against that statement "You are death's," a more powerful assertion is driven inward—"You are Christ's."[85] That is, you belong to Life!

    Thus when Athanasius says that through the Word (who is Jesus Christ) every individual human being was created, or in his own phrase "the presence and love of the

Word had called them into being;"[86] Athanasius means that no one was created for death. On the contrary, Athanasius asserts that the Word (who was completely Divine) became a human being to condemn the law of death.[87] For Athanasius everyone was created for incorruption into the likeness of Christ.[88] The human race, however, rebelled against the plan and commandments of this creation.[89] As a consequence of <u>this</u> rebellion that which was created good became perverted.[90] However with Athanasius this particular sin followed from a <u>definite</u> refusal of man to live as the Triune God had created him. With Athanasius this sin, although enacted by man, is never diverted from the persevering Love of Christ to overcome that sin. In other words, with Athanasius sin is a rebellion against the activity of the Triune God. However, since it is always Christ's intention to overcome and banish sin (with its consequence -- death) a person who sins cannot lock himself up in his sin or in himself <u>and</u> still maintain that he is directly confronting the real and active Love of the Triune God. He could, of course, make up his own "god", accept another "god", declare himself a sinner, and then despair. But he would not then be in relation to the living Love of Jesus Christ.

This twisted projective capacity within everyone is for Athanasius a consequence of the rebellion against the Triune God. To correct this twisted projective capacity the Word (who is Jesus Christ) took on the human body in order to communicate to everyone what the real Love of the true God is.[91] The body itself did not completely contain the Word. Rather, the activity of the Word remained completely active throughout the universe before and while it assumed the human body.[92] This is especially important since it establishes the Triune God's Will as a Will which desires at all times and in all places to overcome that which is twisted and confused.

"Fine, but how does one become aware of this Loving activity?" This brings us finally back to Athanasius' doctrine of the Holy Spirit. For Athanasius anyone who does not have the Holy Spirit simply does not have the Triune God.[93] "Well how does one know that he has the Holy Spirit?" Quite simply, for Athanasius, the Holy Spirit comes with the Father and Son to take up active residence in the human person.[94] The effects of such inward indwelling are 1) freedom from the power of death,[95] 2) a knowledge of immortal and indestructible life in this life,[96] 3) a renewal of the human person (once the projective capacity has been set right) in order that the human person may do the Will of the Triune God Who is with us.[97] This is the meaning of the phrases "the body is a temple of God,"[98] "we are to be taught by God,"[99] and "we are the adopted children of God."[100] Finally, such phrases are really the content of the sentence "He, indeed, assumed humanity that we might become God."[101]

C. Augustine (354-430 A.D.)[102]

The usual process in evaluating the Christian position on suicide is simply to forget about the Bible and the Greek theologians (such as Justin Martyr and Athanasius) and rush forward to a few fragmented utterances of Augustine. Augustine's comments on suicide are then completely ripped out of the context in which he wrote them. Augustine thus appears as a vicious legalist whose name is used to authenticate all "modern" claims denouncing Christianity. I am not attempting to defend or condemn Christianity. I am only attempting to investigate Christ's Freedom. However such descriptions of Augustine as "that great enemy of voluntary death"[103] are not exactly overflowing with information. In order to elucidate Augustine's actual thoughts concerning suicide I have found it necessary to turn to significant passages in his voluminous writings where he can speak for himself. Why Augustine speaks in the manner he does will be briefly explained as far as can be allowed within the scope of this essay.

Augustine, in his Confessions (397-401),[104] portrays his youthful search for wisdom. He relates how he investigated rather brutal theatrical displays,[105] Cicero's Hortensius,[106] his struggles in attempting to understand scripture,[107] and, among other things, his life as a Manichaean investigating astrology.[108] Through much inward turmoil, pain, and confusion, Augustine finds in the Nee-Platonic school some aid in helping to understand the immateriality and invisibility of God.[109] There then occurs a series of mystical experiences[110] which solidify and help to formulate his forthcoming years as one of the most active men who ever lived.

This extremely brief outline of Augustine's life is immensely important in evaluating his attitude toward suicide. It is to be remembered that his Confessions were written during the years 397—401.[111] It is a completed work of a man (age 42) who has already been made a bishop of the church.[112] Many of his formulations have become set. His quest of wisdom is in the process of being fulfilled under definite guidelines. Now bishops are not notorious for committing suicide. Perhaps their enemies might desire that they would kill themselves, but then this is not an essay devoted to the aggressions of the clergy. There is already more than enough written on such a topic and can be found in those volumes concerned with the "Christian" religious crusades, wars, etc. What is the present concern is how Bishop Augustine found his wisdom and how such wisdom is related to suicidal behavior. To really investigate this, some of Augustine's earlier works should be examined.

One of Augustine's earliest works, The Soliloquies (387)[113] was written during the period between his mystical conversion and his baptism.[114] It expresses Augustine's own most private thoughts on the question of wisdom and suicide. Augustine (age 33) is speaking to his own reason. Augustine's reason questions him:

> Reason: If your life was a hindrance to the obtaining of wisdom, would you want it to continue?
> Augustine: No I should flee from it.
> Reason: If you learned that you could reach wisdom equally by continuing in the body or by leaving it, would you greatly care whether you enjoyed what you love in this life or in another?

> Augustine: If I knew that I should encounter nothing that would drive me back from the point to which I have already progressed I should not care.
> Reason: Your reason, then for fearing death now is lest you be involved in some evil which would rob you of the knowledge of God.
> Augustine: Not only lest I should be robbed of such understanding as I have reached, but also lest, retaining what I myself possess, I should be precluded from the society of those whom I eagerly desire to share it.
> Reason: So you do not wish for continued life on its own account but on account of wisdom.
> Augustine: That is so.[115]

"Well how do you come to this wisdom? And what really is this wisdom?" As can be seen from the forgoing dialogue such questions are not fully answered. Who is to be the teacher of wisdom and where is he to be found?

Augustine attempts to answer these questions in another early work, The Teacher, written about 389.[116] In this work he speaks of wisdom, the teacher, and where they are to be found.

> Our real teacher is he who is said to dwell in the inner man, namely Christ, that is the unchangeable power and eternal wisdom of God. To this wisdom every rational soul gives heed, but to each is given only so much as he is able to receive, according to his own good or evil will.[117]

For Augustine Christ is at once Teacher and Eternal Wisdom contained within everyone.

This very Teacher continues to instruct everyone.[118] Augustine means by a rational soul simply that soul found in every human person. Augustine's full analysis of the human soul and body cannot be presented in this essay. Nor is it possible to describe fully his doctrine of the human will. This much can be said: the human soul, the human body, and the human will were created good. All that is physical is also good. Everything and everyone are essentially good because they have been created through the Eternal Wisdom (who is Jesus Christ).[119] Even if the human soul or body became corrupted through a bad will, the human body, the human soul, and the human will are essentially good. Not generally good, not "pleasantly" good, but good essentially because they were created through Jesus Christ within the activity of the Triune God. Varied gnostic cults whose teachings were comparable to the teachings of Marcion (cf. section on Justin Martyr) were still active at the time of Augustine. One such cult, the Manichees or Manichaeans taught a highly complex cosmology of two competing gods one of which was evil and one of which was good. For our purposes it is sufficient to note that the Manichaeans condemned the physical universe as a product of the evil god. Augustine who had once been a Manichaean never ceases denouncing such an attitude. [120] For Augustine, Jesus Christ wills to teach, correct and bring to Himself all that He has created. He does this through an activity of instruction whereby He Himself corrects and revitalizes the human will. For Augustine <u>everyone's will is corrupted in relation to the Teacher</u>. However because of the Power and Love within the Teacher, it is the Teacher's free desire (this free desire is known theologically as "grace") to correct the corrupted will and the consequences following upon such a corrupted will.[121] One of the consequences of such a corrupted will would be the desire to commit suicide. This is affirmed in Augustine's work <u>On Free Choice of the Will</u> (begun between the years 387—388 and completed about the year 395).[122] Augustine contends that an individual is influenced by faulty teachers, opinions and feelings. Because of such faulty teachers, opinions, and feelings a tormented individual might believe that he could overcome his plight by ceasing to exist. But, for Augustine:

> his natural feeling is a longing for peace. What is at peace, however, is not nothing; on the contrary; it exists to a greater degree than something that is not at peace. Restlessness

changes a man's emotions so that one feeling destroys another. Peace, however, is constant and because of this constancy it is said of peace that it exists. Every willful desire for death is directed toward peace, not toward nonexistence.[123]

Augustine was at this time a very restless human being. Peace for him could not be separated from Eternal Wisdom,[124] and Eternal Wisdom could not be separated from the inward Teacher.[125] Further, this Peace, this Wisdom, and this Teacher did not exist just for Augustine. On the contrary, Augustine has stated to himself in The Soliloquies[126] that the reason why he would not kill himself is because he did not want to deny the possibility of the knowledge of God to "the society of those whom I eagerly desire to share it."[127] What man, woman, or child preoccupied with suicidal behavior is not a member of this society? Who is to be denied Augustine's Teacher? What infernal power or teaching will try to disjoin the Teacher's peace from the pupil?

In answering this last question it will be necessary to look at more passages in Augustine which refer to suicide. That is, the more familiar passages which have made Augustine "that great enemy of voluntary death" for our "modern" world should be analyzed. Augustine in the first book of The City of God (413—416 A.D.)[128] is addressing himself to virgins who were raped during the barbarian invasions.[129] The destruction, brutality, and ferocity of these barbarian invasions was manifested in the sack of Rome (410 A.D.) by Alaric and his Goths.[130] The virgins who were violated believed that they were somehow guilty for the atrocities committed against them. (This same form of guilt can be found in suicide wards where young girls wish to kill themselves because some man -- sometimes their own father -- attempted or succeeded in raping them.) What does Augustine say and do? What does any psychiatrist or psychologist say and do? What does any compassionate person say and do? Augustine simply tells the virgins that they have done nothing wrong. He informs them that the law of virginity is not an absolute law. He consoles them by affirming that Christ is not to be compared with the law of virginity. He says that Christ Himself accuses no one who has been violated against her will. Augustine "that great enemy of voluntary death" remains such an enemy when the tortures of individuals' consciences have so attacked them that they see death as the only possible escape.

Maintaining that the peace derivable from Christ is the real source of a higher life, he also attacks Stoic ideals of suicide in book one and book nineteen of The City of God. If the Stoics have really mastered this life with their philosophy, why do they praise so much those who have actually killed themselves?[131] For Augustine a person who had really mastered this life would certainly wish to continue overseeing his conquest. The Stoics maintained that the highest state of man could be learned from the varied movements of nature through reason. Nature and nature's law were for the Stoics the real teachers. Over against this Augustine asserts that the very evils promulgated by nature such as blindness, deafness, and twisted limbs automatically disqualify nature and nature's law as teachers.[132] Further such teachers cannot speak of another life operative in this life which would give an individual mastery over this life.

For Augustine, the other life operative in this life is Jesus Christ or the Life and Light of everyone.[133] This Life and Light overcomes evil and death, and, by so doing, offers everyone an eternal perspective in this life.[134]

Thus Augustine's attitude towards suicide is never an abstract theory written by a legalistic churchman preoccupied with intellectually fleecing his flock. Augustine himself took the question of suicide seriously, very seriously. He was inwardly taught a constant peace by the inward Teacher. This peace was not threatened by natural death. On the contrary, eternal life taught and given vitally and immediately by Jesus Christ, was the basis of this peace. This constant peace does in His Strength overcome human constructs of what is relatively good or evil. Finally this peace quite vehemently denounces any doctrine that would wish to separate the Teacher from His students.

D.   The Council of Chalcedon (451 A.D.)[135]

The simplest and most penetrating way of summarizing and completing our discussion of Justin Martyr's positive attitude toward this world, Athanasius' belief in everyone's possible this-worldly divinity, and Augustine's belief in lasting inward peace is to acknowledge a pronouncement made at the Council of Chalcedon in 451 A.D. The Council of Chalcedon did not concur in order to establish denominational boundaries, fatten ministers' or priests' salaries, or discuss the permissible height of the local church's bell tower. Nor did the Council of Chalcedon concur in order to form dozens of committees which were to busy themselves in angelic nose-picking, needless arguments, and churchly power politics. The central concern of the Council of Chalcedon was to formulate a statement concerning Christ's Person. What is said about Christ's Person will bear a direct influence on the type, degree, and strength of the freedom that will be available from Him. In other words, unless the source of the world's goodness, our potential divinity in this life, and the constant peace in this life are investigated and made clear there will be a great deal of confusion. Confusion is not anyone's freedom, much less Christ's Freedom. Therefore the framers of the formula of Chalcedon tried to do everyone a favor by clarifying the Person of Christ.

For the present purpose which is concerned with Christ's Freedom and suicidal behavior, it is only necessary to bring forth particular phrases in the formula which would be useful. The formula states that Jesus Christ is completely and truly God, and at once completely and truly a human being. As was seen in the discussion of Augustine, everyone's will is corrupted in relation to the Teacher, Jesus Christ. However, this corruption (known theologically as sin) is not the basic determinant of anyone. What is the basic determinant of everyone is that he or she is created by Jesus Christ in conjunction with the Divine Activity. Thus Jesus Christ does not have a corrupted will (or a will controlled by sin). But He does have a complete and true humanity.[136]

Jesus Christ has made Himself known as the manifestation of the Divine Activity's Will. He is completely and truly God and completely and truly a human person "without confusion, without change, without division, without separation."[137] Now these "withouts" may appear to add to confusion instead of aiding clarification. However this formula is not simply a logical, abstract display of theological hocus-pocus. It is to be remembered that the Divine Activity is an activity of Love and Freedom for every single human person. This formula only wishes to display vitally and dynamically such Love and Freedom. The Divine Love and Freedom would be imperiled if the "withouts" were changed to "withs."

Let us say hypothetically that the divine and human natures were described as being joined "with confusion" and "with change." If the two natures were confused and changed such that what was divine co-mingled and lost itself in the human nature, there would be no possibility of the divine nature communicating itself to anyone. What is divine would be lost, bound, and twisted so that it could never really revivify or change what is confused and destructive in every human person. Jesus Christ would actually be something in between God and man. He would no longer be divine but a mythological creature totally isolated from the purity of the Divine Activity. Jesus Christ would also be isolated from everyone. He could only participate with other mythological creatures. What human individual wants to be prodded by a unicorn, rest on the shoulders of a giant, or identify with "a thing I know not what"? Every human being should rebel against such a thing. If God can't become totally a human being and at the same time in every way maintain his divinity, forget about God. Why should such a God be forgotten? Simply because the divine activity would go its own way (I know not where), and the human race would go its own way (which, as "the true empiricist" [who is not the Teacher] has shown, is to the cemetery, the mausoleum, and the crematorium). Something that is "unhuman," "in-human," or "ahuman," simply cannot understand what it means to be human. Nor can "It" show a communicable form of compassion or in any way aid anyone. Thus if "with confusion" and/or "with change" had been adopted at Chalcedon there would have been no real and vital mediation between the Divine Love as Divine Love and humanity as humanity. Jesus Christ would have become "jesus christ," an isolated and very foolish mythological "blurp."

If the words "with division" and "with separation" were substituted for "without division" and "without separation," then all Love and Freedom would break loose. The real activity of Love and Freedom would not encompass, hold fast, and set right the human individual's wretchedness. No lasting unity would be established between the Divine Activity and the human person. What would then be called "god" would simply remain on its own. There would not even be the possibility of a mythological wonder. All that could really be known would be flimsy human speculations and projections about "god." Again, there would be no real and lasting mediation between the Divine Activity and the human person. Again, everyone would be left to himself or herself. Again, the law of death would rule.

Therefore, when the words "without confusion," "without change," "without division" and "without separation," are used to describe the person of Christ, they serve a definite function. They are used to destroy the innumerable phantasms, myths, and twisted constructs which are usually grouped around the word "god." Further they are used to destroy that hideous notion of the "god" is an unapproachable, completely hidden, uncaring zero. What the formula of Chalcedon affirms is that there is nothing essentially wrong with any human person. This is utterly and completely impossible because Jesus Christ who is completely and truly God has become completely and truly a human person. The "withouts" merely wish to express that this union of Divinity and humanity is always to be understood as an unshakable source of Love and Freedom for everyone.

E. Thomas Aquinas (c. 1225-1274 A.D.)[138] and the Roman Catholic Church's Proclamation on Suicide

In analyzing Thomas Aquinas's view of suicide it is best that he speak entirely for himself. Thomas Aquinas, unlike Justin Martyr and Athanasius, did not live a dramatic life. Nor, like Augustine, did he really speak about suicide in relation to Christ's Freedom. Thomas Aquinas's life was simply that of a university professor.[139] His actual thoughts on suicide were probably well meant. Unfortunately these thoughts are horribly legalistic in style and content. These are his words:

> It is altogether unlawful to kill oneself for three reasons. First, because everything naturally loves itself, the result being that everything naturally keeps itself in being, and resists corruptions so far as it can. Wherefore suicide is contrary to the inclination of nature, and to charity whereby man should love himself. Hence suicide is always a mortal sin, as being contrary to natural law and to charity.
> Secondly, because every part, as such, belongs to the whole. Now every man is part of the community, and so, as such, he belongs to the community. Hence by killing himself he injures the community, as the Philosopher declares (Ethic, v.).
> Thirdly because life is God's gift to man, and is subject to His power, Who kills and makes to live. Hence whoever takes his own life, sins against God, even as he who kills another's slave, sins against that slave's master, and as he who usurps to himself judgment of a matter not entrusted to him. For it belongs to God alone to pronounce sentence of death and life, according to Deut xxxii. 39: I will kill and I will make to live.[140]

It is obvious from the incidents recorded at the beginning of this essay, that "naturally" everyone does not love himself. Of course Thomas Aquinas is not aware of possible biochemical secretions which could "naturally" cause suicidal behavior. Of course Thomas Aquinas is not aware of "natural" environmental stresses which could lead to self-destructive activity. Of course Thomas Aquinas is not a biochemist or psychiatrist in the modern sense. Of course -- this is all true and no one should blame Mr. Aquinas for his ignorance. However -- Thomas Aquinas's culpability rests with his referral of suicidal behavior to the abstract, general precepts of "natural" justice. This is derived not from Christ's teachings but from "the philosopher" who is Aristotle (384-322 B.C.). Aristotle in book five, chapter eleven of The Nicomachean Ethics; states:

> Now when a person kills himself in a fit of anger, he acts voluntarily in violation of right reason; and that the law does not permit. Consequently, he acts unjustly. But toward whom? Surely toward the state, not toward himself. For he suffers voluntarily, but no one voluntarily accepts unjust treatment. That is also the reason why the state exacts a penalty, and some dishonor is imposed upon a man who has taken his own life on the grounds that he has acted unjustly toward the state.[141]

In Aristotle's time the penalty which the state exacted was that "the hand with which a suicide was committed was buried apart from the body."[142]

Aquinas has simply transferred Aristotle's thought with respect to his (Aquinas's) first two reasons why one should not commit suicide. Suicide is 1) against nature[143] and, 2) against the state.[144] The third reason Aquinas gives refers simply to Aquinas's view of "god." Aquinas does not in this instance describe God by means of the Bible's description of Jesus Christ, the Holy Spirit, and Christ's Father. On the contrary what is presented is a general "god" who gives life to man and makes man subject to his power.[145] It is not to be ignored that this "god's" relation to the suicidal person is comparable to that of a master to a slave.[146] It is to be noted, and noted well, that there is not one reference to the person and work of Jesus Christ in relation to suicide. Just as Aristotle discussed suicide under the topic of justice,[147] so Aquinas discussed suicide under the topic of justice.[148] Justice is not interpreted as Christ's justice which only means that He claims all of creation as His own. Rather, justice is seen as general legalistic precepts such as "natural law,"[149] "man is part of the community,"[150] and "god relates himself to suicidal people as a master to a slave."[151] Even when Aquinas makes use of Augustine, he does it in such a legalistic manner as not even to mention Augustine's earlier works which were quoted in the last section.[152] Rather, Aquinas simply gives an abstract, non-historical interpretation of Augustine's views of suicide from <u>The City of God</u>.[153]

Thomas Aquinas never once mentions Christ's Freedom in relation to suicidal behavior. He only gives a brutally judgmental cataloging of reasons against suicide based on an amorphous and psychologically detrimental concept of "god." The same legalistic viewpoint had precedents in two councils of the Roman Catholic Church which denounced suicide. At the Second Council of Brage (between 560 and 575 A.D.) those who committed suicide were not to be remembered at the sacrifice of the Mass.[154] Nor were their bodies to be buried accompanied by the singing of Psalms.[155] Suicides were to be treated in the same way as executed criminals.[156] (According to a prior council, the Second Council of Orléans in 533 A.D., executed criminals were to be given the last rites at burial.[157] However, suicides were to be denied such rites.[158]) By the time of Thomas Aquinas (c. 1225-1274 A.D.) suicide is bluntly declared to be a mortal sin.[159] According to Roman Catholicism, a mortal sin carries with it the most horrible of penalties. A penalty which is in fact an impossibility in a universe created through Jesus Christ. But, for historical interest, a mortal sin is such that if it is not forgiven by a priest or through a perfect act of contrition (a perfect act of contrition is one in which a person loves "god" for himself [or itself] apart from all possible punishment) a person is damned to the fires of hell for all eternity.

Essentially this same view of suicide -- the denial of last rites -- mortal sin -- hell eternal is the Roman Catholic Church's position in the Twentieth Century.[160] Just as in Aristotle's time a suicide's hand was to be cut from the physical body as a penalty, so the Roman Catholic Church attempts to cut off its members from its corporate body by denying them burial. However in the Twentieth Century more complex distinctions have been made. Suicides are to be refused burial only if "their act was deliberate and <u>notoriously so.</u>"[161] That is, a human being is to be denied burial in consecrated ground if his act of suicide is a public and manifest act of sin.[162]

> Such notoriety will be rare, and scandal unlikely, where the more or less common opinion prevails that suicide usually results from nervous or mental derangement.[163]

Although the official position of the Roman Catholic Church has perhaps become slightly more humane, the legalism, lack of reference to Christ's Freedom, and severity of some weird god's penal activity in the next life still remain.

It is authoritatively known that such laws about penal action either in this life or in the next do not in the least stop anyone from committing suicide. I say this is "authoritatively known" because the source of this information does not come from philosophers, clergymen, theologians, poets, writers, artists, social scientists, psychologists or psychiatrists. It is "authoritatively known" because the information comes from the actual notes of those who <u>have already committed suicide.</u>[164] I trust that everyone will agree that there is no better source of information. The deductions made from such notes are:

> religious convictions do not appear to be ultimately binding upon the individual as a constraint against suicide, since one tends to interpret religious dogma as one has need to interpret it.[165]

Thus neither religious conviction, church laws, nor all the abstract theories in the world can stop a single suicide. What am I to say? The real authorities have already spoken. It is obvious that I am still writing, and thus I am in all truth disqualified as an authority. However, filled with the vanity of vanities I will continue the essay.

CHAPTER III

Luther's Denunciation of "the accusing christ" and Calvin's Denunciation of "The Vested Wonders"

A.   Martin Luther (1483-1546 A.D.)[1]

In discussing Luther's thought concerning suicide, it is best to recount the story of Luther's friend, John Krause.[2] In this way Luther's own life, style of writing, and suicidal preoccupations will come to light.

The date is a December day, 1527. It is the lunch hour. The eminent councilman, John Krause of Halle, has not yet left his bedroom. His daughter calls to him to come down for the afternoon supper. There is no response. She goes to her father's bedroom door and knocks. John Krause has locked his door and will admit no one. When his daughter inquires about her father's health the only words heard from behind the locked door are: "It is all too much."

After a few more inquiries which are met with silence, John Krause's daughter returns to the supper table.

The hours pass and the councilman does not appear. Finally, after more entreaties are met with silence, workmen are summoned to break down John Krause's locked door.

The councilman's clothes are red with blood. Upon the floor a dagger lies in a small pool of red liquid. At first glance no marks are to be found on councilman Krause's body except for a slash on the jugular vein. On closer inspection dagger marks are found on the chest and shoulder areas.

Luther commenting on the councilman's death inquires, "Who knows what could occur to a person suffering from extreme sorrow, when such a sane and stable man destroys himself?"[3]

John Krause's suicide was to be mentioned often by Martin Luther.[4] Luther remarked that the councilman felt that "the negative christ" was accusing him.[5] That is, John Krause's conscience was attacked and made to feel guilty because he was unable to fulfill the inward laws which activate and attack the conscience.[6] For Luther the inward laws which attack the conscience are a definite power or force.[7] These laws can take such a form as to convince the person being attacked that "christ himself" is accusing him and wishing to lead him to destruction.[8] For Luther, when these laws do trouble a person in such a way the devil, or power of destruction, is at work.[9]

"Oh come now. Really! The devil. The modern world has proven the stupidity of such a myth. What is demonic is simply an erotic drive which should be moulded to participate in the 'creative act'." I admit that there are a variety of devils. Some devils attempt to appear as erotic drives (Medievalism). Such devils are not Luther's devil. Some devils are grandiose and bellow at a cloud-puff heaven (Milton). Such devils are not Luther's devil. Some devils are "cute" and appear in modern upper-middle-class garb and garbage about "the creative act." Such devils are not Luther's devil.

Luther's devil purely and simply attempts to completely destroy everyone and everything in the universe. The devil even uses Christ's name. Luther is well acquainted with this devil because Luther had himself once lived as John Krause behind a locked door. That is, Martin Luther was a

Roman Catholic monk in good standing for sixteen years (1505-1521).[10] For at least ten years of Luther's time in the monastery[11] he felt "christ" periodically attacking him. The source of this christ's attacks was the medieval conception of "a righteous god" who demanded a variety of religious works (i.e., fasting, vigils, prayers, works, etc.) in order that a human person would work his way into heaven. In this monastic medieval context "christ" was pictured as an awesome judge with a sword coming forth out of his mouth.[12] This "christ" was a task-maker who really gave no peace of conscience. Rather, this "christ" perpetually troubled and required of monks: works, prayers, and fasting so that one could earn merits for getting into heaven. Luther could never be satisfied that he had done enough to appease such a "christ's" demands.[13] As a monk Martin Luther did everything in his power to become righteous before "god."[14] In fact, in every sense he was a good monk according to the prescribed discipline of his monastic order.[15] But the righteousness which he tried to obtain by his own efforts could never set things right between himself and "god." The "false christ" continued to demand a righteousness of him which he could not fulfill.

After much inward turmoil and pain[16] Luther came to the realization that the righteousness which The Real Christ expects is not a righteousness which an individual can in any way produce by his own powers. Rather the real Righteousness of God is a Righteousness by which Jesus Christ freely offers Himself and His Benefit of Freedom. This is a completely gratuitous act on Christ's part. Following upon this gratuitous Activity a phenomenon known as "faith" is formed within the individual. Practically and realistically faith is simply trust in what Jesus Christ has done for us.[17] What Christ has done for us is to give us freedom from "the accusing and false christ." For Luther "the false and accusing christ" is really an amalgam of the devil, the law, and sin, which persecutes the conscience. This very "accusing christ" who wishes to lead us to destruction is overcome and driven out by the True Christ whose Activity is one of Love and Freedom.

Luther, however, is no bustling optimist who can say "Well, that's that. Let's get 'creatively' busy and make money, trouble, babies, and books." Although Martin did leave the monastic order, light the match to the powder keg known as the Reformation, have six children, and write well over a hundred volumes, he never denied the possibility and actuality of the re-occurrence of inward turmoil and pain which can be evoked by "the accusing christ." In 1533 Luther makes this blatantly clear as he continues to discuss John Krause's suicide. Luther maintains that it is of course easy to sit back with fine doctrinal distinctions between the "accusing christ" (or the devil, law and sin) and the True Christ (i.e., the Gospel or Christ's Love and Freedom).[18] However, when one is in the center of turmoil and inward pain such fine distinctions are necessary but not sufficient.[19] Such distinctions must be made in order that we understand that Jesus Christ is Love and Freedom for us and not "the accusing christ." However, the Power which solidifies and makes real this distinction is the Power of the Triune God working through Jesus Christ's Love and Freedom. In other words, one cannot overcome inward turmoil and pain simply by abstract theological distinctions. A person must know and completely trust the living and true God who acts through Jesus Christ. This knowledge and trust is not a human work. Rather it is the response of the human person who has been created by the Triune God. The Triune God wills that everyone shall place his or her trust in Christ's Activity alone.

Now it is obvious that everyone places ultimate trust in varied things. Some individuals trust ultimately in the society, the state, or in world government. By so doing they wish to justify their lives. Some individuals trust ultimately in human love, their children, their home, and their social status. This, they believe, will justify their being born. Other individuals ultimately trust in art, science, scholarship, and the "great progress" of the universities. This, they believe, will justify their lives. Some, but not all suicidal people, may wish to overcome and justify their lives by destroying themselves. That is, they destroy themselves to prove that they have ultimate power over their own lives and deaths. The list of possible alternatives which people can and do use to justify themselves ultimately could be extended to fill at least a dozen libraries. (In fact, right now, more than dozens of libraries are so filled.) For Luther, however, there is only one real Power that <u>is able to justify us</u>. That Power is the Power of the Triune God acting in and through the Love and Freedom of Jesus Christ. For Luther this Power and this Power alone is our <u>justification</u> for having been born.

"Well how do you know if you are really confronting this Power?" For Luther everyone is at once a sinner and a justified human person. He or she is a sinner because he or she constantly places his or her trust in someone or something other than Jesus Christ's Activity. He or she is at the same time a justified human person because the Triune God does not sleep but perpetually wills to set things right through Christ's Activity. The turmoil and pain which everyone undergoes through "the false, destructive, and accusing christ" is used to make it clear to everyone Whom he or she should trust. That is, the false hopes of the world, the law, and the devil show us that ultimate trust in such powers do not in any way give us eternal life in <u>this</u> life. Rather such powers lead us to despair of being justified by anything or anyone apart from the True Christ's Activity. However, such powers <u>against their own wills</u> lead us to Christ. They do this because they are unmasked as being unworthy of our ultimate trust since they cannot overcome death and despair. That is, they indirectly lead us to place our full trust in Jesus Christ. This is their function -- to lead us to Jesus Christ's Activity of Love and Freedom. Such leading is a torturous and painful process because most people wish to place their trust in what is visible, gnawable, touchable, and easily comprehended. For Luther, however, the Triune God is not to be put off. This God will have it that everyone shall ultimately trust in Jesus Christ's Activity of Love and Freedom which is eternal life in <u>this</u> life.

Thus the Power of the Triune God's acting through and in Christ's Love and Freedom does not compete with the power of destruction on an equal basis. Rather the Power of the Triune God acting through and in Christ's Love and Freedom uses the power of destruction to show us where our ultimate trust should be placed. It should simply be placed in the Activity of Christ's Love and Freedom. When, through turmoil and pain, one finally does trust in Jesus Christ's Activity there is no doubt that it is Christ's Activity. There is no doubt because the inward scars inflicted during the battle attest to the need of a Real Physician. This Real Physician can be no one else than Jesus Christ.

"Well what about poor John Krause? He didn't get anything but a slit jugular vein." On the question of suicide Luther does not pretend or attempt to give systematic answers. He only says that John Krause was being tortured by "a false and accusing christ."[20] Luther did not believe that anyone who committed suicide was in any way penalized by the activity of the Triune God in another world.[21] For Luther those who commit suicide are like "soldiers dying in battle,"[22] or persons who are "murdered by a robber in the woods."[23] Nor are suicides to be denied any rights of burial by civil or religious authorities.[24] Luther believed that the death of John Krause and all other suicides teach us how insecure every human being really is.[25]

No theological doctrine as a rational speculative teaching can really establish the vital Freedom and Love of Jesus Christ. Nor can any real commentator on Luther do much else than repeat Luther's words that those people who have committed suicide still instruct us to pray for Christ's Love and Freedom since we are not in any way more secure than they were.[26] Luther says this not to add to anyone's anxieties nor is he making moral judgments. He is only stating what seemed true to him and is offering to anyone who is interested his solution which is to pray and trust in Christ's Love and Freedom.

With respect to the relatives of people preoccupied with suicidal behavior, Luther gives some very sound advice. These are his words of November 27, 1532,[27] to a woman whose husband was suffering from suicidal preoccupation:

> Be very careful not to leave your husband alone for a single moment, and leave nothing lying about with which he might harm himself. Solitude is poison to him. For this reason the devil drives him to it. There is no harm in your reading or telling him stories, news, and curiosities, even if some of them are idle talk and gossip or fables about Turks, Tartars, and the like, as long as they excite him to laughter and jesting. Then quickly recite comforting verses from the Scriptures. Whatever you do, do not leave him alone and be sure that his surroundings are not so quiet that he sinks into his own thoughts. It does not matter if he becomes angry about this. Act as if it were disagreeable to you and scold about it, but let it be done all the more.[28]

Although Martin Luther contended that everyone was justified by faith alone in and through Christ's Love and Freedom, Luther never wished to deprecate the created universe, human society, knowledge, food, beer, reason, marriage, children, dogs, cats or four-legged pigs. He simply desired that everyone should know that the right order of creation really begins and continues through the Activity of the Triune God. For Luther God's creation as God's creation is always very, very good. No false deifying or spiritualizing of human projections or capacities is tolerated in his thought. This is very important for the present discussion of suicide. It is important because often suicidal patients believe that "the flesh" is the human body, erotic drives, or dozens of other natural phenomena. Over against "the flesh" many well-meaning but idiotic pastors, priests, and teachers have placed "the spirit." How often has it been bellowed down through the centuries: "the flesh is of no avail," "what is spiritual is true," and "damn those fleshy sinners." In all such instances "the flesh" is taken quite wrongly to mean the human body, natural desires, and created capacities. Further scripture can also be wrongly used to verify such statements, provoke guilt, and violently torture the consciences of many people.

For Luther "the flesh" is simply a failure to trust in the Activity of the Triune God as manifested in Christ's Love and Freedom. The "flesh" does not mean the human body.[29] Once more. For Luther "the flesh" is simply a failure to trust in the Activity of the Triune God as manifested in Christ's Love and Freedom. The "flesh" does not mean the human body. This is an impossibility because the Word of God (who is Jesus Christ) has become a human person having a human body.[30] Further the full humanity of Jesus Christ is never to be separated from the Activity of the Triune God. This simply means that for Luther a "god" without a human body, is no "god" at all.[31] Also for Luther there is only one True Spirit -- the Holy Spirit. But the Holy Spirit is never to be separated from Christ's body. Christ's body is the Spirit's dwelling place and through Jesus Christ "the Spirit comes into all others."[32]

"Well what does all this have to do with suicidal behavior?" Simply this, when Luther wrote to the woman whose husband was stricken with self-destructive moods and thoughts, he advised her to use all the means at her disposal to re-establish her husband's relationship with society, humor, and this world. Comforting lines from scripture were to be used in rehabilitating him. Anger or rage at his wife's chatter was also to be used in aiding him to overcome his suicidal behavior. The source and basis of Luther's advice is not a general naturalistic view of human nature. For Luther the source and basis of his advice is the Divine Will which desires the rehabilitation of all that was created through Jesus Christ. The Divine Will has manifested the essential goodness of all creation by becoming a human person. In Jesus Christ the full embodiment of the Divine Will is completely manifested. Whatever is harmful to any human person is to be overcome through the Love and Freedom embodied in Christ. Thus society, gossip, rage, laughter, anger, scripture and all else which is beneficial to and for anyone is to be freely used in authenticating and completing the Divine Will.

B.   John Calvin (1509-1564)[33]

"What?" "Calvin! What's he doing here?" "This is no time to bring in a dogmatic moralist. You're ruining your essay which is already pretty bad." "Enough, enough!" In order to confront the jeers, guffaws, and hatred surrounding the name of John Calvin, a few comments should be made. If you wish to insult a Greek simply say, "I spit on the grave of your father." If you wish to insult an Italian simply say, "When is your mother going to learn how to cook?" If you wish to insult a "modern" intellectual simply say, "You dirty Calvinist!" Now this is common knowledge. Everyone thinks Calvin had four heads, caused the rise of capitalism, delighted at children going blind in London's nineteenth century textile mills, embroidered the red "A" known as the scarlet letter, and generally discovered and authorized "the busy spirit" of modern Protestantism. Further "the busy spirit" (Calvin's supposed child) has given birth to another "spirit" (Calvin's supposed grandchild) which characterizes "god's elect" as those people who insensitively wallow in their riches indifferent to the sufferings of the economically and psychologically poor. Well fine, common knowledge is after all usually quite common and need not be true. Well fine, who cares about the truth when cocktail conversation is the ruling power? Well fine, that's that and let's move on to the next chapter.

Unfortunately, this writer has met too many people who feel guilty because of a particular world-view attributed to Calvin and this guilt has often been a major cause in their self-destructive behavior. Unfortunately for "modernity" this writer has not found "modern Calvinism" to be in any of Calvin's writings. Unfortunately for the slick commentators on our "modern plight" who have never read Calvin, their conclusions will be proven to be <u>absolutely</u> false.

The reason why this world-view, modernity, and the slick commentators are wrong, is proven by Calvin's analysis of Christ's Freedom. For Calvin as for Luther there is the possibility of misinterpreting the substance of Christ's two commandments found in Chapter I of this essay. For Calvin there is also the possibility of having "an accusing christ" if the two commandments are wrongly applied.[34] For Calvin as for Luther, when a human person is empowered with Christ's Love and Freedom as a manifestation and gift of the Triune God a human person is able most vitally and correctly to use all created goods in the hope of rehabilitating any wretched human being.[35] However with Calvin there is also a third application of Christ's Freedom[36] with respect to "outward things that are of themselves 'indifferent'."[37] For Calvin with respect to outward things that are of themselves "indifferent"

> we are not bound before God by any religious obligation preventing us from sometimes using them and other times not using them, indifferently. And the knowledge of this freedom is very necessary for us, for if it is lacking, our consciences will have no repose and there will be no end to superstitions. Today we seem to be unreasonable because we stir up discussion over the unrestricted eating of meat, use of holidays and of vestments, and such things, which seem to them vain frivolities.
>
> But these matters are more important than is commonly believed. For when consciences once ensnare themselves, they enter a long and inextricable maze not easy to get out of. If a man begins to doubt whether he may use linen for sheets, shirts, handkerchiefs, and napkins, he will afterward be uncertain also about hemp; finally, doubt will even arise over tow. For he will turn over in his mind whether he can sup without napkins, or go without a handkerchief. If any man should consider daintier food unlawful, in the end he will not be at peace before God, when he eats either black bread or common victuals, while it occurs to him that he could sustain his body on even coarser foods. If he boggles at sweet wine, he will not with clear conscience drink even flat wine, and finally he

will not dare touch water if sweeter and cleaner than other water. To sum up, he will come to the point of considering it wrong to step upon a straw across his path, as the saying goes.

Here begins a weighty controversy. For what is in debate is whether God, whose will ought to proceed all our plans and actions, wishes us to use these things or those. As a consequence, some, in despair, are of necessity cast into a pit of confusion; others, despising God and abandoning fear of him, must make their own way in destruction, where they have none ready-made. For all those entangled in such doubts wherever they turn, see offence of conscience everywhere present.[38]

"Well what does all that mean?" As far as Calvin is concerned every individual possesses within him a capacity for projecting, manufacturing, and adoring idols.[39] Apart from Christ's Love and Freedom this capacity for idol-making and idol-worship leads everyone into an inward maze or labyrinth. In this inward maze of ghouls, specters, past voices, human traditions, false constructs of "god," and destructive drives, a human being's conscience perpetually tortures him until the human being is left without clarity, energy, or hope. The Divine Activity manifested in Jesus Christ's Love and Freedom overcomes this state of affairs by affirming that there is really only One Triune God who has but two commandments. This establishes some degree of clarity. Further this same Triune God makes possible the fulfillment of the two commandments through Christ's Love and Freedom. Christ's Love and Freedom are always active through the revivifying work of the Holy Spirit (who is not the general and abstract "busy spirit") which secretly operates to renew the human person. This process of renewal or regeneration establishes a real, vital, and immediate energy and hope which enables the human person to overcome his capacity for making and worshiping idols.

For Calvin the overcoming of idols and the consequences of idol worship is one of the major activities of the Triune God. Further, once the Triune God is active in correcting man's confusion, lethargy, and despair, this same God does not wish a thousand other problems and anxieties to trouble the consciences of those in whom He is working. This would attempt to impede His working and He does not desire this. Thus a type of Christ's Freedom is offered in which the human person's conscience is to be at peace with respect to those things not pertaining to the Activity surrounding the two commandments. This is the Freedom with respect to things indifferent.

In Calvin's time he instructs his listeners simply to be indifferent to such things as foods, fasting, vestments and vain frivolities. This is simply said for the peace of his listeners' consciences. In our day we are served many meals by vested wonders who are also masters of vain frivolities. These "vested wonders" are of course social pressures and success, universities which bellow "Responsibility . . . responsibility for the world" to powerless and confused students, the god-dollar, the newspaper, the "latest," etc. What? What's that I hear? A thousand armed voices chanting "Success, success," "Knowledge, responsibility -- ah, the university," "Money, drugs, sex -- our trinity." What am I to say to the vested wonders? Only that their foods are often digested by those whose end is recorded near the obituary column. I can only say that suicide is the second cause of death among college students. I can only say that the criterion of financial success or failure determines the suicidal behavior for much of the middle-aged population. I can only say that Christ's Freedom offers us the possibility of being indifferent to a multitude of "gods" and vain frivolities which mutilate the human person.

CHAPTER IV

Suicide in the Thought of Kierkegaard, Dostoevsky, Schopenauer, Nietzsche, and Camus

A.   Søren Kierkegaard (1813-1855)[1]

In interpreting Kierkegaard's attitude towards suicide I have selected a series of quotations from his various writings. In this way Kierkegaard can have his own way (which he always demanded). Also, the reader can have his own way with Kierkegaard (which Kierkegaard also always demanded).[2]

Kierkegaard at the age of thirty[3] recounts the suicide of Ludvig Blackfeldt.[4] Ludvig Blackfeldt's name was simply used to describe Kierkegaard's own suicidal impulses which were manifestly active from the age of twenty-three.[5] Thus Kierkegaard is really describing himself in speaking with himself.

> You surely have not forgotten young Ludvig Blackfeldt with whom a few years ago we both of us, and I especially, were in pretty close touch. He certainly was a very talented fellow, his misfortune was that he lost himself in a mysticism which was not so much Christian as Indian. If he lived in the Middle Ages, he doubtless would have found refuge in the cloister. Our age has no such helps. If a man goes astray, he must necessarily perish if he be not entirely healed. We have no such relative salvation to offer him. You know that he ended with suicide. With me he had a sort of intimacy and to that extent contradicted his

pet theory that one should not put oneself in relationship to any man but only to God immediately. Hence his intimacy with me was not great, and he never opened himself to me fully. During the last half year of his life I was an anxious witness of his eccentric movements. It is possible that I stopped him several times. I cannot know this definitely since he never opened himself to anyone. He had an unusual gift for concealing his psychic condition and for giving to one passion the semblance of another. Finally he put an end to his life without anyone being able to explain the reason for it. His physician expressed the opinion that it was due to partial insanity. Well, that was a very sensible thing for him to say. In fact his mind was unimpaired up to the last moment. Perhaps you do not know that there exists a letter which be wrote to his brother, the Councillor of Justice, in which he informs him of his intention. I enclose herewith a copy of it. It has harrowing evidence of genuineness and is a highly objective expression of the last agony of complete isolation.*

*"Honorable Mr. Councillor,

I write to you because in a way you are my nearest of kin, and yet in another way you are not nearer to me than other men. When you receive these lines I am no more. Should anyone ask you the reason, you can say that once there was a princess called Morning Glory, or something else like that; for so it is I myself would reply if I had the joy to survive myself. Should anyone ask you the occasion for it, you can say that it was on the occasion of the great conflagration. Should anyone ask you about the time, you can say that it was in the month of July, so notable for me. Should no one ask you any of these questions, you are to make no reply.

I do not regard suicide as a praiseworthy thing. It is not out of vanity I have resolved upon it. On the contrary, I believe in the correctness of the proposition that no man can bear to behold the infinite. That once became evident to me in an intellectual respect, and the expression for this is ignorance. That is to say ignorance is the negative expression for infinite knowledge. Suicide is the negative expression for infinite freedom. It is a form of the infinite freedom, but the negative form. Hail to him who finds the positive form.

With the highest respect,
I am deferentially yours."6

For Kierkegaard mystical brooding and isolation has no use for this temporal world. The temporal world then becomes a place of boredom. One enmeshed in such negative possibilities for infinitude looks again at his particular life and

> it appears to him that time, that the temporal, is his ruin; he demands a more perfect form of existence, and at this point there comes to evidence a fatigue, an apathy, which resembles the languor which is the attendant of pleasure. This apathy may rest so broodingly upon a man that suicide appears to him the only way of escape. No power can wrest from him his self; it checks him and delays, it arrests the embrace of the spirit with which he grasps his self. He has not chosen himself; like Narcissus he has fallen in love with himself. Such a situation has certainly ended not infrequently in suicide.
> The error lies in the fact that he has not chosen in the right way, not simply in the

sense that he had no eye for his error, but that he has seen himself under the category of necessity -- himself, this personality, with all these manifold characteristics, he has seen as part and parcel of the world-process, he has seen this self confronted by the eternal Power the fire of which pervades it without consuming it. But he has not seen himself in his freedom, has not chosen himself with freedom. If he does that, then the very instant he chooses himself he is in motion; concrete as his self is, he has nevertheless chosen himself in accordance with his possibility, in repentance he has ransomed himself for the sake of remaining in his freedom, but he can remain in his freedom only by constantly realizing it. He therefore, who has chosen himself is eo ipso active.[7]

This "choosing of one's self" is always a choice filled with anxiety. Every individual must of course come to know who he or she is in relation to his or her decision. Often such a choice conjures up another self-image. Such a self-image could then be deified. One could rigidly lock himself or herself into his or her image. Anything that would threaten the self-image would be a further cause of anxiety. However in Kierkegaard's thought, the real basis for the overcoming of the anxiety related both to "the choosing of one's self" and "the chosen self-image" is the Model (i.e., a Model who is more than mere example). This Model is Jesus Christ.

Shortly before Kierkegeard's own natural death, (age 42), he writes a short note commenting on Christ's cry from the cross:

My God, my God, why hast thou forsaken me?
(Matthew 27. 46)
These words indicate that the Model is not Stoicism, stoic self-satisfaction, but that he must and will hold out longer, to the point where the Stoic gives up (in suicide) because

he merely wants to have an idea of himself, and when he can no longer have this he prefers to kill himself, if possible to annihilate his life.

These words are a consolation to disciples. For was there ever a martyr who in the moments of greatest torment, or in a weak moment, was not on the verge of losing his idea of himself, as though he were forsaken by God? Then his life seems to him to be infinite despair: he is lost for this life, he has himself turned it into a torment -- and as for a better world, this must seem an even greater torment to him, to have to live a whole eternity and have the feeling, be persecuted by the memory, that he has lost his idea of himself.

This then is how the Model consoles us, by showing that this suffering is part of the following.

In a certain sense we may say that to feel oneself forsaken by God is part of the complete emptying of the human element in face of God, and that being a martyr is not a matter of human self-satisfaction.

But if this is so, then there is nothing depressing in being reminded that one has endured this human suffering of feeling oneself forsaken by God, of losing one's idea of oneself. For precisely this ultimate suffering restores in an eminent degree the idea of oneself.[8]

Now it is obvious that a great deal has not been said about how Kierkegaard came to hold such a view that a lost self-image under the cross of Christ really indicates a higher positive possible life in this life. Could it be that Kierkegaard came to understand a possibility of individual resurrection in this life which could not be destroyed? Ah, but Kierkegaard wishes no commentator to stand between him and his prospective readers. Consequently I can only refer the reader to some of his works listed in the bibliography and quietly sneak away.

B.   Fyodor Dostoevsky (1821-1881)[9]

As with Kierkegaard, Dostoevsky needs no interpreter between himself and the reader. I merely wish to make a few remarks which refer to Dostoevsky's view of Christ and suicide. In attempting to unravel how Dostoevsky came to understand and believe in Jesus Christ it should be mentioned that Dostoevsky was condemned to death on December 22, 1849 for his participation in a progressive political group of Russian intellectuals.[10] In a letter to his brother, Dostoevsky described his reprieve:

> Today, the 22nd of December, we were all taken to Semjonovsky Square. There the death-sentence was read to us, we were given the Cross to kiss, the dagger was broken over our heads, and our funeral toilet (white shirts) was made. Then three of us were put standing before the palisades for the execution of the death-sentence. I was sixth in the row; we were called up by groups of three, and so I was in the second group, and had not more than a minute to live. I thought of you, my brother, and of yours; in that last moment you alone were in my mind; then first I learnt how very much I love you, my beloved brother! I had time to embrace Plestcheiev and Dourov, who stood near me, and to take my leave of them. Finally, retreat was sounded, those who were bound to the palisades were brought back, and it was read to us that His Imperial Majesty granted us our lives. Then the final sentences were recited.[11]

The final sentence for Dostoevsky was four years in a Siberian prison. During this four year period Dostoevsky, who had already established himself as a novelist,[12] was denied the possibility of writing. Further, the Bible was one of the few books that he and the other prisoners were allowed to read.[13] Specialized Bible studies, sophisticated exegesis, and Biblical languages were of course unavailable to the murderers, thieves, madmen, peasants and political prisoners hovering for warmth around a coal stove.[14] Without the "wondrous" modern theological equipment the prisoners argued perpetually about the existence of God, the meaning of human life, and Jesus Christ.[15]

Upon his release from prison in 1854, Dostoevsky wrote to his brother:

> I won't even try to tell you what transformations were undergone by my soul, my faith, my mind, and my heart in those four years. It would be a long story. Still the eternal concentration, the escape into myself from bitter reality, did bear its fruit. I now have many new needs and hopes of which I never thought in other days.[16]

In March of the same year Dostoevsky writes to Mme. N. D. Fonvisin whose husband had also been imprisoned in Siberia at the same time.[17] With reference to her life of suffering Dostoevsky says:

> I have not lived your life, and much in it is unknown to me, and indeed, no one can really know exactly his fellow-mortal's life; still, human feeling is common to us all, and it seems to me that everyone who has been banished must live all his past grief over again in consciousness and memory on his return home. It is like a balance, by which one can test the true gravity of what one has endured, gone through, and lost. God grant you a long life! I have heard from many people that you are very religious. But not because you are religious, but because I myself have learnt it and gone through it, I want to say to you that in such moments, one does, "like dry

grass," thirst after faith, and that one finds it in the end, solely and simply because one sees the truth more clearly when one is unhappy. I want to say to you, about myself, that I am a child of this age, a child of unfaith and skepticism, and probably (indeed I know it) shall remain so to the end of my life. How dreadfully has it tormented me (and torments me even now) -- this longing for faith, which is all the stronger for the proofs I have against it. And yet God gives me sometimes moments of perfect peace; in such moments I love and believe that I am loved; in such moments I have formulated my creed; wherein all is clear and holy to me. This creed is extremely simple; here it is: I believe that there is nothing lovelier, deeper, more sympathetic, more rational, more manly, and more perfect than the Saviour; I say to myself with jealous love that not only is there no one else like Him, but that there could be no one. I would even say more: if anyone could prove to me that Christ is outside the truth, and if the truth really did exclude Christ, I should prefer to stay with Christ and not with truth.

I would rather not say anything more about it. And yet I don't know why certain topics may never be touched on in society, and why, if anyone does introduce them, it makes the others uncomfortable.[18]

Dostoevsky's creed established through his Siberian exile, his reading of the Bible and his love of the Russian people are blatantly manifested throughout the entirety of his later writings. In The House of the Dead (1861-62)[19] his four years in prison are described. The phenomenon of "the eternal concentration, the escape into myself from bitter reality"[20] is evident in Dostoevsky's novels such as The Insulted and Injured (1861),[21] Notes from the Underground (1864),[22] and A Raw Youth (1875).[23] Crime and Punishment (1865-66)[24] ends with Raskolnikov in Siberia asking for the New Testament.[25]

Dostoevsky's love of the Russian people is evident on every page he wrote but finds its most direct expression in <u>Winter Notes on Summer Impressions</u> (1863),[26] <u>The Idiot</u> (1868)[27] and <u>The Diary of a Writer</u> (1876—77).[28] Despite the fact that Dostoevsky was a compulsive gambler[29] and was thought by Turgenev to be aesthetically the Russian version of the Marquis De Sade,[30] he always attempted to hold to his creed that "If anyone could prove to me that Christ is outside the truth, and if the truth really did exclude Christ, I should prefer to stay with Christ and not with truth."[31] The finest aesthetic expression of this belief is found in the short story, <u>The Heavenly Christmas Tree</u> of 1876.[32] Here are his words:

> I am a novelist, and I suppose I have made up this story. I write "I suppose," though I know for a fact that I have made it up, but yet I keep fancying that it must have happened somewhere at sometime, that it must have happened on Christmas Eve in some great town in a time of terrible frost.
>   I have a vision of a boy, a little boy, six years old or even younger. This boy woke up that morning in a cold damp cellar. He was dressed in a sort of little dressing-gown and was shivering with cold. There was a cloud of white steam from his breath, and sitting on a box in the corner, he blew the steam out of his mouth and amused himself in his dullness watching it float away. But he was terribly hungry. Several times that morning he went up to the plank bed where his sick mother was lying on a mattress as thin as a pancake, with some sort of bundle on her head for a pillow. How had she come here? She must have come with her boy from some other town and suddenly fallen ill. The landlady who let the "corner" had been taken two days before to the police station, the lodgers were out and about as the holiday was so near, and only one left had been lying for the last twenty-four hours dead drunk, not having waited for Christmas.

In another corner of the room a wretched old woman of eighty, who had once been a children's nurse but was now left to die friendless, was moaning and groaning with rheumatism, scolding and grumbling at the boy so that he was afraid to go near her corner. He had got a drink of water in the outer room, but could not find a crust anywhere, and had been on the point of waking his mother a dozen times. He felt frightened at last in the darkness: it had long been dusk, but no light was kindled. Touching his mother's face, he was surprised that she did not move at all, and that she was as cold as the wall. "It is very cold here," he thought. He stood a little, unconsciously letting his hands rest on the dead woman's shoulders, then he breathed on his fingers to warm them, and then quietly fumbling for his cap on the bed, he went out of the cellar. He would have gone earlier, but was afraid of the big dog which had been howling all day at the neighbor's door at the top of the stairs. But the dog was not there now, and he went out into the street.

Mercy on us, what a town! He had never seen anything like it before. In the town from which he had come, it was always such black darkness at night. There was one lamp for the whole street, the little, low-pitched, wooden houses were closed up with shutters, there was no one to be seen in the street after dusk, all the people shut themselves up in their houses, and there was nothing but the howling of packs of dogs, hundreds and thousands of them barking and howling all night. But there it was so warm and he was given food, while here -- oh dear, if he only had something to eat! And what a noise and rattle here, what light and what people, horses and carriages, and what a frost! The frozen steam hung in clouds over the horses, over their warmly breathing mouths; their hoofs clanged against the stones through the powdery snow, and everyone pushed so, and -- oh, dear, how he longed for some morsel to eat, and how wretched he suddenly felt. A policeman walked by and turned away to avoid seeing the boy.

There was another street -- oh, what a wide one, here he would be run over for certain; how everyone was shouting, racing and driving along, and the light, the light! And what was this? A huge glass window, and through the window a tree reaching up to the ceiling; it was a fir tree, and on it were ever so many lights, gold papers and apples and little dolls and horses; and there were children clean and dressed in their best running about the room, laughing and playing and eating and drinking something. And then a little girl began dancing with one of the boys, what a pretty little girl! And he could hear the music through the window. The boy looked and wondered and laughed, though his toes were aching with the cold and his fingers were red and stiff so that it hurt him to move them. And all at once the boy remembered how his toes and fingers hurt him, and began crying, and ran on; and again through another window-pane he saw another Christmas tree, and on a table cakes of all sorts -- almond cakes, red cakes and yellow cakes, and three grand young ladies were sitting there, and they gave the cakes to anyone who went up to them, and the door kept opening, lots of gentlemen and ladies went in from the street. The boy crept up, suddenly opened the door and went in. Oh, how they shouted at him and waved him back! One lady went up to him hurriedly and slipped a kopeck into his hand, and with her own hands opened the door into the street for him! How frightened he was.

And the kopeck rolled away and clinked upon the steps; he could not bend his red fingers to hold it tight. The boy ran away and went on, where he did not know. He was ready to cry again but he was afraid, and ran on and on and blew his fingers. And he was miserable because he felt suddenly so lonely and terrified, and all at once, mercy on us! What was this again? People were standing in a crowd admiring. Behind a glass window there were three little dolls, dressed in red and green dresses, and exactly, exactly as though they were alive. One was a little old man sitting and playing a big violin, the two others were standing close by and playing little violins and nodding in time, and looking at one another, and their lips moved, they were speaking, actually speaking, only one couldn't hear through the glass. And at first the boy thought they were alive, and when he grasped that they were dolls he laughed. He had never seen such dolls before, and no idea there were such dolls! And he wanted to cry, but he felt amused, amused by the dolls. All at once he fancied that some one caught at his smock behind: a wicked big boy was standing beside him and suddenly hit him on the head, snatched off his cap and tripped him up. The boy fell down on the ground, at once there was a shout, he was numb with fright, he jumped up and ran away. He ran, not knowing where he was going, ran in at the gate of someone's courtyard, and sat down behind a stack of wood: "They won't find me here, besides it's dark!"

  He sat huddled up and was breathless from fright, and all at once, quite suddenly, he felt so happy: his hands and feet suddenly left off aching and grew so warm, as warm as though he were on a stove; then he gave a start, why, he must have been asleep. How nice to have a sleep here! "I'll sit here a little and go and look at the dolls again;" said the boy, and smiled thinking of them. "Just as though they were alive! . . . " And suddenly he heard his mother singing over him. "Mammy, I am asleep; how nice it is to sleep here!"

"Come to my Christmas tree, little one," a soft voice suddenly whispered over his head.

He thought that this was still his mother, but no, it was not she. Who it was calling him, he could not see, but some one bent over and embraced him in the darkness; and he stretched out his hands to him, and . . . and all at once -- oh, what a bright light! Oh, what a Christmas tree! And yet it was not a fir tree, he had never seen a tree like that! Where was he now? Everything was bright and shining, and all round him were dolls; but no, they were not dolls, they were little boys and girls, only so bright and shining. They all came flying round him, they all kissed him, took him and carried him along with them, and he was flying himself, and he saw that his mother was looking at him and laughing joyfully. "Mammy, Mammy; oh, how nice it is here, Mammy!" And again he kissed the children and wanted to tell them at once of those dolls in the shop window.

"Who are you, boys? Who are you, girls?" he asked, laughing and admiring them.

"This is Christ's Christmas tree," they answered. "Christ always has a Christmas tree on this day, for the little children who have no tree of their own . . . " And he found out that all these little boys and girls were children just like himself; that some had been frozen in the baskets in which they had as babies been laid on the doorsteps of well-to-do Petersburg people, others had been boarded out with Finnish women by the Foundling and had been suffocated, others had died at their starved mother's breasts (in the Samara famine), others had died in the third-class railway carriages from the foul air; and yet they were all here, they were all like angels about Christ, and He was in the midst of them and held out His hands to them and blessed them and their sinful mothers. . . . And the mothers of these children stood on one side weeping; each one knew her boy or girl, and the children flew up to them and kissed them and wiped away their tears with their little hands, and begged them not to weep because they were so happy.

And down below in the morning the porter found the little dead body of the frozen child on the woodstack; they sought out his mother. . . . She had died before him. They met before the Lord God in heaven.

Why have I made up such a story, so out of keeping with an ordinary diary, and a writer's above all? And I promised two stories dealing with real events! But that is just it, I keep fancying that all this may have happened really -- that is, what took place in the cellar and on the woodstack; but as for Christ's Christmas tree, I cannot tell you whether that could have happened or not.[33]

It is important to remember that this short story was written in 1876. It is important because one of Dostoevsky's more famous works, The Brothers Karamazov, appeared during the years 1879-1880.[34]

The Brothers Karamazov ends at the cemetery where a small dead boy, "Little Ilyusha," is being buried. Kolya, a precocious and thoughtful adolescent, addresses the ex-monk Alyosha Karamazov:

"Karamazov," cried Kolya, "Is it really true that, as our religion tells us, we shall all rise from the dead and come to life and see one another again, all, and Ilyusha?"

"Certainly we shall rise again, certainly we shall see one another, and shall tell one another gladly and joyfully all that has been" Alyosha replied, half laughing, half rapturously.

"Oh, how wonderful it will be!" Kolya cried.[35]

This belief in the actual resurrection of the dead as portrayed in <u>The Heavenly Christmas Tree</u>, (1876) and <u>The Brothers Karamozov</u>, (1879-80) is really Dostoevsky's final illustration of what he really believed his creed to mean. This is true because Dostoevsky dies in 1881. In both of his descriptions of resurrection, the resurrection is described in such terms as to affirm the complete spiritual and physical fulfillment of everyone. That is, in <u>The Heavenly Christmas Tree</u> the small child sees light, sees a Christmas tree, sees other boys and girls, and experiences Love and happiness.[36] At the conclusion of <u>The Brothers Karamozov</u> the description of the final state of everyone is:

"Certainly we shall rise again, certainly we shall see one another, and shall tell one another gladly and joyfully all that has been."[37]

In this instance actual conversation about our lives is used to portray the completeness of Christ-The-Creator's preservation of everyone's physical and spiritual nature regardless of death.

II

Thus far in this brief outline of Dostoevsky's thought an effort has been made to establish what Dostoevsky meant by his creed, his faith, and his attitude toward Jesus Christ. It was seen that his belief came about through suffering. Further it was contended that this faith establishes the recognition of an invulnerable life in which everything within everyone is completely fulfilled through Christ's Love.

However, it is not to be forgotten that Dostoevsky in 1854 also described himself by saying

> ... I am a child of the age, a child of unfaith and scepticism, and probably (indeed I know it) shall remain so to the end of my life.[38]

It has already been seen that he may not have remained such a child to the end of his life. However, Dostoevsky always did understand the age of scepticism and unfaith. This is especially important in relation to the question of suicide. In Dostoevsky's journalistic enterprise, The Diary of a Writer, there is the description of the inward logic of a sceptical materialist. The entry is dated October, 1876.[39] The materialist's argument is simply that the universe is indifferent, meaningless and absurd. Man consciously suffers because of nature's indifference, meaninglessness and absurdity. Therefore there is no reason why one should not kill himself. The materialist decides to annihilate himself. These are his final words

> "Now, therefore, in my unmistakable role of plaintiff and of a defendent, of a judge and of an accused, I sentence this nature, which has so unceremoniously and impudently brought me into existence for suffering, to annihilation, together with myself. . . . And because I am unable to destroy nature, I am destroying only myself, weary of enduring a tyranny in which there is no guilty one.
>
> N.N."[40]

One of Dostoevsky's readers, N. P., wrote to him concerning the materialist's (N.N.'s) suicide. Dostoevsky in the December, 1876 entry of The Diary of a Writer,[41] summarizes N.P.'s attitude concerning the materialist (N.N.).

Dostoevsky further states his view of suicide. Here are Dostoevsky's words in response to his inquiring reader, N.P.:

> He (N.P.) says that the "deliberation" of my suicide is merely "the delirium of a half-crazy man," and that that is "well known." I am very much inclined to believe that the "deliberation" became "known" to him only after he had read my article. As to the "delirium of a half-crazy man" (is this known to Mr. N. P. and the whole collection of the N.P.'s?), it -- i.e. the inference of the necessity of suicide -- is too much to many people in Europe, as it were, the last word of science. I have expressed this "this last word of science" in brief terms, clearly and popularly, with the sole purpose of refuting it -- not by reasoning or logic, since it cannot be refuted by logic (I challenge not only Mr. N. P. but anyone to refute logically this "delirium of the insane"), but by faith, by the deduction of the necessity of faith in the immortality of man's soul; by the inference of the conviction that this faith is the only source of "live life" on earth -- of life health, sane ideas and sound deductions and inferences....[42]

The refutation of <u>this</u> type of suicide

> by faith, by the deduction of the necessity of faith in the immortality of man's soul; by the inference of the conviction that this faith is the only source of "live life" on earth -- of life, health, sane ideas and sound deductions and inferences....[43]

is found throughout all of Dostoevsky's writings which deal with suicide. Before this can be scholarly established it is beneficial to remember that completed faith for Dostoevsky was acquired over a period of years. Further "the immortality of man's soul" has already been seen to be something far more embracing and fulfilling than mere specters hovering in a darkened, melancholic realm. On the contrary, faith and immortality are determined by Christ's Love, Light, and Freedom. Such acquired faith in everyone's immortality is the source of "'live life' on earth -- of life, health, sane ideas and sound deductions and inferences. . . ."[44]

It would now be appropriate to analyze some of Dostoevsky's characters who possessed and were possessed by a variety of "false faiths" all of which contributed to their own self-destruction. That is, their obsessional and confused beliefs in "gods" led them to death, disease, insane ideas and unsound deductions and inferences.

Dostoevsky wrote The Possessed (also translated as The Devils) during the years 1870-72.[45] Within this novel four suicides are described. The first person to actually commit suicide is a young man "not more than nineteen."[46] His parents who lived in the country had apprehensively entrusted him with four-hundred roubles with which he was to buy articles for his sister's trousseau. He was supposed to go to his parents' relatives' house in town, spend the night, and then do the shopping for his sister the next day. However when he arrives in town, the young man decides to get a hotel room, look for gambling houses, and visit gypsies. He returns to his hotel room and orders champagne and a sumptuous dinner. He becomes too drunk to eat the dinner. In the early morning, he writes a note that he has squandered the family fortune. He then shoots himself. When the people of the town break down the door and find the young man, someone notes the expression on the nineteen year old's face.

> There was no trace of the anguish of death in the face; the expression was serene, almost happy as though there were no cares in his life.[47]

Many people of the town who had come into the room in order to relieve their boredom commented that this suicide was of course "the best way out of it" and that "he had had a good time if only for a moment."[48] However someone suddenly blurted out the inquiry why people had begun shooting themselves among us of late, as though they had suddenly lost their roots, as though the ground were giving way under every one's feet. People looked coldly at this <u>raisonneur</u>.[49]

The second actual suicide described in <u>The Possessed</u> is the suicide of a twelve year old girl. However Dostoevsky does not always allow the commentator to be strictly systematic. I will thus be forced to discuss her suicide in connection with Stavrogin, the fourth suicide described in <u>The Possessed</u>.

The third suicide is that of Kirillov. Kirillov had once traveled to the United States in order to discover the "American dream." However the American dream had proven itself to be a nightmare.[50] Kirillov then returned to Russia, began associating with Nihilists and continued to live a life of isolated brooding. The source of his brooding is the question of God and the question of suicide. Kirillov is for Dostoevsky a prime example of the idealistic and confused thinker whose conclusions are unsound, diseased, and wrong. Although Kirillov has the highest aspiration -- to become God -- neither his method nor his basis for becoming God is in any way sound. Now there is nothing wrong in wanting to become God. Athanasius (of Chapter II) actually did believe that man was to become God. However the method, basis and source of Athanasius saying that Christ "assumed humanity that we might become God" is not at all the same method, basis and source of Kirillov. Kirillov contends that human beings will become "gods" when they commit suicide. For Kirillov there are two types of suicides:

> those who kill themselves either from great sorrow or from spite, or being mad, or no matter what . . . they do it suddenly. They think little about pain, but kill themselves suddenly. But some do it from reason -- they think a great deal.[51]

For Kirillov superstition, pain, and fear have stopped people from killing themselves.[52] Kirillov's "god" is simply the fear of death, a deterrent force that keeps human beings bound to a life of servitude.[53] When this "god" is overcome through man's suicide, man will become "god."[54] Kirillov's "god" has tortured him all his life and Kirillov wishes to rebel against and destroy this "god."[55]

Finally after Kirillov has been partially goaded by the Nihilists' leader, Pyotor Stepanovitch, Kirillov actually does kill himself.[56] Although Kirillov <u>thinks</u> he is committing suicide by his own completely free will[57] the Nihilist Pyotor Stepanovitch's (Pyotor Stepanovitch was for Dostoevsky the personification of the devil) influence is an unmistakable factor in Kirillov's suicide.[58] Before his suicide Kirillov makes a few comments on whom he thought Christ to be. He asks Pyotor Stepanovitch:

> "Believe in whom? In <u>Him</u>? Listen." Kirillov stood still, gazing before him with fixed and ecstatic look. "Listen to a great idea: there was a day on earth, and in the midst of the earth there stood three crosses. One on the Cross had such faith that he said to another, 'Today thou shalt be with me in Paradise.' The day ended; both died and passed away and found neither Paradise nor resurrection. His words did not come true. Listen: that Man was the loftiest of all on earth. He was that which gave meaning to life. The whole planet, with everything on it, is mere madness without that Man. There has never been any like Him before or since, never, up to a miracle. For that is the miracle, that there never was or never will be another like Him. And if that is so, if the laws of nature did not spare even Him, have not spared even their miracle and made even Him live in a lie and die for a lie, then all the planet is a lie and rests on a lie and on mockery. So then, the very laws of the

planet are a lie and the vaudeville of devils. What is there to live for? Answer, if you are a man."[59]

Although Kirillov admires an ideal type of "christ" which for Kirillov is the unique occurrence in the history of the world, this ideal type of "christ" was bound and destroyed by natural laws. That is, Kirillov <u>does not believe</u> in the actual resurrection of Jesus Christ. Although Kirillov's thought is more idealistic than the sceptical materialist (see footnote 40, Chapter 4 of this essay), Kirillov does not attempt a fight for faith in the resurrection. That is, Kirillov does not attempt a real refutation of suicide

> by faith, by the deduction of the necessity of faith in the immortality of man's soul; by the inference of the conviction that this faith is the only source of "live life" on earth -- of life, health, sane ideas and sound deductions and inferences. . . .[60]

The second and fourth suicides in <u>The Possessed</u> are the suicides of a twelve year old girl and Nikolay Stavrogin. Nikolay Stavrogin is the son of an aristocrat. As far as natural gifts are concerned he possesses wealth, good looks, intelligence, physical strength, and enough political connections as a birth right to become a great hope for Russia. However Stavrogin is susceptible to giving in to strange impulses. He pulls one dignitary by the nose, bites a bureaucrat's ear, and, at a party, kisses rapturously the wife of his host with the purpose of offending everyone. As the novel progresses Stavrogin's strange behavior is discovered to have its basis in the debauched manner in which he spent his early twenties. However, Stavrogin always wishes to take full responsibility for his activity.[61] Further he desires to make a public confession of his wretched past.[62] He goes to the Russian monk, Tihon, and gives the monk his written confession.[63] In the confession Stavrogin relates how he, out of boredom, seduced a twelve year old girl. The young girl, being confused and overcome, was apparently not altogether unwilling.[64] However soon after her seduction, she hanged herself.⁶⁵ After this Stavrogin thought of shooting himself. But a "better" idea occurred to him one night while he was drunk. He decided to marry a pathetic crippled woman. The next day he married her. However he soon deserts her and begins to wander about the world dreaming about a Platonic heaven while he remains living in a morbidly real hell.

After the monk, Tihon, has been informed of Stavrogin's past, the monk advises Stavrogin not to make his confession public. Tihon says this because in his opinion Stavrogin is only interested in publishing his confession in order that he may boast of his sins. The monk feels that Stavrogin's real intention is to mock everyone. Tihon then gives Stavrogin some "churchly" advice which Stavrogin mocks. He and the monk part company.⁶⁶

Stavrogin decides not to publish his confession. As the novel continues Stavrogin by tacit assent allows his crippled wife to be murdered.⁶⁷ He runs off with another woman who is also later murdered at the scene of Stavrogin's crippled wife's murder.⁶⁸ Stavrogin finally goes away alone, despairs, and hangs himself.⁶⁹ Dostoevsky ends <u>The Possessed</u> with these words:

> The strong silk cord upon which Nikolay Vsyevolodovitch* had hanged himself had evidently been chosen and prepared beforehand and was thickly smeared with soap. Everything proved that there had keen premeditation and consciousness up to the last moment.
> At the inquest our doctors absolutely and emphatically rejected all idea of insanity.⁷⁰

Dostoevsky never denies that there is a moral law operative in the universe. However this moral law is not a general humanistic moral law. Rather it is a law empowered and fulfilled by Jesus Christ's Activity of Love and Freedom

---

* i.e., Stavrogin

as manifested The Heavenly Christmas Tree and at the conclusion of The Brothers Karamazov. Thus there is no possibility that Stavrogin will have to endure further torments in another life. However, this life . . . yes, that was a problem. . . .

In Dostoevsky 's novel of 1875, A Raw Youth, a young student named Kraft shoots himself with elements of the same type of obsessional logic and deductions as Kirillov.[71] In Dostoevsky's short story of 1876, A Gentle Spirit, a girl between the age of sixteen and eighteen kills herself after an egotistical (egotistical for both herself and her husband) battle of the sexes between herself and her husband.[72] In The Diary of a Writer, entry for October 1876, Dostoevsky records a suicide note written in boredom by a twenty-three or twenty-four year old girl who did commit suicide. Here is her note:

> "I am undertaking a long journey. If I should not succeed, let people gather to celebrate my resurrection with a bottle of Cliquot. If I should succeed, I ask that I be interred only after I am altogether dead, since it is very disagreeable to awake in a coffin in the earth. It is not chic!"[73]

Finally in The Brothers Karamazov, (1879-1880), Dostoevsky portrays the suicide of Smerdyakov, the epileptic servant of the Karamazov household who masterminded old man Karamazov's murder. The basis of Smerdyakov murdering old man Karamazov and his own suicide is directly connected with Ivan's nihilism,[74] (Ivan is Karamazov's atheistic son) and Ivan's idealistic and moralistic "false christ" (i.e. , "christ" as example not Christ as Power, Love, and Freedom) as displayed in the chapter entitled "The Grand Inquisitor."[75] Further Ivan's thought that "all is permitted" since there is no "god" with its corollary that there is no "god" because little children suffer and die, are all influences which motivate the epileptic Smerdyakov to murder old man Karamazov. Smerdyakov then kills himself [76] and Ivan meets the devil.[77] The devil is of course the direct outcome of Ivan's "false christ," nihilism, and his conclusions based upon supposedly dead children. As was seen in Dostoevsky's creed, The Heavenly Christmas Tree. and the end of The Brothers Karamazov, Dostoevsky did not himself hold any other view except that everyone is finally completely fulfilled by, through, and with Jesus Christ's Activity. Indeed, for Dostoevsky, the True God and the True Jesus Christ are that Love, Power, and Freedom which shall ultimately and finally overcome all suffering, pain, and death for everyone. This is Dostoevsky's faith assertion, an assertion he was finally able to make despite his own scepticism and unbelief.

But what have I done? I promised the reader that I would only make a few comments and let Dostoevsky speak for himself. Given the vastness of Dostoevsky's thought simply on one subject -- suicide -- I have done only that.

C. Schopenhauer, Nietzsche, and Camus

a. Arthur Schopenhauer (1788-1860)[78]

For Schopenhauer there is a graded scale of suicidal behavior. The "lowest" on this "suicide scale" is the individual who commits suicide out of despair thinking that he will escape life's sufferings.[79] The "highest" type of suicide is one in which a person would ascetically starve himself to death.

> Between this voluntary death arising from extreme asceticism and the common suicide resulting from despair there may be various intermediate species and combinations, though this is hard to find out.[80]

For Schopenhauer the world into which we are born is a world ruled by a wild and uncontrollable force known as the "will-as-thing-in-itself." This "will-as-thing-in itself" manifests itself in the aimless birth and decay of nature. However the phenomena of natural birth and death are not the complete manifestations of the "will-as-thing-in-itself." The "will-as--thing-in-itself" cannot really be known directly. What can be known indirectly about the "will-as-thing-in-itself" is the suffering, meaninglessness, and folly which are also some of the "will-as--thing-in-itself's" manifestations. However the "will-as-the-thing-in-itself's" activity does in certain instances strike human consciousness in such a way as to yield through philosophy and the arts an intuition of the "will-as-thing-in-itself's" surging power.

Thus through human consciousness some human beings can become aware of the "will-as-thing-in-itself's" activity. That is, for a select few, human consciousness is a philosophical and aesthetic means for obtaining freedom from the "will-as-thing in-itself's" activity. The more knowledge, the more ideas, the more art created through human intuition about the "will-as-thing-in-itself," the more freedom there is.

As one attempts to gain knowledge about the "will-as-thing-in-itself" one discovers that another manifestation of the "will-as-thing-in-itself" is "the will to live." For Schopenhauer this "will to live" is really the will to chaos, bondage, and despair. That is, for Schopenhauer, this "will to live" is a will to suffering. For an individual to escape this suffering caused by the "will to live" he must pursue knowledge and fast, refrain from sexual intercourse, and in every way deny his natural appetites.

Schopenhauer attempts to be consistent. To kill oneself rashly as an act of despair is really an act motivated by the "will to live." That is, such a suicide would really be a chaotic and rash act with its basis in the "will to live." However to patiently starve oneself to death by denying the "will to live," and by accepting the suffering involved in starving to death, one really does, for Schopenhauer, rise above the "will to live."

> No other death than that by starvation is in this case conceivable . . . for the intention to cut short the torment would itself be a stage in the assetion of will.*[81]

---

* i.e., the "will to live"

Well, I suppose that is a consistency of sorts.

Schopenhauer does do an admirable job of destroying religious and secular legalism which could offend the consciences of those people stricken with suicidal behavior.[82]

But what does he put in its place? In its place Schopenhauer establishes a graded scale ranging from ascetic death by starvation to the suicide of despair. One of Schopenhauer's sources for the ascetic suicide is a man who was led into the woods by some "spirit" and starved to death in the woods reading a Bible.[83] I do not know about this ascetic's reading habits or how weak he became, but after Christ was in the desert he was found among men, women and children, drinking wine, curing diseases, giving life more abundantly, etc. But for Schopenhauer "jesus" is just another ascetic.[84]

What am I to say? Obviously there is something not quite right with Schopenhauer's view of life. Obviously Jesus Christ had something completely different in mind. But I do not wish to drag this contrast out too far and bore the reader. I would only like to tell a brief story about a gangland killing that happened fifty years ago. Obviously for Schopenhauer murder would also be a part of the "will to live."

The killing occurred near a large city in the United States. One of the gang called "T" had betrayed the gang's rather dubious honor. "T's" allotted henchman gave "T" an alternative. These are the henchman's words:

> "If you stand here I'll stab you to death. If you run I'll shoot you to death. But, if you go and drown yourself in the river, I'll forgive you."*

---

* Unrecorded source.

b.   Friedrich Nietzsche (1844-1900)[85]

In order to analyze Nietzsche's thought on suicide, it is best to become briefly acquainted with what Nietzsche believed to be the justification of life. In his first book, The Birth of Tragedy (1872),[86] Nietzsche asserts "it is only as an aesthetic phenomenon that existence and the world are eternally justified."[87] For Nietzsche the will to life manifested in the birth and death of natural phenomenon is a source for artistic expression. In the process of this expression one is to mold through one's own individual will not only aesthetic works (i.e., tragedies, music, poems, sculpture) but also one's self. Unlike Schopenhauer, Nietzsche wills to hurl himself into the vortex of the will to live. Further, for Nietzsche, the natural will to live is an overloaded tree of fruits. The "great creators" (or "overmen") such as Leonardo da Vinci, Goethe, and Beethoven had, through suffering and genius, learned how to pick such fruits and mold them into high forms of aesthetic production. Further, such men had molded themselves into "higher" types of men.

One of Nietzsche's final works, a collection of notes entitled The Will to Power (1884-1888),[88] ends with:

> This world is the will to power -- and nothing besides! And you yourselves are also this will to power -- and nothing besides.[89]

For Nietzsche everyone wills to be either controlled (despicable herd or slave morality) or control (noble overman morality). Those overmen who succeed in mastering either purely aesthetic forms (example Beethoven) or aesthetic politics (ex. Caesar and/or Caesar Borgia) are men above criticism. They are beyond good and evil.

Thus for Nietzsche the aesthetic justification for the world has its concomitant in the will to power which is the activity of perpetually molding artistic expression, one's self, and the world. Further this process of molding is really left up to the "superior man's" choice as to what he will select from the heavy laden tree of "creativity."

Of course for Nietzsche there are some "inferior" people who do not really belong on this tree but are forced to hang upon it. In the first part of Thus Spoke Zarathustra (1883)[90] Nietzsche says:

> All-too-many live, and all-too-long they hang on their branches. Would that a storm came to shake all this worm-eaten rot from the tree![91]

Nietzsche believes that he is the first wind of such a storm, He advocates voluntary death at the right (?) natural time.

> One must cease letting oneself be eaten when one tastes best: that is known to those who want to be loved long. There are sour apples, to be sure, whose lot requires that they wait till the last day of autumn: and they become ripe, yellow, and wrinkled all at once. In some, the heart grows old first: in others, the spirit. And some are old in their youth: but late youth preserves long youth.
> For some, life turns out badly: a poisonous worm eats its way to their heart. Let them see to it that their dying turns out that much better. Some never become sweet: they rot already in the summer. It is cowardice that keeps them on their branch.[92]

Thus for Nietzsche to die at the right time (?) is best; "second to this, however, is to die fighting and to squander a great soul."[93]

Also for Nietzsche:

> Some become too old even for their truths and victories: a toothless mouth no longer has the right to every truth.[94]

This same attitude of "voluntary death" at the right (?) time is also mentioned in Human, All-Too-Human (1878).[95] In The Dawn of Day(1881),[96] Nietzsche advises that incurable criminals be allowed to kill themselves.[97] In The Joyful Wisdom (1832)[98] Nietzsche discusses

> Christianity and Suicide. -- Christianity made use of the excessive longing for suicide at the time of its origin as a lever for its power: it left only two forms of suicide, invested them with the highest dignity and the highest hopes, and forbade all others with dreadful threatenings. But martyrdom and the slow self-annihilation of the ascetic were permitted.[99]

For Nietzsche "the Hebrew jesus" is really a melancholic figure whose truth has been far surpassed by Nietzsche's own wisdom.[100] Nietzsche in The Twilight of the Idols (1888),[101] decides to counsel medical doctors:

> A moral for doctors: -- The sick man is a parasite of society. In certain cases it is indecent to go on living. To continue to vegetate in a state of cowardly dependence upon doctors and special treatments, once the meaning of life, the right to life, has been lost, ought to be regarded with the greatest contempt by society. The doctors, for their part, should be the agents for imparting this contempt, -- they should no longer prepare prescriptions, but should every day administer a fresh dose of disgust to their patients. A new responsibility should be created, that of the doctor -- the responsibility of ruthlessly suppressing and eliminating degenerate life, in all cases in which the highest interests of life itself, of ascending life, demand such a course. . . . [102]

Nietzsche's aesthetic justification of life begins to show rather ugly tendencies when he attempts to give medical advice. Medical advice is of course advice with social ramifications. Further that which affects society will quite frequently infect politics. And, well, no matter how much Nietzsche scholars would like to look the other way, Doctor Hitler (a fan of Nietzsche) used a more than "ugly" scalpel on the body-politic.

Finally in the name of "superior men," the tree of fruits, and "the ascending life," Nietzsche concludes his thoughts on suicide with a reference to pessimism "one should in the first place deny <u>Schopenhauer</u>."[103] Fine, but should anyone accept Nietzsche?

c. Albert Camus (1913-1960)[104]

Albert Camus' <u>The Myth of Sisyphus</u> was written in 1940 when Camus was twenty-seven years old.[105] Camus at the age of thirty—eight[106] explains the methodology of <u>The Myth of Sisyphus</u>:

> When I analyzed the feeling of the Absurd in <u>The Myth of Sisyphus</u>, I was looking for a method and not a doctrine. I was practicing methodical doubt. I was trying to make a "<u>tabula rasa,</u>" on the basis of which it would then be possible to construct something.[107]

This should be noted because I have been recently informed of a California student who has killed himself with sleeping pills. He was eighteen. Apparently his first philosophy book was <u>The Myth of Sisyphus.</u> His final known thoughts were that he did not feel that he had the strength or endurance to take the tragic stance of Sisyphus with respect to this world. Camus wrote a book at the age of twenty-seven. At the age of thirty-eight he maintains that he was <u>not</u> asserting a doctrine.

On November 15, 1945[108] Camus states:

> The only book of ideas that I have published, The Myth of Sisyphus, was directed against so-called existentialist philosophers.[109]

I do not know how Camus comes to his conclusions concerning the thought of some of the "so-called existentialist philosophers" which Camus thinks he has written against. In common intellectual lore Kierkegaard, Nietzsche, and Dostoevsky are typed as "existentialist philosophers." Fine, let's take a look at how Camus wishes to interpret them.

1) Kierkegaard. Camus' basic contention is that Kierkegaard leaped forth into some type of weird "christian absolute,"[110] sacrificed his intellect,[111] and, in order to overcome his despair,[112] was swallowed up in his "god."[113] I could say that Kierkegaard spent at least his whole life trying to explain what "this leap" meant (but for Camus it is a weird "christian absolute" to which he leaps). I could say that Kierkegaard wrote over thirty highly complex volumes ranging from depth psychology to the confrontation with Christ Himself (but for Camus Kierkegaard "sacrificed his intellect"). I could say that for Kierkegaard despair, death, and anxiety are always held by the individual in dialectical tension with Christ's contemporaniety with us (but for Camus Kierkegaard was "swallowed up in his god" in a rather [all said and done] sniveling manner). Alas, using one of Cicero's nasty rhetorical tricks* I have said all of that. But I am not happy that I have said all of that because Kierkegaard always wanted to speak for himself. In total embarrassment I recommend to the interested reader two of Kierkegaard's works: Training in Christianity and Judge for Yourselves. (By all means, judge for yourselves!) Finally, Camus does not mention what Kierkegaard actually thought about suicide.

2) Nietzsche. It is astounding that in The Myth of Sisyphus only the positive aspects of Nietzsche's aesthetic justification for life are mentioned.[114] Not one of Nietzsche's

---

* Cicero, Orations Against Cataline.

twisted thoughts in relation to suicide can be found. Of course Camus at the age of thirty-eight states that Hegel, Marx, and Nietzsche are the evil geniuses of contemporary Europe.[115] When Camus is asked if Nietzsche was one of his "spiritual" ancestors, Camus replies:

> He is, undoubtedly. What is admirable, in Nietzsche, is that you always find in him something to correct what is dangerous elsewhere in his ideas. I place him infinitely higher than the two others.[116]

Now this is written by a man who was a member of the French Resistance against the Nazis. Yes, if you have the time to read through a great deal of Nietzsche, have aesthetic ability, and have the opportunity to forcibly combat Doctor Hitler; well, yes, there are many things in Nietzsche. But if you are a toothless, overripe fruit? But if you are not "a great creator"? But . . . if you are a Jew?

3) Dostoevsky. For Camus Ivan Karamazov's statement "Everything is permitted" is not to be taken in the "vulgar sense."[117] Well now! In Dostoevsky's thought Ivan's statement leads Smerdyakov to kill old man Karamazov. Smerdyakov commits suicide, and Ivan begins an insane conversation with the devil. Vulgar? A great deal more than "vulgar" or "not vulgar."

One of Camus' statements about Dostoevsky's muddled characters, Kirillov of The Possessed, is that "he (i.e., Kirillov) is not mad or else Dostoevsky is."[118] As can be seen from section B in this chapter, this is no interpretation of Dostoevsky. Dostoevsky quite clearly saw the flaws in Kirillov's argument. The character of Kirillov is simply used by Dostoevsky to illustrate a completely false attitude towards Jesus Christ. This is affirmed not only by quotations from The Diary of a Writer and the conclusion of The Brothers Karamazov (which Camus makes partial use of), but also by Dostoevsky's own creed formulated after his release from Siberia and The Heavenly Christmas Tree. It is therefore obvious that Kirillov's madness or sanity <u>is not</u> Dostoevsky's madness or sanity.

For Camus Stavrogin (another character of <u>The Possessed</u>), leads an "ironic" life.[119] What irony! Stavrogin seduces a twelve year old girl who later hangs herself because of Stavrogin's seduction. What irony! Stavrogin in a drunken reverie marries a crippled woman and is then implicated in her murder. What irony! Stavrogin finally with a soap-slicked cord, hangs himself, <u>What</u> "irony"?

Camus never mentions the many varied types of suicide in Dostoevsky's writings which might not be "philosophically or artistically" interesting. Of course Camus says:

> I am not interested in philosophical suicide, but rather in plain suicide. I merely wish to purge it of its emotional content and know its logic and integrity.[120]

But where, (oh where?) in <u>The Myth of Sisyphus</u> is there a plain suicide? And where (oh where?) on the face of this earth has there been, is there, or will there be found a suicide purged of "its emotional content"? After all, a horse without legs, a head, a neck, a torso, or a tail is not much of a horse. Dostoevsky never followed such a presumptuous intellectual method. On the contrary his writings also describe the suicides of many simple and plain people who might not be considered philosophically or artistically interesting.

Towards the end of The <u>Myth of Sisyphus</u> Camus makes this comment with respect to the affirmation of everyone's personal resurrection as found in Dostoevsky's conclusion of <u>The Brothers Karamazov</u>:

> what contradicts the absurd is not its Christian character, but rather its announcing a future life.[121]

Here is a quotation which may be of aid in distinguishing what pertains to the "Christian character" of anything and what pertains to Christ's Freedom. This quotation is from Paul the Apostle:

> Why am I in peril every hour? I protest, brethren, by my pride in you which, I have in Christ Jesus our Lord, I die every day! What do I gain if, humanly speaking, I fought with beasts at Ephesus? If the dead are not raised, "Let us eat and drink for tomorrow we die." Do not be deceived: "Bad company ruins good morals."[122]

What Camus means by the "Christian character" of anything is anyone's guess. But, for the Apostle Paul, Christ's Freedom is never to be separated from the faith assertion of individual, personal resurrection. Anyone or anything that asserts something other than such a resurrection is simply asserting something other than Christ's Freedom. In this present discussion the "beasts at Ephesus" and "bad company" are the beasts and bad company derived from "false christs." False christs, as has been seen throughout this essay, definitely "ruin good morals." And a "false christ" or false view of Christ is such a "christ" or view of Christ which would deny or attempt to hide Paul's assertion of the actual, individual and personal resurrection of the dead.

Camus of course denies the "illusion" of another world.[123] Actually as Camus himself states, the entirety of his argument for the absurd depends on death.[124] That is, for Camus the universe is closed[125] by death and the man devoid of "illusions" must live "without appeal"[126] before death. For Camus such a life is one of revolt, freedom, and passion.[127] But such revolt, freedom, and passion is determined by death.

Thus the heavy stone which Sisyphus pushes is really the consciousness of death. But if there is no longer death then there is no longer a heavy stone. If there is no longer a heavy stone then <u>The Myth of Sisyphus</u> is, as many myths, absurd. Further the morality based upon death which crops up throughout The Myth of Sisyphus in such statements as:

> Schopenhauer is often cited, as a fit subject for laughter, because he praised suicide while seated at a well-set table. This is no subject for joking. That way of not taking the tragic seriously is not so grievous, but it helps to judge a man,[128]

need not offend anyone's conscience even if he or she is not "all that tragic." (Camus, as in other cases, does not really inform us as to Schopenhauer's view of suicide.) Further no one is bound to accept Camus' view of this world or judgments since Camus is not speaking doctrinally (although Camus' thought could be interpreted doctrinally). Nor should anyone destroy himself because of Camus' would-be view of a world determined by death. After all, there are innumerable debates about immortality in every culture at all times and there is no reason why one should accept one man's opinion. If one does not know whether there is a resurrection of the dead or not, one should in all honesty simply say, "I don't know." Wisdom in ignorance and ignorance in wisdom are valid philosophical principles. But to say that there is no resurrection of the dead and that another world is an illusion, well, that is simply an illusory statement.

CHAPTER V

Three Notes on General Culture and Suicidal Behavior

1.

It is finally 1972. According to the Chinese calendar it is "The-Year-of-the-Rat." Plastic artificial trees are being "planted" along the freeways in Los Angeles, California. Apparently the air is so bad no one knows if the plastic trees will survive. The politicians of the world are playing "hot potato" with hydrogen bombs. Drug abuse claims a variety of victims daily. The number of actual suicides continues to increase.

Of course the upward trend in actual suicides is not an isolated factor. What is a plastic tree? Only a dire testimony of man's self-destructive behavior in relation to ecology. What is the political game of "hot potato" with hydrogen bombs? Only another manifestation of man's suicidal behavior in relation to politics. What is the misuse of drugs? Simply a premature flirtation with one's own coffin.

In this modern age of the plastic tree, the hydrogen bomb, the pill bottle, and unnatural death, another monstrosity has occurred which attempts to add the final destructive touch to our "wondrous" era. I am of course speaking of "the suicidal christ-figure." If an age is suicidal it does not follow that the Triune God's Activity as manifested in Jesus Christ's Love and Freedom must also be suicidal.

The consequences of such a false suicidal "christ figure" are abominable. Surprisingly these consequences were partially foreseen in the nineteenth century by Friedrich Schleiermacher (1768-1834).[1]

> We must not set forth Christ's surrender of Himself to death as a free decision on His part in any other sense than that which is here taken as fundamental, namely, that His self-surrender was identical with His persistence in redemptive activity.[2]

For Schleiermacher there are three phases of consciousness which describe human consciousness. First, there is the <u>confused-animal phase</u> of human self-consciousness.[3] The <u>confused-animal phase</u> of human consciousness is that phase of self-consciousness in which natural unconscious and libidinal drives, projections, and magical figures predominate. In the history of religions the confused-animal phase of human self-consciousness is outwardly manifested as idol-worship.[4]

The second phase of human self-consciousness is the <u>sensible-reciprocal phase</u> of human self-consciousness. The sensible-reciprocal phase of human self-consciousness describes the activity of human persons in the give and take of human social activity. That is, the sensible-reciprocal phase of human self-consciousness is related to the "social and moral feelings"[5] which are active in human life. Since this phase of human self-consciousness has a variety of motivations and bases for motivation, its outward expression in the history of religions is polytheism.[6]

The third phase of human self-consciousness is described as <u>the feeling of absolute dependence</u>.[7] The feeling of absolute dependence indicates a basic harmony underlying both the confused-animal phase of human self-consciousness and the sensible-reciprocal phase of human self-consciousness. That is, the feeling of absolute dependence is the most passive and developed phase of human self-consciousness. However the passivity of the feeling of absolute dependence is not the same passivity as is found in the confused-animal phase because the feeling of absolute dependence does not have its basis or "whence" in nature or confused libidinal drives. Rather the feeling of absolute dependence has its basis or "whence" in God.[8] Since the feeling of absolute dependence is passive in character it cannot be the same as the sensible-reciprocal phase of human self-consciousness because the latter is an active phenomenon. However the harmonious feeling of absolute dependence is never found in an isolated state but is always found in conjunction with the confused-animal phase of human self-consciousness and the sensible-reciprocal phase of human self-consciousness. The manifestation of the feeling of absolute dependence in the history of religions is found among the monotheistic type of religion (i.e., Judaism, Christianity, and Mohammedanism).[9]

For Schleiermacher the stability, endurance, and continuity of an individual's harmonious feeling of absolute dependence will be in direct proportion to the "god" on whom one is dependent. Schleiermacher contends that Christianity offers the most viable form of harmonious stability, endurance and continuity because in Christianity "everything is related to the redemption accomplished by Jesus of Nazareth."[10] Schleiermacher believed that Jesus Christ

> is like all men in virtue of the identity of human nature, but distinguished from them all by the constant potency of His God-consciousness, which was a veritable existence of God in Him.[11]

"Just a minute. Now just a minute here. What is redemption?" For Schleiermacher redemption

> signifies a general passage from an evil condition which is represented as a state of captivity or constraint, into a better condition -- this is the passive side of it. But it also signifies the help given in that process by some other person, and this is the active side of it.[12]

This means that the captivity of the human person imprisoned by magical thinking, grotesque projections, and idol-worship which has its basis in the confused-animal self-consciousness could describe an evil condition. This also means that the social constraints, pressures, and norms which have their basis in the sensible-reciprocal self-consciousness could also describe an evil condition. Further a lack of stability, endurance, and continuity in the feeling of absolute dependence could also describe an evil condition. To overcome or "redeem" such evil conditions a Power is needed. Such a Power must also be Love[13] which not only desires to redeem everyone but also wishes to preserve[14] in Wisdom[15] the redeemed. For Schleiermacher the fullness of this Power, Love, and Wisdom is found in the Person and Activity of Jesus Christ who is the "Redeemer." The passage from darkness, confusion, and despair to light, clarity, and hope is accomplished by and through Jesus Christ. The passive side of this Activity is what occurs to us and in us through Jesus Christ. The active agent is Jesus Christ in His vital and immediate Activity.

Thus for Schleiermacher Jesus Christ who is Power, Love, and Wisdom offers to everyone a real and viable serenity in this life. "Serenity? We are modern men. Who needs serenity?" Well now! Come with me. Let us go and look at the butchered consciousness of suicidal people. Come with me. Let us look at the darkest night of despair. Come with me. Let us look at sheer confusion, pain and death. Then let us mock serenity. Then let us mock peace. Then let us mock Christ!

Yes, let us really mock Christ by saying that because of suicidal, confused, and modern cultural gush "christ killed himself." Let's throw up (indeed, we are vomiting) more "suicidal christ-figures" so that an anguished tear can splash off another ice cube in the world's cocktail glass. Let's resort to tragic and melancholic images of the local idol in order to vindicate "christianity" in the modern day.

Then with such "suicidal christ-figures" let us try to explain Christ's Power, Love, and Wisdom to a suicidal world. Sure, if "christ" killed himself why shouldn't everybody kill themselves? After all, they are only imitating "god." What nonsense! What idiocy! What blasphemy!

However if we are to seek Christ's Freedom from suicidal behavior through Christ's Love, Power, and Wisdom, we had best not attempt to destroy the Basis, Source, and Whence of our redemption with "confused, tragic, and suicidal 'christs'." Instead, with Schleiermacher, we should simply say that Christ accepted His death

> as a duty involved in His vocation to appear in the holy city for this feast, in spite of the foreknowledge He possessed;* and beyond question it was an element in the development of this great crisis that Christ met His death in His zeal for His vocation relatively to His Father's law, just as truly as His opponents -- at least the best among them -- condemned Him to death in their professional zeal for the law.16

This simply means that Jesus Christ's death was absolutely unique. It has happened once and for all. It cannot be repeated by anyone, any time, anywhere because no one else is completely and fully God and completely and fully man. Further Jesus Christ's death cannot be arbitrarily repeated by anyone who might believe that the "father" is calling him or her to die. Whoever or whatever this "father" may be it is not Christ's Father because Christ's Father is unknowable apart from Christ's Will, and Christ's Will is that no human person should destroy herself or himself. Finally Christ's death is never to be separated from His resurrection which, as has been seen confirms the preservative Will of the Triune God for everyone in that no one dies but all are Loved eternally.

---

* Matthew 16:21.

2

Among other things modern culture lives with a number of delusions concerning the "divine progress" of human knowledge. Yes, there has been progress. Due to the advancement of modern technology more civilians are killed in each new war. Three men go to one moon; over four-hundred persons jump from one bridge. The infant mortality rate is down but the suicide rate is up. And then there is the plastic tree.

It is commonly thought that the modern sciences of sociology and psychology will eventually bring forth a new utopian era. This common and rather smug thought is not the opinion of many sociologists and psychologists.

For example, Emile Durkheim in his Suicide, A Study of Sociology contended rather dogmatically that the more a specific religion had a common, integrated, and family-like intellectual and psychological ethos, the less chance there was of suicide.[17] That is, the warmer the psychological womb of accepted belief, the stronger the umbilical cord to life.[18] For Durkheim Catholicism presented such a warm womb and strong umbilical cord. Protestantism, however, gave too much freedom to the individual and thus increased the possibility of suicide. Durkheim's sources for these conclusions were the official suicide statistics for different countries in nineteenth century Western Europe. Using this method, Italy was typed Catholic, most of Germany was typed Protestant, etc. Catholic countries were found to have fewer suicides. Protestant countries were found to have more suicides. Using official statistics and this method Durkheim drew his conclusions.[19]

However according to Jack Douglas, a contemporary sociologist and historian of the sociology of suicide:

> In general at the present time there seems to be no adequate justification for using official statistics on suicide to build or test a scientific theory of suicide. There seems to be every reason for not using them.[20]

According to Douglas there are too many possible interpretations of the official statistics on suicide. There are also too many variants and flaws in such statistics. Durkheim's sources, method, and conclusions were too simplistic to be considered valid by modern statistical techniques. With respect to Durkheim's sources, method and conclusions Douglas comments:

> Unfortunately, the concrete examples Durkheim gives us will not support the notion that his common sense was superior, as a scientific instrument, to anyone else's.[21]

To illustrate Douglas' criticism of Durkheim let us say that in a small nineteenth century Italian village a father comes home from a hard day's work. He discovers that his nineteen year old daughter, who has been suffering from melancholia, has jumped from the roof and killed herself. No one knows of his daughter's suicide but the man's wife who is hysterically sobbing in the next room. What is the man supposed to do? Report the suicide to the local priest and have his daughter denied the rites of burial? Are he and his wife supposed to accept social disgrace and social guilt? So, the man reports his daughter's death was an accident. And no one (not even Durkheim) knows anything about this suicide. Did such a thing ever happen? I don't know there are no "official statistics." However others besides Durkheim are blessed (and cursed) with common sense.

In the twentieth century the same problems of gathering "official statistics" on suicide and classifying what is or what is not suicidal behavior[22] are necessary scientific endeavors. However the modern classification of suicidal behavior is still being developed.[23] The statistics which can be obtained are open to constant revision. And conclusions based upon such statistics, well, one must still resort to common sense.

The same sort of scientific insecurity found in the sociological study of suicide is also found in the psychotherapeutic treatment of suicide. This is especially true with respect to many psychotic disorders which may or may not result in suicide.[24] Despite the blind faith of the modern world in psychotherapy:

> We realize that no treatment (including psychotherapy, drugs, electroshock therapy, and prolonged hospitalization) guarantees the patient against suicide. In the therapy of many patients, there are certain unavoidable periods of suicide risk. The most competent psychotherapists have had patients who have committed suicide.[25]

It is also interesting to note psychotherapists' attitudes towards themselves after the actual suicide of one of their patients. Litman commenting on the seldom mentioned response of the psychotherapist[26] after a patient has committed suicide maintains that out of the 200 psychotherapists he interviewed two responses could be determined. First psychotherapists reacted much the same as other people. That is, the psychotherapist felt personal failure, grief, occasional anger, guilt, and denial. Second, in their professional roles psychotherapists attempted to constructively re-examine the individual histories of their former patients. This was done both to overcome their own pain and to increase their knowledge and sensitivity for the future.[27]

It is also important to note that:

> My colleagues and I have never interviewed a therapist who advanced the notion that the suicide of his patient was philosophically acceptable to him and congruent with his theoretical expectations regarding the methods and goals of therapy.[28]

In other words the involvement of the psychotherapist with the patient is more than is usually observed externally. The ethical therapeutic concern for another's life is unable to be handled by professional indifference after a patient has committed suicide. Nor is it possible to treat the whole matter with disgust if one is actually drawn into a real confrontation with suicidal behavior.

This responsibility and concern for the preservation of human life <u>could</u> be interpreted as a given and immanent view of history. This view of history applies not only to sociologists and psychotherapists attempting to correct suicidal behavior, but also to the numerous individuals and secular and religious organizations which attempt to overcome suicidal behavior. Such organizations as The Suicide Prevention Center of Los Angeles,[29] The Suicide Prevention Center of Vienna,[30] and The Samaritans,[31] as well as all the suicide prevention centers and Samaritans of the world <u>could</u> give some indication of a possible particular view of history. Perhaps such a history could be summarized in this way:

> There is also no absolute ethical transformation of material nature or of human nature; all that does exist is a constant wrestling with the problems which they raise. Thus the Christian ethic of the present day and of the future will also only be an adjustment to the world-situation, and it will only desire to achieve that which is practically possible. This is the cause of that ceaseless tension which drives man onward yet gives him the sense that he can never realize his ethical ideal. Only doctrinaire idealists or religious fanatics can fail to recognize these facts. Faith is the source of energy in the struggle of life, but life still remains a battle which is continually renewed upon ever new fronts. For every threatening abyss which is closed, another yawning gulf appears. The truth is--and this is the conclusion of the whole matter--the Kingdom of God is within us.[32]

This statement of Ernst Troeltsch (1865-1923)[33] made in 1912[34] does not attempt to claim as a "christian" anyone who is repulsed by such a problematic label. It simply attempts to offer a description of a view of history which might embrace the human being's undying effort to overcome destruction despite innumerable setbacks and naive public delusions about "perfect" sciences. Like all views of history it can be accepted or rejected according to the reader's tastes. But it is obvious from what has been said throughout this essay about Christ's attitude towards the human body that anyone who attempts to preserve, cure, or aid in any way a human being stricken with suicidal tendencies is participating in Christ's Activity. Thus the notorious word which has been ignored in this essay, the word "church" would apply to that life-sustaining Activity of Christ in relation to suicidal behavior. That is, in this discussion, Christ's Church is simply that Activity which attempts to overcome suicidal behavior.

3

"All right. Not bad; not really good; but all right. So much for the good people. But not everyone is imbued with . . . what's his name's . . . Troeltsch's idea of history. What about the politicians who forget about the people in the suicide ward and allocate tax money for wars, freeways, and plastic trees? What about the wrong kind of social indifference? What about destructive societies? How is anyone going to survive in this colossal wreck of a world?" Now it is obvious that no one can speak for all. At the most, what can be said is that one should attempt to find a solid and stable enough basis of serenity, peace, and love, in order to continue the battle against destruction. Many persons have different interpretations and descriptions of Jesus Christ, and, although there are different ways of expressing Christ's Freedom as the basis for our freedom no one is bound to anyone's interpretation of this basis. In this essay numerous descriptions of Christ's Freedom have been offered in contrast to "false christs."

CHRIST AND FREEDOM

In conclusion I wish to quote a poem from Dietrich Bonhoeffer (1906-1945)[35] as a final description of Christ's Freedom. Dietrich Bonhoeffer was a German theologian imprisoned for his implication in the attempted assassination of Adolf Hitler. He was executed by the Nazis in 1945. Here is his poem of July 16, 1944.

Who Am I?

Who am I? They often tell me
that I walk from my cell
deliberately, calmly, firmly,
like a nobleman from his castle.

Who am I? They often tell me
that I speak with the jailers
freely, friendly, clearly,
as if I were the one in command.

Who am I? They also tell me
that I bear the days of misfortune
quietly, cheerfully, proudly,
as one who has lived for victories.

Who am I really? What the others tell me?
Or am I only that which I know of myself?
turbulent, longing, sick, like a bird in a cage,
grappling with life's breath as it strangles me,
hungry for colors, for flowers, for the
singing of birds,
thirsting for kind words, for human surroundings,
trembling with rage over both despotism
and paltry insult,
spun 'round in expectation of great events,
powerlessly fearing for friends at an infinite distance;
exhausted and empty at praying, thinking, and
creating,
lifeless: and ready for the final leave-taking.

Who am I? This or the other?

Am I this one today and tomorrow the other?
Am I both together? Before men--a hypocrite
and before myself--a scorned and wretched
    weakling?
Or yet, is there still something within
    me resembling a beaten army,
which is already retreating from hard-won victory?

Who am I? They mock me, these lonely
    questions of mine.
Whoever I am, Thou knowest me, O God,
    I am Thine.[36]

FOOTNOTES

Chapter I

1. Mt. 22:37-40. The abbreviation means The Gospel According to Matthew, chapter 22, verse 37-40. For the most part Biblical quotations are taken from The Revised Standard Version of the Bible.
2. Mk. (i.e. The Gospel According to Mark) 12:31.
3. Idem.
4. Mt. 22:40.
5. Mt. 1:23.
6. Jn. (i.e. The Gospel According to John) 1:1-3.
7. Idem.
8. Mt. 23:8.
9. Basescu, "The Threat of Suicide in Psychotherapy," p. 104.
10. Chapman, "Suicide During Psychiatric Hospitalization," p. 35.
11. Schriber and Herman, "How to Cure Depression," p. 72.
12. Mt. 3:11.
13. Idem.
14. Young, Analytical Concordance to the Bible, p. 70.
15. Arndt and Gingrich, A Greek-English Lexicon of the New Testament and Other Early Christian Literature, pp. 131-132. Washing is interpreted as the removal of that which stands against God.
16. Cor. (i.e. The First Letter of Paul to the Corinthians) 2:10.
17. Mt. 1:20. Lk. (i.e. The Gospel According to Luke) 1:35.
18. Mt. 3:11.
19. Jn. 1:13.
20. Jn. 5:30-38.
21. Jn. 10:30.
22. Mt. 6:9-13.
23. Mt. 23:8,10.
24. Mt. 23:9.
25. Jn. 1:14-34.
26. Mt. 3:16-17; Mk. 1:9-11; Lk. 3:21-22.
27. Mt. 4:1-2.

[28] Mk. 5:2-6.
[29] Mt. 17:14-18.
[30] Mt. 12:22.
[31] Mt. 4:3-11.
[32] Mt. 4:4.
[33] Genesis 1:31.
[34] Mt. 4:7.
[35] Mt. 4:10.
[36] Jn. 2:19-22.
[37] 2 Cor. (i.e. The Second Letter of Paul to the Corinthians) 6:16.
[38] The Gospel of Matthew, Chapter 23.
[39] Mt. 23:37-38.
[40] Jn. 2:16.
[41] Mt. 23:4.
[42] Jn. 8:44.
[43] Conflated from Jn. 2:14-16; Mt. 21:12-13; Mk. 11:15-17; Lk. 19:45-46; and the entirety of the New Testament especially with reference to Mt. 12:28.
[44] I Jn. (i.e. The First Letter of John) 4:18.
[45] Jn. 2:19.
[46] Jn. 12:31-33.
[47] Idem.
[48] Jn. 12:27.
[49] Jn. 10:18.
[50] Exodus 3:13. This means no one forces the Triune God to do anything against His Will.
[51] Idem.
[52] Jn. 8:48-59; Jn. 10:31-39.
[53] Lk. 22:42.
[54] I Cor. 15:42-50.
[55] I Cor. 15:51-55 and the Book of Revelations 7:17.
[56] I Jn. 2:25.
[57] Mt. 19:17.
[58] I Cor. 15:28: Eph. (The Letter of Paul to the Ephesians) 1:9-10.
[59] Idem.
[60] Idem.
[61] Mt. 15:19.
[62] I Cor. 3:23.
[63] Mt. 9:13.

Chapter II

¹Justin Martyr, The Ante-Nicene Fathers, vol. 1, pp. 160-161.
² Frend, Martyrdom and Persecution in the Early Church, p. 59.
³ Ibid., p. 174.
⁴ Ibid., pp. 185-186.
⁵ Justin Martyr, op. cit., (Dialogue with Trypho, a Jew, chap. 2), p. 95.
⁶ Idem.
⁷ Idem.
⁸ Idem. See also Bernard, Justin Martyr, p. 38.
⁹ Justin's disagreement with Stoicism was based upon the Stoic doctrines of materialism and fate.
¹⁰ For Justin human reason in itself is not the source of truth. Justin Martyr, op.cit., (Second Apology, chap. 13), pp. 192-193.
¹¹ For Justin the devils were the source of destruction. Justin Martyr, op.cit. (First Apology, chaps. 14, 56, 57, 58), pp. 167-168, p. 182.
¹²Justin Martyr, op.cit., (Second Apology, chap. 13), pp. 192-193.
¹³Idem. See also First Apology, chap. 46.
¹⁴ Justin Martyr, op. cit., (First Apology, chap. 63), p. 184.
¹⁵ Ibid., (First Apology, chap. 2), p. 163.
¹⁶ Ibid., (Second Apology, chap. 4), p. 189.
¹⁷ Barnard, op. cit., chap. 5.
¹⁸ Idem.
¹⁹ Justin Martyr, op. cit., (Second Apology, chap. 13), pp. 192-193. See also Dorner, History of the Development of the Doctrine of the Person of Christ, vol. 1, pp. 264-277.
²⁰ Justin Martyr, op. cit., (Dialogue with Trypho, a Jew, chap. 2), p. 195.
²¹ Idem. For Justin those philosophers who worry about fees are not philosophers.
²² Arndt and Gingrich, A Greek-English Lexicon of the New Testament and Other Early Christian Literature, pp. 494-495.
²³ Ibid., p. 495.
²⁴ Ibid., p. 493.
²⁵ Justin Martyr, op. cit., (Dialogue with Trypho, a Jew, chap. 95), p. 247.
²⁶ Ibid., (Second Apology, chap. 13), p. 192-93.
²⁷ Barnard, op. cit., p. 13. Frend, op. cit., p. 189.
²⁸ Barnard, loc. cit.

[29] Frend, op. cit., p. 189. See also Justin Martyr, op. cit., (Second Apology, chap. 3), p. 189.
[30] Justin Martyr, loc. cit.
[31] Frend, loc. cit.
[32] Ibid., pp. 190-191.
[33] Idem.
[34] Idem.
[35] Idem.
[36] See footnote sixteen in chapter two.
[37] Idem.
[38] Justin Martyr, op. cit., (First Apology, chap. 26), p. 171.
[39] Hans Jonas, The Gnostic Religion, pp. 141-142.
[40] Ibid., p. 141.
[41] Idem.
[42] Ibid., p. 142.
[43] Idem.
[44] Ibid., p. 138. Jonas's source is Tertullian Adversus Marcionem.
[45] Ibid., p. 142.
[46] Idem.
[47] Idem.
[48] Idem.
[49] Idem.
[50] Ibid., p. 139.
[51] Ibid., p. 144.
[52] Justin Martyr, op. cit., (Second Apology, chap. 10), pp. 191-92.
[53] Idem.
[54] Walker, A History of the Christian Church, p. 54.
[55] Ayer, A Source Book for Ancient Church History, p. 102. Ayer's source is Irenaeus, Against Heresies, I, 27:1-3.
[56] Justin Martyr, op. cit., (First Apology, chap. 14), p. 167.
[57] Altaner, Patrology, p. 312.
[58] Idem. See also Campenhausern, The Fathers of the Greek Church, p. 72.
[59] Altaner, op. cit., p. 314.
[60] Athanasius, The Incarnation of the Word of God, tr. by a religious of C.S.M.V.S.Th., p. 93.
[61] Dorner, op. cit., vol. 2, p. 233.
[62] Idem.
[63] Ibid., p. 234.
[64] Idem.

[65] Ibid., p. 239.
[66] Ibid., p. 236.
[67] Ibid., p. 237.
[68] Ibid., pp. 240, 243.
[69] Altaner, op. cit., p. 315. According to Altaner the fourth oration was added by an anonymous writer.
[70] Ibid., p. 317.
[71] Athanasius, The Letters of Saint Athanasius Concerning the Holy Spirit, pp. 134-135.
[72] Athanasius, The Orations of S. Athanasius Against the Arians, p. 12.
[73] Athanasius, The Letters of Saint Athanasius Concerning the Holy Spirit, pp. 59-60.
[74] Idem.
[75] Ibid., pp. 112, 184.
[76] Athanasius, The Orations of S. Athanasius Against the Arians, p. 27.
[77] Idem.
[78] Idem.
[79] Ibid., pp. 37-38.
[80] Ibid., p. 38.
[81] Ibid., p. 37.
[82] Ibid., p. 27.
[83] Ibid., p. 147.
[84] I Cor. 5:55.
[85] Ibid., 3:23.
[86] Athanasius, The Incarnation of the Word of God, p. 30.
[87] Ibid., p. 32.
[88] Ibid., p. 30.
[89] Ibid., pp. 30-31.
[90] Ibid., p. 31.
[91] Athanasius, The Orations of S. Athanasius Against the Arians, p. 27.
[92] Athanasius, The Incarnation of the Word of God, pp. 45-46.
[93] Athanasius, The Letters of Saint Athanasius Concerning the Holy Spirit, p. 410.
[94] Ibid., pp. 113, 142, 143, 176.
[95] Athanasius, The Incarnation of the Word of God, p. 44.
[96] Athanasius, The Letters of Saint Athanasius Concerning the Holy Spirit, p. 172.
[97] Ibid., p. 82.
[98] Ibid., p. 126.

[99] Ibid., p. 172.
[100] Ibid., p. 112.
[101] Footnote 60, chapter 2.
[102] Altaner, op. cit., p. 487.
[103] Shneidman, Essays in Self-Destruction, cf. M. D. Faber, "Shakespeare's Suicides: Some Historic, Dramatic and Psychological Reflections," p. 36.
[104] Portalié, A Guide to the Thought of St. Augustine, p. 403.
[105] Augustine, Confessions in Augustine: Confessions and Enchiridion, Library of Christian Classics, bk. 3, chap. 2.
[106] Ibid., bk. 3, chap. 3.
[107] Ibid., bk. 3, chap. 5.
[108] Ibid., bk. 4, chaps. 2 and 3.
[109] Ibid., bk. 7.
[110] Ibid., bks. 8, 9.
[111] Portalié, loc. cit.
[112] Portalié, op. cit., p. 22. Portalié sets the date for the beginning of Augustine's bishopric at 395-396.
[113] Ibid., p. 401.
[114] Augustine, Augustine: Earlier Writings, p. 19.
[115] Ibid., p. 36. (Soliloquies, bk. 1, chap. xii, sec. 20).
[116] Ibid., p. 64.
[117] Ibid., p. 95. (The Teacher, chap. xi. Sec. 38).
[118] Ibid., p. 100. (The Teacher, chap. xiv, sec. 46).
[119] Ibid., pp. 327-329. The Nature of the Good Against the Manichees, chaps. iv-xiii).
[120] See all of Augustine's Anti-Manichaean writings.
[121] Portalié, op. cit., pp. 176-229. In these pages Portalié attempts to work out Augustine's full doctrine of grace and sin with reference especially to the Pelagian controversy. It appears that with Augustine one would always be free to reject the Teacher's instruction and aid if these were construed as the free gift of grace. However Augustine, in the earlier works, is not really attempting to define the possibility of rejecting or accepting grace. He is really attempting to describe Eternal Wisdom and His Creation. The issue is not so much grace's acceptance or rejection but who or what any human person is as a creature of Christ.

In these earlier works, the seeds of Augustine's mature Christological thought are also present. For Portalié this mature thought is that "The true and apostolic opinion is that Christ is the savior of all men." (p. 167) Apparently when Augustine stated that "the effects of Redemption were restricted to the elect, he has to be understood as speaking of efficacious graces which were not given to all." (p. 167) Thus all are saved but not all receive efficacious graces. Of course in the earlier works the inward Teacher never appears as a miser who would deny a single student His aid. Thus no one could ever say that the Teacher would really deny anyone His grace. At later times and in other contexts Augustine's views of election may differ, but that is beyond the concern of this essay.

[122] Augustine, On Free Choice of the Will, tr. By Anna S. Benjamin, and L. H. Hackstaff, p. ix.
[123] Ibid., pp. 105-106. (On Free Choice of the Will, bk. 3, chap. viii, secs. 83-84.)
[124] See footnote 117, chapter two.
[125] Idem.
[126] See footnote 115, chapter two.
[127] Idem.
[128] Portalié, op. cit., p. 404.
[129] Augustine, The City of God, bk. 1, pp. 21-28.
[130] Ibid., p. ix.
[131] Ibid., bk. xix, p. 678.
[132] Idem.
[133] Gospel According to John, 1:4.
[134] Augustine, The City of God, bk. xix, p. 678.
[135] Grillmeier, Christ in Christian Tradition, pp. 479-480.
[136] Ibid., p. 481. This paragraph refers to the first paragraph of the Chalcedonian formula.
[137] Idem., paragraph two of the Chalcedonian formula.
[138] Copleston, Aquinas, pp. 9-10.
[139] Ibid., p. 9.
[140] Aquinas, The Summa Theologica, second part of the second part, question 64, article 5, pp. 203-204.
[141] Aristotle, Nicomachean Ethics, bk. 5, chap. 11, p. 143.
[142] Ibid., p. 143, footnote 76.
[143] Aquinas, loc. cit., see footnote 140, chapter 2 of this essay, first reason.
[144] Idem. (See second reason.)
[145] Idem. (See third reason.)
[146] Idem.
[147] Aristotle, op. cit., p. ix.
[148] Aquinas, op. cit., p. v.
[149] Ibid., pp. 204-205.
[150] Ibid., p. 204.
[151] Idem.

[152] Ibid., p. 203-206.
[153] Idem.
[154] Hefele, (ed.), Histoire Des Conciles, vol. 3, first part, p. 180, canon 16.
[155] Idem.
[156] Idem.
[157] Hefele (ed.), op. cit,. vol. 2, second part, p. 1135, canon 15.
[158] Idem.
[159] Thomas Aquinas, op. cit., pp. 203-204.
[160] A. Michel, "Suicide," in the Dictionnaire de Theologie Catholique, 194, vol. 14, 2, pp. 2739-2749. See also Bouscaren, Canon Law, A Text and Commentary, 1957, p. 669.
[161] Idem.
[162] Idem.
[163] Idem.
[164] Jacobs, "A Phenomenological Study of Suicide Notes," in Social Problems, vol. 15, 1967, pp. 60-72.
[165] Ibid., p. 72.

Chapter III

[1] Bainton, Here I Stand, pp. 17-20.
[2] Luther, Briefwechsel, #1180, series 4, vol 4, p. 294. This is the basis for the following incident. The letter is dated December 10, 1527.
[3] Idem.
[4] Ibid., p. 296, footnote 8.
[5] Ibid., p. 294; Luther, Tischreden #590, vol. 1, p. 277, dated summer and fall, 1533.
[6] Luther, Tischreden, #590, vol. 1, p. 277, dated summer and fall, 1533.
[7] Ebeling, "Reflections on the Doctrine of the Law," in Word and Faith, p. 272.
[8] Luther, Tischreden #590, vol. 1, p. 277.
[9] Idem.
[10] Bainton, op. cit. Luther entered the Augustinian Cloister at Erfurt on July 17, 1505 (p. 17). Up until the Diet of Worms in April, 1521 he still possessed the possibility of being considered a Roman Catholic monk (p. 19).
[11] From 1505 until his Lectures on Romans (1515-1516) Luther's conscience is in active turmoil attempting to discover the gracious God.
[12] Bainton, op. cit., see page 43 for illustration.

[13] Ibid., pp. 37-58.
[14] Idem.
[15] Ibid. p. 45.
[16] The German word "Anfectung" (assault or attack) has many contexts and meanings for Luther. In this discussion the effects produced by such attacks or assaults (i.e. they create internal turmoil) are being emphasized.
[17] Luther, Lectures on Galatians (1535), p. 88.
[18] Luther, Tischreden, #590, vol. 1, p. 277.
[19] Idem.
[20] See footnote 5 in chapter III of this essay.
[21] Luther, Tischreden, #222, vol. 1, p. 45, dated April 7, 1532.
[22] Idem.
[23] Luther, Letters of Spiritual Counsel, p. 58.
[24] See footnote 21, chapter III of this essay.
[25] Luther, Tischreden, #590 and #222, vol. pp. 277, 95.
[26] Idem.
[27] Luther, Letters of Spiritual Counsel, pp. 90-91. Letter to Mrs. Jonas von Stockhausen, November 27, 1532.
[28] Idem.
[29] Luther, That These Words of Christ "This Is My Body," Etc., Still Stand Firm Against the Fanatics, 1527, p. 95.
[30] Ibid., pp. 5-150. See also Luther, Confession Concerning Christ's Supper, pp. 153-372.
[31] Idem.
[32] Luther, That These Words of Christ "This Is My Body," Etc., Still Stand Firm Against the Fanatics, 1527, p. 95.
[33] Walker, A History of the Christian Church, pp. 348-357.
[34] Calvin, Institutes of the Christian Religion, bk. 3, chap. 19, sections 2&3, pp. 834-836.
[35] Ibid, bk. 3, chap. 10, pp. 719-725; bk. 3, chap. 19, section 4, pp. 836-837; bk. 3, chap. 19, section 8, pp. 839-840.
[36] This third application of Christ's Freedom would definitely be in accord with Martin Luther's thought. (c.f. Luther, Eight Sermons by Dr. Martin Luther, "Sermon 3," pp. 397-406.) However as of yet I have not discovered Luther using the exact phrasing of Calvin's "freedom regarding outward things that are of themselves 'indifferent.'" (Calvin, op. cit., bk. 3, chap. 19, section 7, pp. 838-839).
[37] Ibid., bk. 3, chap. 19, section 7, p. 838.
[38] Ibid., pp. 838-839.
[39] Ibid., bk. 1, chap. 11, pp. 99-116; bk. 1 chap. 12, pp. 116-120.

CHAPTER IV

[1] Lowrie, Kierkegaard, vol. 1, p. 19, vol. 2, p. 583.

[2] This statement is made in reference to Kierkegaard's note "When I am dead, all that is mine will also be exploited by assistant professors" (Kierkegaard, Søren Kierkegaard's Journals and Papers, vol. 2, F-K, p. 513). Kierkegaard had an extremely low opinion of professorial professionalism established in the name of Christ (Lowrie, op. cit., vol. 2, pp. 507-509). Kierkegaard's method was an attempt to indirectly communicate with the reader so that the reader would directly confront himself or herself. This method, however, permits no systematization. Thus I have decided to let Kierkegaard simply be Kierkegaard. I shall only attempt to give a light touch of unsystematic coherence to Kierkegaard's thoughts on suicide.

[3] Kierkegaard, Either/Or, vol. 1, p. ix, published in 1843.

[4] Ibid., vol. 2, p. 250.

[5] Ibid., vol. 2, p. 250, p. 361 note 28; Walter Lowrie, op. cit., pp. 145-146.

[6] Kierkegaard, Either/Or, vol. 2, p. 250-251.

[7] Ibid., vol. 2, p. 236.

[8] Kierkegaard, The Last Years, The Kierkegaard Journals, 1853-1855, p. 111

[9] Dostoevsky, Letters of Fyodor Dostoevsky, pp. xix-xxiv.

[10] Ibid., p. 53, letter to his brother Michael dated December 22, 1849.

[11] Idem.

[12] Ibid., pp. xx and 25-35, (letters to his brother Michael dated October 8 and November 16, 1845; and February 1, 1846).

[13] Dostoevsky, The House of the Dead, pp. 60, 67, 95, 114, 140, 152. In this usually unread novel Dostoevsky relates the squalor, misery, and wretchedness of his Siberian exile.

[14] Idem.

[15] Idem.

[16] Dostoevsky, Letters of Fyodor Dostoevsky, p. 63. (Letter to his brother Michael dated February 22, 1854).

[17] Ibid., p. 69, n. 2. Mme. N. D. Fonvisin was the "wife of the Decembrist M. A. Fonvisin. Dostoevsky had met her in Tobolsk in 1850." During his captivity, Dostoevsky was not allowed to correspond with his brother. Mme. N. D. Fonvisin was his only communication with the outside world.

[18] Ibid., pp. 70-71.

[19] Ibid., p. xxii.

[20] See footnote 16 of this chapter of this essay.
[21] Dostoevsky, Letters of Fyodor Dostoevsky, p. xxii.
[22] Dostoevsky, Notes from the Underground in The Laurel Dostoevsky, p. 13.
[23] Dostoevsky, A Raw Youth in The Laurel Dostoevsky, p. 18.
[24] Dostoevsky, Letters of Fyodor Dostoevsky, p. xxiii.
[25] Dostoevsky, Crime and Punishment, pp. 492-493.
[26] Dostoevsky, Letters of Fyodor Dostoevsky, p. xxii.
[27] Ibid., p. xxiii.
[28] Ibid., p. xxiv.
[29] Dostoevsky, The Gambler, in Penguin Books, intro. By Jessie Coulson, pp. 7-15.
[30] Dostoevsky, Letters of Fyodor Dostoevsky, p. 336. This is Turgenev's letter to Saltykov, dated September 24, 1882:
"I also read Michailovsky's article on Dostoevsky. He has rightly divined the characteristic mark of Dostoevsky's creative work. In French literature, too, there was a like case -- namely, the famous Marquis de Sade. This latter depicts in 'Tourments et Suplices' the sensual pleasure afforded by the infliction of refined tortures. And Dostoevsky, in one of his books, enlarges on th same sort of delights. . . . And when one thinks that all the Russian Bishops said masses for the soul of this Marquis de Sade, and even preached sermons about his great love for all mankind! Truly, we live in a remarkable age."
[31] See notes 17 and 18 of this chapter of this essay.
[32] Dostoevsky, The Heavenly Christmas Tree in The Short Stories of Dostoevsky, p. 535.
[33] Ibid., pp. 535-541. This same short story is in The Diary of a Writer, entry for January, 1876, entitled A Little Boy at Christ's Christmas Tree.
[34] Dostoevsky, The Letters of Fyodor Dostoevsky, p. xxiv.
[35] Dostoevsky, The Brothers Karamazov, vol. 2, p. 912.
[36] Dostoevsky, The Heavenly Christmas Tree, pp. 540-541.
[37] Dostoevsky, The Brothers Karamazov, vol. 2, p. 912.
[38] See footnotes 17 and 18 of this chapter of the essay.
[39] Dostoevsky, The Diary of a Writer, p. 459.
[40] Ibid., p. 473.
[41] Ibid., p. 527.
[42] Ibid., p. 545.
[43] Idem.
[44] Idem.
[45] Dostoevsky, The Possessed, p. vi.

⁴⁶ Ibid., p. 333 in the chapter entitled, "On the Eve of the Fête," section ii, pp. 332-334.
⁴⁷ Ibid., p. 334.
⁴⁸ Idem.
⁴⁹ Idem.
⁵⁰ Ibid., p. 137, chapter entitled, "The Cripple," section iv.
⁵¹ Ibid., p. 113, chapter entitled, "The Sins of Others," section viii.
⁵² Ibid., pp. 113-116, chapter entitled, "The Sins of Others," section viii.
⁵³ Idem.
⁵⁴ Idem. See also p. 241, chapter entitled, "Night," section v.
⁵⁵ Idem. (i.e. both references in footnote 54).
⁵⁶ Ibid., pp. 620-636, chapter entitled, "A Busy Night," section ii.
⁵⁷ Ibid., p. 630, chapter entitled, "A Busy Night," section ii.
⁵⁸ Ibid., pp. 620-636, chapter entitled, "A Busy Night," section ii.
⁵⁹ Ibid., p. 629, chapter entitled, "A Busy Night," section ii.
⁶⁰ See footnotes 42 and 43, chapter four of this essay.
⁶¹ Dostoevsky, The Possessed, pp. 691-730, chapter entitled, "At Tihon's."
⁶² Idem.
⁶³ Idem.
⁶⁴ Idem.
⁶⁵ Idem.
⁶⁶ Idem.
⁶⁷ Ibid., p. 542, chapter entitled, "A Romance Ended," section ii.
⁶⁸ Ibid., p. 550, chapter entitled, "A Romance Ended," section iii.
⁶⁹ Ibid., p. 688, chapter entitled, "Conclusion."
⁷⁰ Idem.
⁷¹ Dostoevsky, A Raw Youth, part 1, chapter 9, section ii, p. 189.
⁷² Dostoevsky, A Gentle Spirit, in The Short Stories of Dostoevsky, pp. 545-590. This same story is recorded in The Diary of a Writer under the title A Meek One, November, 1876.
⁷³ Dostoevsky, The Diary of a Writer, p. 469, entry for October, 1876.
⁷⁴ Dostoevsky, The Brothers Karamazov, part 4, chapters 6-8.
⁷⁵ Ibid., part 2, chapter 5.

[76] Ibid., part 4, chapter 10.
[77] Ibid., part 4, chapter 9.
[78] Castell, An Introduction to Modern Philosophy, p. 137.
[79] Schopenhauer, The World as Will and Idea, vol. 1, bk. 4, section 69, pp. 519-520.
[80] Idem.
[81] Ibid., p. 518.
[82] Schopenhauer, "On Suicide," in Studies in Pessimism in The Essays of Arthur Schopenhauer, pp. 399-404.
[83] Schopenhauer, The World as Will and Idea, vol. I, bk. 4, section 69, pp. 519-520.
[84] Ibid., vol. I, bk. 4, section 68, p. 490.
[85] Kaufmann, Nietzsche: Philosopher, Psychologist, Antichrist, pp. 31-58.
[86] Nietzsche, The Birth of Tragedy, p. 4.
[87] Ibid., section 5, p. 52.
[88] Nietzsche, The Will to Power.
[89] Ibid., p. 530, entry #1067 (1885).
[90] Nietzsche, Thus Spoke Zarathustra, intro. By Elizabeth Förster Nietzsche in The Complete Works of Friedrich Nietzsche, vol. 11, p. xviii.
[91] Nietzsche, Thus Spoke Zarathustra, bk. I, chapter 21, p. 73, Kaufmann translation.
[92] Idem.
[93] Ibid., p. 92.
[94] Idem.
[95] Nietzsche, Human, All-Too-Human, intro. By J. M. Kennedy, vol. 6, pp. vii, 85-88; vol. 7, pp. 286-287; The Complete Works of Friedrich Nietzsche.
[96] Nietzsche, The Dawn of Day, vol. 9, p. v. The Complete Works of Friedrich Nietzsche.
[97] Ibid., vol. 9, pp. 205-208.
[98] Nietzsche, The Joyful Wisdom, vol. 10, p. vii, The Complete Works of Friedrich Nietzsche.
[99] Ibid., bk. 3, #131, p. 173.
[100] Nietzsche, Thus Spoke Zarathustra, Bk. 1, chap. 21.
[101] Nietzsche, The Twilight of the Idols, vol. 16, p. vii, The Complete Works of Friedrich Nietzsche.
[102] Ibid., p. 88.
[103] Ibid., p. 90.
[104] Camus, Lyrical and Critical Essays, p. 367.
[105] Camus, The Myth of Sisyphus, p. v.

[106] Camus, Lyrical and Critical Essays, "Interview with Gabriel d'Aubarède" May 10, 1951, p. 356.
[107] Idem.
[108] Ibid., p. 348, "Interview with Jeanne Delpech," November 15, 1945.
[109] Ibid., p. 345.
[110] Camus, The Myth of Sisyphus, p. 35.
[111] Ibid., p. 28.
[112] Ibid., pp. 17, 29-30.
[113] Ibid., p. 33.
[114] Ibid. pp. 3, 48, 50, 61, 69.
[115] Camus, Lyrical and Critical Essays, p. 354, "Interview with Gabriel d'Aubarède" May 10, 1951.
[116] Idem.
[117] Camus, The Myth of Sisyphus, p. 50.
[118] Ibid., p. 79.
[119] Ibid., pp. 80-81.
[120] Ibid., p. 37.
[121] Ibid., p. 83.
[122] Paul the Apostle, First Letter to the Corinthians, chap. 5, verses 31-38.
[123] Camus The Myth of Sisyphus, p. 87.
[124] Ibid., pp. 47, 83.
[125] Ibid., p. 25.
[126] Ibid., p. 45.
[127] Ibid., p. 47.
[128] Ibid., p. 6.

Chapter V
[1] Schleiermacher, The Christian Faith, vol. 1, p. xi.
[2] Ibid., vol. 2, paragraph 104, p. 462.
[3] Ibid., vol. 1, paragraph 3, pp. 118-19.
[4] Ibid., vol. 1, paragraph 8, p. 35.
[5] Ibid., vol. 1, paragraph 5, p. 19.
[6] Ibid., vol. 1, paragraph 8, p. 35.
[7] Ibid., vol. 1, paragraph 5, p. 19.
[8] Ibid., vol. 1, paragraph 4, p. 16.
[9] Ibid., vol. 1, paragraph 8, p. 34-37.
[10] Ibid., vol. 1, paragraph 11, p. 52.
[11] Ibid., vol. 2, paragraph 94, p. 385.
[12] Ibid., vol. 1, paragraph 11, p. 54.
[13] Ibid., vol. 2, paragraph 167, p. 730.

[14] Ibid., vol. 1, paragraph 46, p. 170.
[15] Ibid., vol. 2, paragraph 168, p. 732.
[16] Ibid., vol. 2, paragraph 104, p. 462-463.
[17] Durkheim, Suicide, A Study of Sociology, pp. 158-1589.
[18] Ibid., chaps. 2 & 3.
[19] Idem.
[20] Douglas, "Suicide: Social Aspects" in International Encyclopedia of the Social Sciences, vol. 15, p. 380.
[21] Ibid., p. 381.
[22] Shneidman, "Orientations Toward Death: A Vital Aspect of the Study of Lives," in Resnik (ed.) Suicidal Behaviors, pp. 19-49. This same article of Shneidman's is published in the International Journal of Psychiatry, vol. 2, 1966, pp. 167-200 with an analysis of Shneidman's views by other authors.
[23] Idem.
[24] Kaplan, Comprehensive Textbook of Psychiatry, pp. 593-705.
[25] Litman, "Psychotherapists Orientations Toward Suicide," in Resnik, Suicidal Behaviors, part 3, article 27, p.357. Robert E. Litman, M.E., is "Clinical Professor of Psychiatry, University of Southern California School of Medicine: Co-Director and Chief Psychiatrist, Suicide Prevention Center, Los Angeles," Resnik, op. cit., p. vii.
[26] Litman, "When Patients Commit Suicide," in American Journal of Psychotherapy, vol. 19, 1965, pp. 570-576.
[27] Ibid., p. 576.
[28] Litman, "Psychotherapists' Orientations Towards Suicide," in Resnik, op. cit., p. 361.
[29] Resnik, Suicidal Behaviors, pp. 369-380.
[30] Ibid., pp. 381-390.
[31] Ibid., pp. 405-417.
[32] Troeltsch, The Social Teaching of the Christian Churches, vol. 2, p. 1013.
[33] Reist, Toward A Theology of Involvement, pp. 14-16.
[34] Ibid., p. 16.
[35] Bethge, Dietrich Bonhoeffer, pp. 5, 11.
[36] Bonhoeffer, Widerstand Und Ergebung, pp. 242-243, this translation is my own. Although Bonhoeffer did have some fragments on suicide in his Ethics, I have not found them to be significant at this stage of the essay. That is, what is worthwhile in his fragments on suicide has already been described. What is harmful has already been denounced. I am of the opinion that Bonhoeffer's main contribution to this discussion of suicide is his own struggling with the question of

personal identity. Such a question is not only relevant in the twentieth century but in _any_ century.

SELECTED BIBLIOGRAPHY

Achté, K.A.; Steinbäck, A.; and Teräväinen. "On Suicides Committed During Treatment in Psychiatric Hospitals." Acta Psychiatrica Scandinavica, 1966, vol. 12, pp. 272—284.

Altaner, Berthold. Patrology, tr. by Hilda C. Graef. Freiburg, West Germany: Herder and Edinburg-London: Nelson, 1960.

Althaus, Paul. The Theology of Martin Luther, tr. by Robert C. Schultz. Philadelphia: The Fortress Press, 1966.

Aquinas, Thomas. The "Summa Theologica" of St. Thomas Aquinas, part two, (second part), second number, (question 64, i.e. "Of Murder"). London: R. & T. Washbourne, Ltd., 1918.

Aristotle. Nicomachean Ethics, tr. with intro, by Martin Ostwald. New York: The Bobbs-Merrill Company, Inc., 1962.

Arndt, William F. and Gingrich, F. Wilbur. A Greek-English Lexicon of the New Testament and Other Early Christian Literature. Chicago and Cambridge: University of Chicago Press and The Syndics of the Cambridge University Press, 1957.

Athanasius. The Incarnation of the Word of God, tr. by a religious of C. S. M. V. with an intro, by C. S. Lewis. New York: The Macmillan Company, 1946.

_____ The Letters of Saint Athanasius Concerning the Holy Spirit, tr. by C. R. B. Shapland. New York: Philosophical Library, 1951.

_____ The Orations of S. Athanasius Against the Arians. London: Griffith Farran & Co., n.d.

Augustine. Augustine: Earlier Writings, ed. & tr. by John H. S. Burleigh. Philadelphia: The Westminster Press, The Library of Christian Classics, vol. 6, 1953.

_____ The City of God, tr. by Marcus Dods. New York: The Modern Library, 1950.

_____ Confessions, tr. by Albert C. Outler. Philadelphia: The Westminster Press, The Library of Christian Classics. vol. 7, pp. 1-333.

_____ On Free Choice of the Will, tr. by Anna S. Benjamin and L.H. Hackstaff. New York: The Bobbs-Merrill Company, The Library of Liberal Arts, 1964.

_____ The Writings Against the Manichaeans and Against the Donatists. Grand Rapids, Michigan: Wm. B. Eerdmans Publishing Company, A Select Library of the Nicene and Post-Nicene Fathers of the Christian Church, 1956, vol. 4.

Ayer, Joseph Cullen. A Source Book for Ancient Church History. New York: Charles Scribner's Sons, 1913.

Bainton, Roland. Here I Stand Nashville, Tennessee: Abingdon Press, 1950.

Barnar, L.W. Justin Martyr. His Life and Thought. Cambridge: Cambridge University Press, 1967.

Barter, James T., M.D.; Swaback, Dwight O., M.D.; Todd, Dorothy, M.S.W. "Adolescent Suicide Attempts." Arch. Gen. Psychiat., vol. 19, Nov. 1968, pp. 523—527.

Basescu, Subert. "The Threat of Suicide in Psychotherapy." American Journal of Psychotherapy, 1965, vol. 19, pp. 99-105.

Bethge, Eberhard. Dietrich Bonhoeffer, tr. by Eric Mosbacher, et.al. New York: Harper and Row, 1970, pp. 1-150.

Block, Jeanne; and Christiansen Bjørn. "A Test of Hendin's Hypotheses Relating Studies in Scandinavia to Child-Rearing Orientations." Scan. J. Psych., 1966, vol. 7, pp. 267-288.

Boisset, Jean. Sagesse et Sainteté dans la Pensée de Jean Calvin. Paris: Presses Universitaires de France, 1959.

Bolin, Robert K. et al. "Survey of Suicide Among Patients on Home Leave From a Mental Hospital." The Psychiatric Quarterly, 1968, vol. 12, pp. 81-89.

Bonhoeffer, Dietrich. Ethics, ed. by Eberhard Bethge, tr. by Neville Horton Smith. New York: The Macmillan Company, 1965.

_____ Widerstand und Ergebung. München: Chr. Kaiser Verlag, 1959, pp. 242-243.

Bornkamm, Heinrich. Luther and the Old Testament, tr. by Erich W. and Ruth C. Gritsch. Philadelphia: Fortress Press, 1969.

Bouscaren, Lincoln T. and Ellis, Adam C. Canon Law, A Text and Commentary. Milwaukee, Wisconsin: The Bruce Publishing Company, 1957, sections referring to suicide.

Calvin, John. Calvin: Institues of the Christian Religion ed. by John T. McNeill and tr. by Ford Lewis Battles. Philadelphia: The Westminster Press, The Library of Christian Classics, vols. 20 and 21, 1960.

Camus, Albert. Lyrical and Critical Essays. tr. by Ellen Conroy Kennedy. New York: Alfred A. Knopf, 1968.

_____ The Myth of Sisyphus and Other Essays, tr. by Justin O'Brien. New York: Vintage Books, 1955.

Castell, Albury. An Introduction to Modern Philosophy. New York: The Macmillan Company, 1963.

Chapman, Richard F. "Suicide During Psychiatric Hospitalization." Topeka, Kansas, Menninger Clinic Bulletin, 1965, vol. 29, pp. 35-44.

Cochrane, Charles Norris. Christianity and Classical Culture, New York: Oxford University Press, 1968.

Cohen, Earl, M.D. "Suicide in San Francisco." California Medicine, 1965, vol. 102, pp. 426-430.

Copleston, F. C. Aquinas. Baltimore, Maryland: Penguin Books, 1967.

Dean, R.A.; Miskimins, Wm.; De Cook, Richard; Wilson, Lowell T.; Maley, Roger F. "Predictions of Suicide in a Psychiatric Hospital." Journal of Clinical Psychology. vol. 23, 1967, pp. 296-301.

Devries, Alcon G.; and Shneidman, Edwin S. "Multiple MMPL Profiles of Suicidal Persons." Psychological Reports, 1967, 21, pp. 401-405.

Dorner, J.A. The History of the Development of the Doctrine of the Person of Christ, tr. by D. W. Simon. Edinburgh: T. & T. Clark, 1861, vols. 1 & 2.

Dorport, Theodore, M. D.; Jackson, Joan K., Ph.D.; and Ripley, Berbert S., M.D. "Broken Home and Attempted and Completed Suicides." Arch. Gen. Psychiat., vol. 12, Feb., 1965, pp. 213—216.

Dostoevsky, Fyodor. The Brothers Karamazov, tr. by David Magarshack. Hammondsworth, Middlesex: Penquin Books, 1963, vols. 1 & 2.

_____ Crime and Punishment, tr. by Constance Garnett. London: Everyman's Library, 1963.

_____ The Diary of a Writer, tr. by Boris Brasol. New York: George Braziller, 1954.

_____ The Double and Notes From the Underground in Three Short Novels of Dostoevsky, tr. by Constance Garnett. New York: Anchor Books, 1960.

_____ A Funny Man's Dream. tr. by Olga Shartes. Moscow: Foreign Languages Publishing House, n.d.

_____ *The Gambler*, tr. by Jessie Coulson. Baltimore, Maryland, Penguin Books, 1966.

_____ *The Idiot*, tr. by Constance Garnett. Toronto and New York: Bantam Books, Ltd., 1965.

_____ *The Insulted and Injured* tr. by Constance Garnett. New York: Grove Press, Inc., 1962.

_____ *Letters of Fyodor Michailovitch Dostoevsky to His Family and Friends* tr. by Ethel Colburn Mayne. New York: McGraw-Hill Book Company, 1964.

_____ *The Possessed*, tr. by Constance Garnett. New York: The Modern Library, 1963.

_____ *A Raw Youth*, tr. By Constance Garnett, New York: Dell Publishing House, 1961.

_____ *The Short Stories of Dostoevsky* tr. by Constance Garnett and ed. by William Phillips. New York: The Dial Press, 1946.

_____ *Winter Notes on Summer Impressions*, tr. by Richard Lee Renfield. New York: McGraw-Hill Book Company, 1965.

Douglas, Jack D. "Suicide: Social Aspects." *International Encyclopedia of the Social Sciences,* vol. 15, pp. 375-385.

Durkheim, Emile. *Suicide*, tr. by John A. Spaulding and George Simpson. New York: The Free Press, 1951.

Ebeling, Gerhard. *Word and Faith*, tr. by James W. Leitch. Philadelphia: Fortress Press, chaps. 2, 3, 8, 16, 17.

Egan, George A. The Armenian Version of The Letters of Athanasius to Bishop Serapion Concerning the Holy Spirit. Salt Lake City, Utah: University of Utah Printing Service, Studies and Documents, 1962.

Eisenthal, Sherman. "Suicide and Aggression." Psychological Reports, 1967, 21, pp. 745-757.

Ettlinger, Ruth W. "Suicides in a Group of Patients Who Had Previously Attempted Suicide." Acta Psychiatrica Scandinavica, 1965, vol. 40, pp. 363-378.

Faber, M.D. "Suicide and the 'Ajax' of Sophocles." The Psychoanalytic Review, 1967, vol. 54, pp. 49(441)-60(452).

Farberow, Norman L. "Suicide: Psychological Aspects (2)." International Encyclopedia of the Social Sciences, vol. 15, pp. 390-396.

Farberow, Norman L.; and Devries, Alcon G. "An Item Differentiation Analysis of MMPIs of Suicidal Neuropsychiatric Hospital Patients." Psychological Reports, 1967, 20, pp. 607-617.

Flood, R. A.; and Seayer, C. P. "A Retrospective Examination of Psychiatric Case Records of Patients who Subsequently Committed Suicide." Brit. J. Psychiat. (1968), 114, pp. 443-450.

Freedman, Alfred M. (ed.). Comprehensive Textbook of Psychiatry. Baltimore, Maryland: The Williams & Wilkins Company, pp. 593-705.

Frend, W. H. C. Martyrdom and Persecution in the Early Church. New York: New York University Press, 1967.

Freud, Sigmund. "Mourning and Melancholia" in The Collected Papers of Sigmund Freud tr. by John Riviere. New York: Basic Books, vol. 4, pp. 152-170.

Furst, Sidney S.; and Ostow, Mortimer. "The Psychodynamics of Suicide." New York Academy of Medicine Bulletin, 1965, vol. 41, pp. 190-204.

Gerrish, B.A. Grace and Reason. Oxford: Oxford University Press, 1962.

Gilson, Etienne. The Christian Philosophy of Saint Augustine, tr. by E. M. Lynch. New York: Random House, 1960.

_____ Reason and Revelation in the Middle Ages. New York: Charles Scribner's Sons, 1938.

Gittleson, N. L. "The Relationship Between Obsession and Suicidal Attempts in Depressive Psychosis." Brit. J. Psychit., 112, pp. 889-890, 1966.

Glaser, Kurt. "Attempted Suicide in Children and Adolescents: Psychodynamic Observations." American Journal of Psychotherapy, 1965, vol. 19, pp. 220-227.

Gould, Robert E., M.D. "Suicide Problems in Children and Adolescents." American Journal of Psychotherapy, 1965, vol. 19, pp. 228-246.

Greer, S. "Parental Loss and Attempted Suicide: A Further Report." Brit. J. Psychiat., 1966, 112, pp. 465-470.

Grillmeier, Aloys. Christ in Christian Tradition, tr. by J. S. Bewden. London: A.R. Mowbray & Co., 1965.

Haider, Ijaz. "Suicidal Attempts in Children and Adolescents." Brit. J. Psychiat., 1968, 114, pp. 1113-1134.

Hefele, Charles Joseph (ed.). Deuxième concile d'Orléans en 533 in Histoire Des Conciles, Paris: Letouzey et Ané, 1908, vol. 2, part 2, pp. 1130-1135.

_____ Conciles entre 560 et 575 in Histoire Des Conciles. Paris: Letouzey et Ané, 1909, vol. 3, part 1, pp. 174-197.

Hillman, James. Suicide and the Soul. New York: Harper & Row, 1965.

Hick, John. Evil and the God of Love. London: Macmillan, 1966.

_____ The Holy Bible Revised Standard Version. New York: Thomas Nelson & Sons, 1952.

Indin, Burt M. M.D. "The Crisis Club: A Group Experience for Suicidal Patients." Mental Hygiene, 1966, vol. 50, pp. 280-290.

Jacobs, Jerry. "A Phenomenological Study of Suicide Notes." Social Problems, 1967, vol. 15, pp. 60-72.

Joest, Wilfried. Ontologie der Person bei Luther. Gottingen: Vanderhoeck & Ruprecht, 1967.

Jonas, Hans. The Gnostic Religion. Boston: Beacon Press, 1963.

Justin Martyr. <u>The First Apology. The Second Apology, and The Dialogue with Trypho, A Jew</u>. Buffalo: The Christian Literature Publishing Company, <u>The Ante Nicene Fathers</u>, 1885, vol. 1, pp. 159-270.

Kaufmann, Walter. <u>Nietzsche: Philosopher. Psychologist. Antichrist</u>. Cleveland, Ohio: Meridian Books, 1966.

Keith-Spiegel, Patricia; and Spiegel, Donald E. "Affective States of Patients Immediately Preceding Suicide." <u>Journal of Psychiatric Research</u>, 1957, vol. 5, pp. 89-93.

Kierkegaard, Søren. <u>Christian Discourses</u>, tr. by Walter Lowrie. London: Oxford University Press, 1952.

_____ <u>The Concept of Dread</u>, tr. by Walter Lowrie. Princeton: Princeton University Press, 1957.

_____ <u>Edifying Discourses</u>, tr. by David F. Swenson and Lilian Marvin Swenson. Minneapolis, Minnesota: The Augsburg Publishing House, 1962, vol. 2.

_____ <u>Edifying Discourses: A Selection</u>, tr. by David F. and Lilian Marvin Swenson. New York: Harper & Row, 1958.

_____ <u>Either/Or</u>, tr. by David F. and Lilian Marvin Swenson. New York: Anchor Books, 1959, vols. 1 & 2.

_____ <u>Fear and Trembling and The Sickness Unto Death</u>, tr. by Walter Lowrie. New York: Doubleday Anchor Books, 1954.

_____ For Self Examination and Judge for Yourselves, tr. by Walter Lowrie. Princeton: Princeton University Press, 1968.

_____ The Journals of Kierkegaard, tr. and ed. by Alexander Dru. New York: Harper Torchbooks, 1959.

_____ Judge for Yourselves, in For Self-Examination and Judge For Yourselves, tr. by Walter Lowrie. Princeton: Princeton University Press, 1968.

_____ Kierkegaard's Concluding Unscientific Postscript, tr. by David F. Swenson and Walter Lowrie. Princeton: Princeton University Press, 1968.

_____ The Last Years, Journals 1853-1855. tr. by Ronald Gregor Smith. New York: Harper & Row, 1965.

_____ Philosophical Fragments tr. by David F. Swenson. Princeton, New Jersey: Princeton University Press, 1962.

_____ The Point of View for My Work as an Author, tr. by Walter Lowrie. New York: Harper Torchbooks, 1962.

_____ The Present Age, tr. by Alexander Dru. New York: Harper Torchbooks, 1962.

_____ Repetition. An Essay In Experimental Psychology, tr. by Walter Lowrie. New York: Harper Torchbooks, 1964.

_____ Sören Kierkegaard's Journals and Papers, ed. and tr. by Howard V. Hong and Edna H. Hong.

Bloomington, Indiana: Indiana University Press, 1967.

_____ Stages on Life's Way, tr. by Walter Lowrie. New York: Schocken Books, 1967.

_____ Training in Christianity, tr. by Walter Lowrie. Princeton: Princeton University Press, 1967.

Klugman, David I.; Litman, Robert E.; Wold, Carl I. "Suicide: Answering the Cry for Help." Social Work, vol. 10, 1965, pp. 43-50.

Kockelman, Joseph J. "On Suicide: Reflections Upon Camus' View of the Problem." The Psychoanalytic Review, 1967, vol. 54.

Koller, K. M.; and Castanos, J. M. "The Influence of Childhood Parental Deprivation In Attempted Suicide." The Medical Journal of Australia, March 9, 1968, vol. 1, pp. 396-399.

Leonard, Calista V. Understanding and Preventing Suicide. Springfield, Illinois: Charles C. Thomas, 1957.

Lesse, Stanley. "Apparent Remissions in Depressed Suicidal Patients." The Journal of Nervous and Mental Disease, 1967, vol. 144, no. 4, pp. 291-296.

Lester, David. "Fear of Death of Suicidal Person." Psychological Reports 1967, 20, pp. 1077-1078.

_____ "Henry and Short on Suicide: A Critique." Journal of Psychology, 1968, 70, pp. 179-186.

_____ "Psychology and Death." Continuum,1967, vol. 5, pp. 550-558.

_____ "Suicide as an Aggressive Act: A Replication with a Control for Neurotics." Journal of General Psychology, 1968, 79, pp. 83-86.

Levi, David L. "Separation and Attempted Suicide." Archives of General Psychiatry, 1966, vol. 15, pp. 158-164.

Litman, Robert E. "When Patients Commit Suicide." American Journal of Psychotherapy, 1965, vol. 19, pp. 571-576.

Loewenich, Walther V. Luthers Theologia Crucis. München: Chr. Kaisar Verlag, 1954.

Lowrie, Walter. Kierkegaard. New York: Harper & Brothers, 1962, vols. 1 & 2.

Luther, Martin. The Abomination of the Secret Mass. 1525, tr. by Abdel Ross Wentz. Philadelphia: The Muhlenberg Press, Luther's Works, vol. 36, pp. 307-328, 1959.

_____ The Adoration of the Sacrament. 1523. tr. by Abdel Ross Wentz. Philadelphia: Muhlenberg Press, Luther's Works, vol. 36, pp. 209-306, 1959.

_____ Against the Heavenly Prophets in the Matter of Images and Sacraments, 1525, part I tr. by Bernhard Erling, part II tr. by Conrad Bergendoff. Philadelphia: Muhlenberg Press, Luther's Works, vol. 40 pp. 74-223.

_____ Briefwechsel #1180 in D. Martin Luthers Werke, Weimar: Hermann Nachfolger, vol. 4, pp. 294-95, 1933.

_____ Catholic Epistles tr. by Martin H. Bertram. St. Louis: Concordia Publishing House, Luther's Works, vol. 30, pp. 1-40.

_____ Confession Concerning Christ's Supper. 1528, tr. Robert H. Fischer, Philadelphia: Muhlenburg Press, Luther's Works 1961, vol. 37, pp. 151-372.

_____ De Servo Arbitnio, tr. by Philip W. Watson, Philadelphia: The Westminster Press, Library of Christian Classics, vol. 17, pp. 101-334, 169.

_____ Der Prophet Jona Ausgelegt. Berlin: Weimar Edition, vol. 19, pp. 169—251, 1883.

_____ Eight Sermons by Dr. Martin Luther. 1522, tr. by A. Steimle. Philadelphia: A.J. Holman Co., Works of Martin Luther, vol. 2, pp. 391-428.

_____ How Christians Should Regard Moses, 1525, tr. by Theodore Bachmann. Philadelphia: Muhlenberg Press, Luther's Works vol. 35, pp. 155-74, 1960.

_____ Lectures on Galatians. 1535, tr. by Jaroslav Pelikan. St. Louis: Concordia Publishing House, Luther's Works, 1963, vol. 26.

_____ Lectures on Romans (1515-1516), ed. and tr. by Wilhelm Pauck. Philadelphia: The Westminster Press, Library of Christian Classics, 1961, vol. 15.

CHRIST AND FREEDOM

_____ Luther: Letters of Spiritual Counsel, tr. and ed. by Theodore G. Tappert. Philadelphia: The Westminster Press, The Library of Christian Classics vol. 18, 1955.

_____ The Magnificat (1520-1521), intro, and tr. by A. T.W. Steinhaeuser. Philadelphia: A. J. Holman Company, Works of Martin Luther, 1930, vol. 3, pp. 119-200.

_____ The Misuse of the Mass. 1521, tr. by Frederick C. Ahrens. Philadelphia: The Muhlenberg Press, Luther's Works, 1959, vol. 36, pp. 127—230.

_____ The Martin Luther Christmas Book, tr. and arranged by Roland H. Bainton. Philadelphia: The Fortress Press, 1958.

_____ On Translating: An Open Letter, 1530, intro, and tr. by C. M. Jacobs. Philadelphia: A.J. Holman Co. Works of Martin Luther, 1931, vol. 5, pp. 9-27.

_____ Psalm 51. 1532. tr. by Jaroslav Pelikan. St. Louis: Concordia Publishing House, Luther's Works, 1955, vol. 12, pp. 303-410.

_____ Receiving Both Kinds in the Sacrament, 1522, tr. by Abdel Ross Wentz. Philadelphia: The Muhlenberg Press, Luther's Works, 1959, vol. 36, pp. 231—268.

_____ The Sacrament of the Body and Blood of Christ -- Against the Fanatics, 1526, tr. by Frederick C. Ahrens. Philadelphia: Muhlenberg Press, Luther's Works, 1959, vol. 36, pp. 329-362.

_____ That These Words of Christ. "This Is My Body." etc.. Still Stand Firm Against the Fanatics, 1527, tr.

by Robert H. Fischer. Philadelphia: Muhlenberg Press, Luther's Works, 1961, vol. 37, pp. 3-150.

_____ Tischreden #222, in D. Martin Luthers Werke. Weimar: Hermann Böhlaus Nachfolger, 1912, vol. 1, p. 95.

_____ Tischreden #590, in D. Martin Luthers Werke- Weimar: Hermann Böhlaus Nachfolger, 1912, vol. 1, pp. 276-277.

_____ Tischreden #4782 in D. Martin Luthers Werke. Weimar: Hermann Böhlaus Nachfolger, 1916, vol. 4, pp. 496-498.

_____ A Treatise on the New Testament, that is the Holy Mass. 1525. tr. By Jeremiah J. Schindel. Philadelphia: Muhlenberg Press, Luther's Works, 1960, vol. 35, pp. 75-111.

McSorley, Harry I. Luther: Right or Wrong? New York: Newman Press and Minneapolis: Augsburg Publishing House, 1969.

Metzger, Günther. Gelebter Glaube, Gottingen: Vandenhoeck & Ruprecht, 1964.

Michel, A. "Suicide" in Dictionnaire de Théologie Catholique. Paris: Libraireie Letouzey et Ané, 1941, vol. 14, part 2, pp. 2739-2749.

Niebuhr, Richard R. Schleiermacher on Christ and Religion. New York: Charles Scribner's Sons, 1964.

Nietzsche, Friedrich. Beyond Good and Evil, tr. by Marianne Cowan. Chicago: Henry Regnery Company, 1955.

_____ The Birth of Tragedy, tr. by Walter Kaufmann. New York: Vintage Books, 1967, pp. 1-144.

_____ The Dawn of Day, tr. by J. M. Kennedy. New York: Russell & Russell, Inc., The Complete Works of Friedrich Nietzsche. 1964, vol. 9, pp. v, 205.

_____ Human, All-Too-Human, tr. by Helen Zimmern. New York: Russell & Russell, Inc., The Complete Works of Friedrich Nietzsche, 1964, vol. 6, pp. vii, 85, 88; vol. 7, p. 286.

_____ The Joyful Wisdom. tr. by Thomas Common. New York: Russell & Russell, Inc., The Complete Works of Friedrich Nietzsche, 1964, vol. 10, pp. vii, 173.

_____ On the Genealogy of Morals, tr. by Walter Kaufmann and R.S. Hollingdale. New York: Vintage Books, 1967.

_____ Thus Spoke Zarathustra, tr. by Walter Kaufmann. New York: The Viking Press, 1966.

_____ The Twilight of the Idols, tr. by Anthony Ludovici. New York: Russell & Russell Inc., The Complete Works of Friedrich Nietzsche, 1964., vol. 16, pp. vi, 89.

_____ The Will to Power tr. by Walter Kaufmann and R. J. Hollindale. New York: Random House, 1971.

Nilsson, Kjell Ove. Simul, Gottingen: Vandenhoeck & Ruprecht, 1966.

Obendiek, Hermannus. Der Teufel bei Martin Luther. Berlin: Furche Verlag, 1931.

Otto, Ulf. "Changes in the Behavior of Children and Adolescents Preceeding Suicidal Attempts." Acta Psychiatica Scandinavica, 1965, vol. 40, pp. 386-400.

Philip, A. E. and McCulloch, J.W. "Social Pathology and Personality in Attempted Suicide." Brit. J. Psychiat., 1967, 113, pp. 1405-1406.

_____ "Some Psychological Features of Persons Who have Attempted Suicide." British Journal of Psychiatry, 1968, 114, pp. 1299-1300.

Pokorny, Alex D., M.D. "A Follow-Up Study of 618 Suicidal Patients." The American Journal of Psychiatry, 1966, vol. 12, pp. 1109-1116.

Portalié, Eugene. A Guide to the Thought of Saint Augustine, tr. by Ralph J. Bastian. Chicago: Henry Regnery Company, 1960.

Prenter, Regin. Spiritus Creator tr. by John M. Jensen. Philadelphia: The Fortress Press, 1953.

Preus, James Samuel. From Shadow to Promise. Cambridge, Massachusetts: Harvard University Press, 1969.

Reist, Benhamin A. Toward A Theology of Involvement. Philadelphia: The Westminster Press, 1966.

Resnik, H.L.P. (ed.). Suicidal Behaviors. Boston: Little Brown and Company, 1968.

Rupp, Gordon. Patterns of Reformation. Philadelphia: Fortress Press, parts 2 & 3, 1969.

Ryle, Anthony. "A Repertory Grid Study of the Meaning and Consequences of a Suicidal Act." British Journal of Psychiatry, 1967, 113, 1393-1403.

Schleiermacher, Friedrich. Brief Outline on the Study of Theology, tr. by Terrence N. Tice. Richmond, Virginia: John Knox Press, 1966.

_____ The Christian Faith, tr. from the German by H. R. Mackintosh, J.S. Stewart, et al. New York: Harper & Row, 1963, 2 vols.

_____ Christmas Eve. Dialogue on the Incarnation, tr. from the German by Terrence N. Tice. Richmond, Virginia: John Knox Press, 1967.

_____ On Religion. Speeches to its Cultured Despisers, tr. from the German by John Oman. New York: Harper & Row, 1958.

_____ Schleiermacher's Soliloquies, tr. from the German by Horace Leland Friess. Chicago: The Open Court Publishing Company, 1957.

Schopenhauer, Arthur. Studies in Pessimism, in Essays of. Arthur Schopenhauer, tr. by T. Bailey Saunders. New York: A. L. Burt Company, n. d.

_____ The World as Will and Idea, tr. by R. B. Haldane and J. Kemp. London: Kegan Paul, Trench, Trübner & Co. Ltd., 1907.

Schreiber, Flora Rehta and Herman, Melvin. "How to Cure Depression." Science Digest, 1967, vol. 61, pp. 12-15.

Shneidman, Edwin S. (ed.). Essays in Self-Destruction. New York: Science House, Inc., 1967.

Shneidman, Edwin S. "Orientations Towards Death: A Vital Aspect of the Study of Lives." International Journal of Psychiatry, 1966, vol. 2, pp. 167-200.

_____ "Suicide: 'Psychological Aspects (I)'." International Encyclopedia of the Social Sciences, vol. 15, pp. 385-390.

Troeltsch, Ernst. The Social Teaching of the Christian Church tr. by Olive Wyon. New York: Harper Torchbooks, vols. 1 & 2, 1960.

Walker, Williston. A History of the Christian Church, revised edition. New York: Charles Scribner's Sons, 1959.

Williams, Glanville. "Suicide." The Encyclopedia of Philosophy, (Paul Edwards, ed.). New York: The Macmillan Company, 1967, pp. 43-46.

Young, Robert. Analytical Concordance to the Bible. New York: Funk & Wagnalls, n.d.

ACKNOWLEDGEMENTS

ACKNOWLEDGEMENT is made to the authors and publishers cited below for permission to quote from the following copyrighted works.

Canon Law: A Text and Commentary (Revised Edition) by Rev. T. Lincoln Bouscaren, S.J., Rev. Adam C. Ellis, S.J., and Rev. Francis Korth, S.J., Copyright (C) The Bruce Publishing Company 1947, 1951, 1957, 1963, 1966, reprinted by permission of The Macmillan Company.

The Gnostic Religion (Second Edition, Revised) by Hans Jonas, copyright 1963 reprinted by permission of Beacon Press, Inc.

On Free Choice of the Will by Saint Augustine, translated by Anne S. Benjamin and L. H. Hackstaff, copyright 1964, reprinted by permission of the Bobbs-Merrill Company, Inc.

Nicomachean Ethics by Aristotle, translated by Martin Ostwald, copyright 1962, reprinted by permission of the Bobbs-Merrill Company, Inc.

Selections from Vol. II Søren Kierkegaard, Either/Or, translated by Walter Lowrie, with Revision and a Foreward by Howard A. Johnson (copyright 1944, 1959 by Princeton University Press: Princeton Paperback, 1971), pp. 250, 251, and 236. Reprinted by permission of Princeton University Press.

"Psychotherapists' Orientations Toward Suicide" by Robert E. Litman, in Resnik's <u>Suicidal Behaviors</u> copyright 1968, reprinted by permission of Robert E. Litman and Little Brown and Company.

Reprinted by permission of the publisher Horizon Press, New York from <u>Letters of Fyodor Michailovitch Dostoevsky To His Family and Friends</u>, copyright 1961.

"Suicide: Social Aspects" by Jack Douglas from <u>The International Encyclopedia of the Social Sciences</u> edited by David L. Sills, copyright 1968, reprinted by permission of the Macmillan Company.

<u>The Possessed</u> by Fyodor Dostoevsky, translated by Constance Garnett, copyright 1936 by the Modern Library, Inc., and renewed, 1963 by Random House, Inc., reprinted by permission of Alfred A. Knopf, Inc. and Random House, Inc.

<u>Lyrical and Critical Essays</u> by Albert Camus, translated by Ellen Conroy Kennedy, copyright 1968, reprinted by permission of Alred A. Knopf, Inc. and Random House, Inc.

<u>The Myth of Sisyphus</u> by Albert Camus, translated by Justin O'Brien, copyright 1955, reprinted by permission of Alfred A. Knopf, Inc. and Random House, Inc.

<u>The Will to Power</u> by Friedrich Nietzsche, translated by Walter Kaufmann and R.J. Hollingdale, copyright 1967, reprinted by permission of Alred A. Knopf, Inc. and Random House, Inc.

<u>The Birth of Tragedy</u> by Friedrich Nietzsche, translated by Walter Kaufmann, copyright 1967, reprinted by permission of Alfred A. Knopf, Inc. and Random House, Inc.

Page 912 of Fyodor Dostoevsky: <u>The Brothers Karamazov</u> translated by David Magarshack. Translation copyright (C) David Magarshack, 1958, reprinted by permission of Penguin Books Ltd.

The Letters of Saint Athanasius Concerning the Holy Spirit, translated by C. R. B. Shapland, published 1951, reprinted by permission of The Philosophical Library, Inc.

Page 173, vol. 10 and page 88 vol. 16 of The Complete Works of Friedrich Nietzsche date of reissue, 1964, reprinted by permission of Russell & Russell Publishers.

Calvin: Institutes of the Christian Religion, vol. xx, The Library of Christian Classics, edited by John T. McNeill and translated by Ford Lewis Battles. Published in the U.S.A. by the Westminster Press. Copyright MCMLX, by W.L. Jenkins, used by permission.

Luther: Letters of Spiritual Counsel, vol. xviii, The Library of Christian Classics, edited by Theodore G. Tappert. Published in the U. S. A. by the Westminster Press, 1955, used by permission. (British Commonwealth Rights granted by permission of SCM Press Ltd.)

The Portable Nietzsche translated by Walter Kaufmann. Copyright 1954 by Viking Press, Inc. Reprinted by permission of The Viking Press, Inc.

The Diary of a Writer by Dostoevsky, translated by Boris Brasol, copyright 1949, reprinted by permission of Charles Scribner's Sons.

"The Heavenly Christmas Tree" from An Honest Thief and Other Stories by Fyodor Dostoevsky, translated from the Russian by Constance Garnett, copyright 1919, reprinted by permission of The Macmillan Company. (British Commonwealth Rights granted by permission of William Heinemann Ltd., Publishers.)

Augustine: Earlier Writings, vol. vi, The Library of Christian Classics, edited by John H.S. Burleigh. Published in the United States, 1953, used by permission of The Westminster Press. (British Commonwealth Rights granted by permission of SCM Press Ltd.)

PART II

INTRODUCTION

A lesbian, a drug addict . . .
The products of a
SECULAR CITY.
the lost despising,
groping, wanting --
and the psychiatrist
enters
and the talk begins
and all are sensitive
and emotive and modern.
And then the old
woman comes
and she cries and
she cries
and her words live
a second before
they die.

Small things are said
of great proportions,
of lost love
and partial abortions,
of a girl with a lover
bound to her sex,
of the single one's sailing
and the colossal wreck.

And the old woman
comes
And she cries and she cries,
And makes of our
truths
A table of lies.

One has used poison,
Another a knife,
One uses a bullet
to quit with all strife.
All are shattered

their memories laid bare . . .
It's hard first to listen;
it's harder to care.

but the old woman
comes and she cries,
and she cries
and to mention "not caring"
is to mention but lies.

We've spoken of
beauty in scholarly
spheres.
Much talk over
coffee and society's
cares.

We've all had our
anguish -- when
anguish was right.
We've fought for
right truth
with <u>scholarly</u> might . . .

But sit down awhile
in a suicide ward,
Sit down a while
as she opens the door.
Sit down with sobs
and all petty concerns . . .

For the old woman
comes
And she cries
and she cries . . .
She weeps over
cities that have
broken all ties,
She weeps over
truths that for
her are all lies.

CHRIST AND FREEDOM

She weeps
in her groping
and hasn't a light. . . .
She weeps through
the scraps
of modernity's night.

SAUL

CAST OF CHARACTERS

Samuel, age 55

Saul, age 40

Amasa, his servant, age 27

Jessica (i.e., Hebrew for "the rich one"), age 30

Marian (i.e., Hebrew for "the bitter one"), age 35

Jobina (i.e., Hebrew for "the afflicted one")

Jonathan, age 18. Jonathan is Saul's son.

David, age 18

Servants, soldiers, workers, etc.

ACT I

Scene I

(The setting is a desert. Three women are on a hill speaking with each other. Jessica is the more attractive of the three. She is thin, tall, and is graceful in her movements. Marian is less attractive but possesses that quality of feminine independence which makes her enticing. Jobina is inordinately homely. She is overweight and conciliatory.)
Jessica: It's a fine day.
Marian: It could be finer.
Jobina: How so?
Marian: We've only been singing and talking to ourselves.
Jobina: I suppose you're tired of us.
Marian: Yes I am.
Jobina: I suppose you would like something more.
Marian: Wouldn't you?
Jobina: Why don't you accept what we're given? The simplicity of work is good enough for us all.
Marian: Nothing is good without some degree of passion.
Jessica: I still say that it's a fine day.
Marian: But it could be finer.

Scene 2

(On the plains of the same desert two men are speaking. Saul is over six feet tall and is extremely handsome. Amasa, his servant, is of average height, about 5' 5", and is overweight.)
Saul: Where have they fled to?

Amasa: I don't know. What's the importance of a few mules running across the sand?
Saul: My father wishes us to gather them again.
Amasa: Well, we can't spend the entire day looking for beasts of burden. Besides if we burden ourselves looking for beasts of burden, who are we?
Saul: (puzzled but with authority) Look, let's just find the mules.
Amasa: Okay.
Saul: (attempting to relieve the tension) Do you know any songs?
Amasa: Just one.
Saul: Well, sing it.
Amasa: It's called "The Burden."
Saul: Let's hear it.
Amasa:
>We work the desert
>for its sand
>To find the sand
>and thirst.
>
>We find the thirst
>to seek again
>Water and a curse.
>
>With our curse
>We seek again . . .

Saul: Stop. That's a terrible song.
Amasa: The song's terrible? (Amasa implies that everything is terrible.)
Saul: Listen, we need harmony. I'll sing for you.

>Man's plight is softened
>Before His God
>Who loves him by the hour.
>
>Like in a fortress
>Before a siege
>God is the watchful tower.

Amasa: That's terrible.
Saul: Why?

Amasa: Because it isn't true.

Scene 3

(Same as scene 1)

Jessica: I heard something.
Marian: The wind no doubt.
Jessica: No, I heard a man's voice.
Jobina: (excited) A man's voice! Where?
Jessica: It rose up from the plain.
(Marian steps back indifferently. Jobina rushes to the front of the stage and looks out at the audience.)
Jobina: There is someone down there. Yes, it is a man; in fact, two men. Wonderful.
Marian: But there are three of us.
Jobina: (disappointed) That's true.
Jessica: How do I look?
Marian: Not bad.
Jobina: You look fine, Jessica.
(Jobina runs to the front of the stage.) They're coming our way.
Marian: (somewhat bored) Fine.
Jobina: What should we tell them?
Jessica: Do we have to tell them something?
Jobina: Yes, or they will not stay long.
Marian: Because of you. Remember there are two of us.
Jobina: But . . .
Jessica: Don't worry.
Jobina (smoothing her hair) Here they come.
(Enter Saul and Amasa.)
Saul: (rather bashfully) Hello. Have you seen any mules?
Marian: (with mockery) That's quite a greeting.
Jessica: No we haven't.
Jobina: I think mules are beautiful.
Amasa: What?
Jobina: They really are.
Amasa: Oh, come now.
Marian: Really, what are you two looking for?
Saul: The mules. They belong to my father and they have strayed away.

Marian: (disgusted) Couldn't you be pursuing something else?
Saul: (confused and embarrassed) What else should a man pursue?
Jessica: (smiling) Why beauty or truth.
Amasa: (laughing) Really. You ask us to pursue the air.
Saul: (defensively) What my father tells me to do, I do.
Marian: But are you satisfied with that?
Saul: (becoming angry) It is not important whether I am satisfied or not.
Jobina: Wouldn't you rather pursue God as wise men do?
Saul: But I am not a wise man.
Amasa: (starting to go) Let's find the mules.
Saul: (perplexed and looking at Jobina) Wait.
Amasa: Don't be a fool! Let's go.
Jobina: (to Saul) But you could be a wise man.
Saul: How?
Jobina: Why. (A pause. She finds it hard to give the right answer.) Why, there is a wise man in the town not far from here. You will know him when you see him.
Jessica: But . . .
Jobina: (hastily) You will be able to find him.
Saul: (to Amasa) Let's go to the town.
Marian: (to herself) Oh, no!
Amasa: But . . .
Saul: We'll talk about it on the way. (Saul and Amasa exit.)
Jessica: Why did you tell him that?
Jobina: Because I did not want him to leave right away. He was so handsome. He was like a pomegranate fallen on the desert.
Marian: (out loud) Oh, no!
Jessica: But there is no wise man in the nearest town.
Jobina: (confused) But I did not want him to go just then.
Marian: Well, there is no need to worry now. Anyone who goes seeking a wise man will at least find men. From them the seeker will make his own wisdom or madness.

(Darkness)

ACT II

Scene I

(The same desert.)
Amasa: But Saul, what about the mules?
Saul: (irritated) Forget about the mules.
Amasa: What has come over you?
Saul: It just occurred to me. I am not a man.
Amasa: What?
Saul: I am not a man because I do not do what I will.
Amasa: Oh, I see. Our fair friends have touched your vanity, You want to become one of those raving madmen in the village square! Take my advice and go back and seduce one of them. You'll feel better.
Saul: Then I'd only be exchanging the mules for a woman.
Amasa: Well, what else is there?
Saul: Let me find out.

Scene 2

(A public square. Five workers are assembled and are yelling. An old man is trying to maintain order.)
Workers: A king . . . a king! Let us have a king.
Samuel: (the old man) Order! At all cost, order! God is still our father. What do you need a king for? God will feed us as he fed Moses and the people in the wilderness. The covenant must still be respected. The covenant is our contract with God. If we will be His people, He will be our God. Please let us have order. Remember that God is our king.
First Worker: Where is the promised land?

Second Worker: (with mockery) We're supposed to be in it.
Third Worker: Then why are we threatened by the thieving and murderous Philistines?
Fourth Worker: There is no peace!
Fifth Worker: There is no security!
First Worker: There is no promised land. God has led us into another desert.
Second Worker: I break my back for a bowl of honey.
Third Worker: I break mine for a bowl of milk.
Fourth Worker: God needs help. The prophets are not enough.
Fifth Worker: A king! We need a king! God cannot defend us against the Philistines.
Samuel: This is all wicked. A king will only enslave you. God defends each breath you take. Believe in Him and do not hope for a king who breathes like yourself. Believe in God who has freed us in the past and who will free us now and in the future.
First Worker: A king. We need a king!
All the Workers: A king! We need a king!
(The workers are now in a frenzy waving their fists and shouting "king!" Saul and Amasa enter.)
Saul: (to third worker) What is happening?
Third Worker: We are demanding a king.
Saul: Why do you demand a king? Seek truth first. Seek God.
Second Worker: You humble fool! We need a king to protect us from the Philistines.
Saul: But God is our king. We need no other. Hold to the covenant and live. You people demand too much. Trust in God and live simply.
Amasa: Good advice. Let's find the mules.
Saul: But . . .
Samuel: (who has been listening attentively) You, sir. What is your name?
Saul: It is Saul.
Samuel: And where do you come from?
Saul: From the tribe of Benjamin. A tribe of mule chasers and lowly men.
Samuel: And you trust in God's guidance?
Saul: There is no other guidance.
Samuel: And do you trust his prophets?
Saul: I have never known one of his prophets.

Samuel: I am one of his prophets.
Saul: I trust God and his prophets of the past. I do not know your teaching.
Samuel: (perplexed, but realizing the immediacy of the hour) What is your feeling towards the Philistines?
Saul: They are against God and must be crushed.
First Worker: Down with the Philistines; we must have a king.
Third Worker: Who will defend us?
Fourth Worker: A king, a king!
All the workers: We must have a king!
Saul: (becoming carried away with his new-found independence) Yes a king, but one who obeys God.
Samuel: And his prophets.
First Worker: The real prophets are dead. We must have a king. He will be both prophet and conqueror.
Second Worker: Make Saul king.
Third Worker: Saul!
Fourth Worker: Saul!
Fifth Worker: Saul!
(The workers grab Saul and start a circular dance. Saul is drawn into this vortex and cannot escape.)
Workers: Saul! Saul! Saul!
(They begin chanting and praising him with shouts and noises. Samuel and Amasa watch this. Saul becomes intoxicated under the powerful movement. When the workers stop, Saul is still spinning and dancing. Amasa goes to Saul and brings him to a stop.)
Samuel: Saul shall be our king.
Saul: But I am from a lowly tribe.
Samuel: God has spoken for you through the people, and therefore you have been anointed by their demands and their dance.
Saul: But I came seeking God.
Samuel: And you have found Him. These are His people, and I am His prophet. His guidance for the people will come through the two of us. Let us retire now and discuss God's will.
(Saul is somewhat dumbfounded. Samuel places his arm around him and leads him off stage. Four of the workers

disperse joyously. The fifth worker is looking for something on the ground but he also is quite happy.)

Amasa: What are you looking for?

First Worker: Some sheckels fell out of my trousers during the dance. Oh, here they are. (He picks up the sheckels and exits. There is a silence.)

Amasa: And I think something far more important has just fallen out of Israel.

(Darkness)

ACT III

Scene 1

(A large fortress is seen in the background. In front Amasa is dressed in a soldier's uniform. The other workers of the second act are also dressed in uniforms.)

Amasa: This place is so dry, my tongue feels like it's made of cotton.
First Worker: There hasn't been a wind here for days.
Second Worker: Everything is quiet. Not a trace of a breeze.
Third Worker: Only Goliath's ravings can be heard.
Fourth Worker: Has he presented himself again today?
Fifth Worker: No, but he soon will.
Second Worker: How are we supposed to go up against him?
Fourth Worker: Not even Saul has challenged him to combat.
Amasa: Something has overcome Saul ever since he disobeyed Samuel's command to hack Agag to pieces after the battle with the Amalekites.
Fourth Worker: And then the breezes died.
First Worker: Yes, all the breezes died.

Scene 2

(A room in the fortress. Jonathan, Saul's son, is apprehensively watching Saul.)

Saul: (stalking back and forth) Can no one here sing? Can no one fight? We have beaten the Philistines before. Why is there so much fear among the people?
Jonathan: They have seen Goliath. His muscles are as big as our shields, the shaft of his spear is like an ancient tree, the size of his sword . . .
Saul: (waving his hands furiously) That's enough.

Jonathan: But you asked and . . .

Saul: Silence! Where is my old servant?

Jonathan: Father, don't you remember? Amasa is now your general. I will go and get him.

Saul: Wait, don't get him.

Jonathan: But you asked for him.

Saul: I did not ask for him. I only asked where he was. Why has he not fought with Goliath?

Jonathan: Because you have forbidden him to do so.

Saul: I did? When did I do that?

Jonathan: Each day you have told him not to fight Goliath. You have ordered him to remain with the troops and keep order.

Saul: (raging) Silence! (Waits for a few seconds trying to control his rage.) Jonathan, find someone to sing to me. I must have music. Somehow the sun has crept into my head and it glows brighter each time I speak. There is no shade and I begin shaking in the white heat. I must be soothed and shaded. (Begins yelling) I must be soothed and shaded! (Jonathan watches him and then runs out.)

Saul: (He speaks in a voice which fluctuates between fear and rage.) God has deserted me. He has deserted me before I had a chance of really knowing Him. And then the orange ball grew inside and melted slowly each part of me. How am I to rid myself of this? I have no one to lean upon. No one knows . . . no one . . . (Begins mumbling and crying) A mule . . . to a woman . . . to the High God -- Who rules the sun and makes the king . . .

The king -- the sun

The sun -- the . . .

Oh . . . Oh . . . (He begins to recognize his ramblings.)

The sun cannot disobey . . .

But the king can.

Scene 3

(A court within the fortress. An eighteen-year-old young man is looking skyward. He has a sling over his shoulder and is

carrying a small bundle. He is whistling and appears quite complacent.)
(Jonathan enters.)
Jonathan: Can I help you?
David: I have never seen a house this large.
Jonathan: (smiling) This is the king's fortress.
David: Oh. Why do all the men in armor have such worried looks on their faces?
Jonathan: They fear the Philistine, Goliath.
David: The Israelites should fear none but God.
Jonathan: That is an easy saying for a young man.
David: (irritated) What has age to do with it? Our God makes light of such concerns. Who is this Philistine that he dares to challenge the Israelites?
Jonathan: He is Goliath. He is the giant of the Philistines.
David: And no one has fought with him?
Jonathan: No one.
David: Does no one trust in God?
Jonathan: They trust my father, Saul.
David: Has Saul fought the Philistine?
Jonathan: My father is not in his right mind. He says things and then forgets them. He cannot distinguish, and he cannot choose.
David: But does he trust in God?
Jonathan: He cannot tell who God is. He is unable to distinguish the path which he must take. His heart has become like the weather. It is as dry as the sand and needs to be soothed.
David: Let me speak with him.
Jonathan: He does not wish to speak with anyone. He only wishes to hear music from the lyre.
David: I can play the lyre.
Jonathan: Can you play it well?
David: Yes.
Jonathan: Then come quickly.

Scene 4

(The interior of the fortress. Saul has his head down on the table. hands are coupled over his head. Jonathan and David enter.)

Jonathan: Father, I have brought you a minstrel.
Saul: (looks up painfully) Then have him play. (Softly almost pleading) Please have him play.
(A servant brings a lyre and exits. David and Jonathan sit down. David begins singing softly as he plays the lyre.)
David:
I wandered across the meadow
just seeking my father's sheep.
A sling, a lyre, and a quickened step
is all that a boy can keep. (He begins seeking a form and a meaning for his song.)

Then I came to the town from the meadows,
with bread and cheese for my brothers . . .
but a king had been stricken
and my heart was quickened,
to help his maddened soul.

A song is needed
when the soul is too heated
and needs the evening shade.
A lyre and a singer
is God s joy-bringer
for the soul to be re-made.

(There is a brief pause. David has found his form and that which he wishes to convey.)

Think of the maidens
and the chilling of wine.
Think of your youth
and your laughing at time,
and the problems at present
will fade from your view,
like a young buck at morning
you'll romp in the dew.
(Saul falls on the floor in hysterical laughter.)
Saul: You're a terrible poet. "You'll romp in the dew." What a line!
(Saul continues to laugh.)
Jonathan: (to David) It's working.
David: (singing with more confidence)
If the poet is bad
and you laugh at his song,
then all is not lost
though an image be wrong.
Saul: (continues to laugh) I feel better. That's enough for now. What is your name? I will pay you handsomely.
David: My name is David and I am from Bethlehem. I came to give my brothers some cheese and bread from my father.
Saul: Just as in the song . . . And you just made that up? Just like that?
David: Yes.
Saul: Well, that's very good, very good indeed. In that case you're not such a bad poet.
David: Thank you.
Saul: Now what would you like as a gift?
David: The love of the king.
Saul: You have that.
David: And that I may sing for the king if it pleases him.
Saul: (still laughing) You must always sing for me.
David: And I would like to fight the Philistine giant.
Saul: (stops laughing) You wish to what?
David: To fight Goliath.

Saul: But you are barely a man. He is four times your size. No, stay here and sing for me. You cannot sing well from beneath the earth.

David: Often times I killed bears and wolves with my sling when they attacked my father's sheep. Let me fight the wolf and bear of the Israelites. Before God there can be little difference.

Saul: (recollecting and somewhat dumbfounded) Are you serious?

David: I am as serious as my faith in God is serious. Please, let me fight Goliath.

Saul: (impressed and jolted) I will get you some armor.

David: Let me see the armor.

(Jonathan exits.)

Saul: But if I do not have your songs, how will I maintain myself?

David: Do not worry. Before the day is over you shall have the head of Goliath and my songs.

(Jonathan returns with a servant carrying the armor.)

Jonathan: Would you like to try it on?

David: (David picks up the breast plate and tries to put it on.) It is too heavy. I would not be able to move quickly. (He puts the breastplate down.) Let God be my armor, and let me fight the Philistine.

Saul: Go with my blessing. (David leaves with Jonathan and the servant.) Oh Lord, I thank thee for this gift today. Guard this boy in his battle and let him be victorious. (He stops.) Oh . . . oh -- the heat is starting again. (He rushes after the servant, Jonathan and David.) David . . . David!

(Darkness)

ACT IV

Scene 1

(Amasa and workers dressed as soldiers are gathered upon a plain.)
Amasa: What a battle! What a fight!
First Soldier: Did you see them run! Hurray for David! With a few pebbles and a piece of leather he slew the giant!
Second Soldier: Here he comes with Saul. We have our king back and a new warrior.
(Saul and David enter. Saul is carrying a spear over his shoulder. David is carrying a sling.)
Saul: They'll be running like rabbits for days. Ha! (He puts his arm around David.) What a man you are!
David: Not nearly the man you are, my king.
Saul: And God is your armor?
David: He is also yours, my king.
Amasa: Hurray for King Saul and David!
All the soldiers: Hurray for the king and David!
Saul: Prepare a feast. We shall celebrate for weeks. David, rest a while, but not for too long, I must hear your songs again.
David: Yes, my king.
Saul: Wonderful, wonderful.
Amasa: Here come some women. Let's go to the fortress.
Saul: No, wait.
David: I think my king needs rest.
Saul: No wait. They're singing. Let us hear their song.
(Enter Jessica, Marian, and Jobina with cymbals and tambourines. The tone of their voices is mischievous, and they wish to flirt with David.)
Jessica: A king had lost control.
Marian: But a young man has kept his wits.

Jobina: David has saved the day and cured the kingly fits.
Jessica, Marian, and Jobina: (in chorus)
    And Saul has slain his thousands,
    But David has slain ten thousand.
Jessica: For David killed Goliath.
Marian: And the Philistines scattered like rats.
Jobina: And ten thousand run, like the rats who shun the first scratchings of the cat.
The three together (smiling and becoming more flirtatious towards David):
    For Saul has slain his thousands
    But David has slain ten thousand.
Jobina: Young women have said that few
    are more handsome than Saul,
Marian: But judgments by youth have seldom
    been right.
Jobina: (giggling)
    Since their hearts will be yearning
    for David tonight.
The three together:
    For Saul has slain his thousands,
    But David has slain ten thousand.
Saul: (becoming enraged) Who taught you that song?
Jessica: The present.
Marian: And the future.
Amasa (furious): All right, you bitches, you can leave now. You're finished!
Marian: But we're not finished.
Amasa: I said LEAVE! (He draws his sword.) Damn you! You've troubled the king!
David: (unsure of himself) Yes, please leave.
Jessica: (flirtatiously) Yes, we must obey David.
Marian: If David says leave, then we must.
Jobina: Yes, we must.
(Jessica, Marian, and Jobina, all laughing, exit.)
David: (turning to Saul timidly) I am sorry that women are so stupid.
Saul: Silence!
David: But . . .
Saul: (raging) Keep silence. They'll not obey me or my captain, but they'll obey you. Who do you think you are?

David: But . . .
Saul: (He gestures with his spear, raising it above his head.) Silence . . .
(David sees the gesture and runs off stage. Saul hurls the spear after him.)
Amasa: King. My king. He meant nothing.
Saul: He is trying to destroy me. (He stops.) The sun is growing hotter and is growing needles. Shade . . . shade . . . please soothe me. David! . . . and bring him back. Bring him back quickly!
Amasa: (on the verge of weeping) Yes, my king. (He leaves with the other soldiers.)
Saul: (He is alone. He is looking at the sky and is in a frenzy.) Will I be bound to this youth and demand distance from him? Is this Your Wrath to bind me to one who shall undo me? Who are You that You leave me in this eternal boiling? I pray to You and You send me thorns in the heat. Why do you torment me? Where is Your graceful shade? (He flourishes his fist at the sky.) I will find You and crush You! I will find You! (He draws his sword and begins hacking the air.) I will find You! (He runs madly about the stage.) I will find You!

Scene 2

(David is weeping in the fortress courtyard. Jonathan enters.)
Jonathan: Why these tears? You are Israel's hero.
David: Saul wishes me dead.
Jonathan: He is not well, but I thought he was becoming cured. What happened?
David: Some women came along with cymbals and tambourines and began making too much of me.
Jonathan: They didn't compare you with him?
David: Yes.
Jonathan: You had better leave immediately.
David: But Saul needs my songs to soothe his pain.
Jonathan: You are right. (Amasa enters.)
Amasa: The king needs you right away.
David: It would be easier to face Goliath again.

Jonathan: Fear not, the Lord is with you.
David: Then I must go to the king.
Jonathan: I will come with you.
David: Thank you, Jonathan. You must be my friend always.
Jonathan: I am, forever. (They embrace each other and move off stage. Amasa follows them.)

Scene 3

(A room in the fortress. Saul is pacing and holding his head. A lyre is on the table. A spear is placed vertically at the same table.)

Saul: Where is he? Where is he? What have I done? The breezes had picked up for awhile but now they have died. The thorns are growing longer inside of my head. DAVID GET THEM OUT! (Screeching) DAVID GET RID OF THEM! (He begins weeping and covers his head with his hands. David enters cautiously with Jonathan and Amasa. David quietly picks up the lyre and begins singing softly.)

David:
    A king shall Saul always be.
    No woman can threaten his state.
    He'll rule us with wisdom,
    he'll strengthen our dominions,
    a king shall Saul always be.

                    (Saul, who has been sitting
                      at a table, looks up.)

    A lion shall Saul always be.
    He'll rage when he must,
    but we are his men,
    and to question is sin.
    A lion shall Saul always be.

    And soothed our good king shall be.
    The heat of the battle
    and feminine prattle
    has shaken his mind once more.
    But soothed our good king shall be.

Saul: (He begins to laugh good-naturedly again.) Stop . . . please stop. David. I did not mean to harm you. I . . . I don't know. Please sing some more. Sing anything. It doesn't matter.

David: (mournfully)
I fear a boy from
the rolling hills shall never
be a king's healer.

I fear the Lord
In His mighty rein
has other designs for a shepherd.

But believe me, oh king . . .
If to you peace I could bring
By thy side I should always be.

(David puts down the lyre. Saul is weeping, he goes over to him and embraces him.)

Saul: My son, my son, you must never leave me. It is just that the heat and the thorns and . . . oh, no, there are voices ... now voices . . . please, play . . . please, play. Wait (Saul begins speaking as if he were possessed.) I hear them. I HEAR THEM. (He grabs his head in his hands and begins speaking as if he were possessed.) I hear them. I HEAR THEM. (Saul is weeping and then screeches.)
"Saul has killed his thousands,
But David has killed ten thousand."
(He stops and then begins raging.) BUT I WILL KILL DAVID! (He grabs the spear. David runs off the stage. Saul hurls the spear after him.)
They are after me! (He begins whirling in circles.) Where is David? Have I killed him? I could have killed him. (Raging) Does he live? DOES HE LIVE? (Amasa goes to him and helps him to sit down.)

Scene 4

(The courtyard of the fortress)
Jonathan: David, you must run to the mountains and hide.
David: But the king might need me.
Jonathan: Wait until he has calmed himself. I will come to you if he needs you. Believe in God and in our friendship.
David: I am sorry I ever came to this place.
Jonathan: Everything is not finished. Now that the Philistines have been pushed back, my father will be able to rest. Go and hide. I will come part way with you and we can speak of a hiding place.
(They leave speaking softly to one another.)

(Darkness)

ACT V

Scene 1

(The same room in the fortress. Saul is alone and pacing back and forth. His fits of rage seem to have subsided.)
Saul: How will I find God's favor again? There must be some way. Yes . . . yes that is the answer. Servant . . . servant . . . SERVANT!
Servant: (enters frightened) Yes, oh . . . (He is cut off.)
Saul: Silence! Where were you?
Servant: I was in the next room.
Saul: Why didn't you come when I called you?
Servant: I came . . . (He is cut off again.)
Saul: Silence. Go get my general. (The servant exits.)
Saul: (continues pacing) I must again have favor with God. What . . . what would please him? What sin offering can I give? My disobedience concerning Agag and the Amalekites seems so petty. God will forgive. (He begins having crying fits.) He must forgive.
(Amasa enters.)
Amasa: You sent for me?
Saul: (attempting to restrain himself) Yes. We must appease God.
Amasa: I do not know if that is possible.
Saul: It must be possible. Let us think of what would please Him.
Amasa: (thinking) There are many witches in the land. It is against the law that they should live.
Saul: (Thinking, pacing and then yelling as a madman who has just seen his last glimmer of hope.) Destroy them! DESTROY THEM! That will please Him. That will please Him.
Amasa: Saul, we do not know if that will please Him.

Saul: Damn what we know or don't know. If it is against the law then it is against God. Kill the witches. Kill them!

Amasa: I will, my king. (He exits.)

Saul: This must work. I must have the shade and I cannot tolerate David. God will then return to me. (He stops) Oh, no . . . oh, no. (He grabs his head with both hands.) The heated thorns and voices. (He whirls around) What do you say? What do you say? (He begins mumbling to himself.)

If the witches are dead
and David is gone . . .
Who will soothe you
with cures or with song?

(Saul speaks to himself but he is also speaking to the words he has just uttered.)

God . . . God must.

(He is stopped and forced to listen. He speaks again.)

But obedience is more pleasing than the fat of rams. Let Saul beware of Saul . . . Beware of Saul!

(Saul falls to his knees and begins weeping. He calls again.) Servant . . . Servant.

(The servant enters immediately.) Yes, oh king.

Saul: Has Amasa left?

Servant: He left immediately with ten men.

Saul: Catch up with him and tell him to kill all the witches but one. Have him bring one witch to me.

Servant: But . . .

Saul: Silence. I have told you what to do. (The servant exits.)

Saul: (desperately) There must be some hope left. This whirling of the orange ball in my head gives me only confusion. I must know my future so that I can act. I must know my future!

Scene 2

(The same room in the fortress. Enter Amasa with Jobina and two soldiers.)

Amasa: (to the soldiers) You are dismissed. I must talk to Saul alone. (The two soldiers leave.)

Jobina: (smiling coquettishly) Where is Saul?
Amasa: Who are you to ask such a question? I'll see you dead before the day is over. (He looks at her again.) Haven't I seen you someplace before?
Jobina: You have.
Amasa: It was on the desert a long time ago before we came to the town.
Jobina: It was.
Amasa: And then again after David had conquered Goliath.
Jobina: Yes, we were singing the praises of David.
Amasa: (furiously) And now you are caught practicing magic.
Jobina: I tried to learn magic. But I didn't learn much.
Amasa: (Outraged, he draws his sword.) You slut of the devil, I'll hack you to pieces!
(Saul enters.)
Saul: Stop . . . stop. Who are you to disobey my orders?
Amasa: But Saul . . . this witch is the same one who led us to the town and sang the songs praising David.
Jobina: (kneels before Saul) Have mercy . . . have mercy!
Saul: (to Amasa) Put your sword away.
Amasa: Saul will you compromise again? How will you please God if . . .
Saul: (raging) Damn God! (Amasa is horror struck. Saul immediately reflects on what he has just said. He speaks with authority to Amasa.) Now leave.
Amasa: Yes, my king. (He exits.)
Saul: (After a brief pause he stares at Jobina and begins laughing.) Oh no . . . oh no.
Jobina: What are you laughing about?
Saul: It isn't true. It can't be true.
Jobina: (innocently) What can't be true?
Saul: Your being a witch.
Jobina: (shamefaced) I know. I was trying to learn magic when the soldiers came. They killed the old woman but brought me here.
Saul: (smiling at first) So you're not even a witch?
Jobina: No.
Saul: Then all the witches are dead?
Jobina: Yes, I imagine they are.
Saul: (looks intently at her) Then how shall I know the future?

Jobina: Do you need to know the future?
Saul: Yes, so that I may act.
Jobina: You do not need such knowledge to act.
Saul: Then how shall I know what God has planned to be my end?
Jobina: Forget about God.
Saul: But . . .
Jobina: Would you have me lie to you and tell you that I could summon the voice of a prophet in order to guide you?
Saul: (desperately) That is an idea, even if it were a lie.
Jobina: But how could I distinguish the dead voice from my own?
Saul: But I would know something.
Jobina: I lied to you once. I do not wish to lie to you again. I lied to you upon the desert by telling you that there was a wise man in the town. But there was no wise man.
Saul: But I found Samuel and was made king. The people made me king.
Jobina: People need idols. You were just another idol.
Saul: Why did you lie then?
Jobina: Because I am ugly and I wanted you, and I did not want you to leave just then.
Saul: But . . .
Jobina: And you wanted something more than the wretchedness of a man after a mule.
Saul: And so I received more wretchedness.
Jobina: Yes but you enjoy this wretchedness and would not give it up for anything.
Saul: Yes . . . yes.
Jobina: And that is why I fear for you now.
Saul: Fear for me?
Jobina: Yes because you have tasted the love of suffering, the bright sun, and the growing thorns. You have tasted the white flame of power and hate, and nothing will satisfy you until you either rule yourself or rule the land.
Saul: I cannot rule myself until I rule the land.
Jobina: I know.
Saul: But there is no end to this. No peace. To conquer once means to conquer again.
Jobina: Such is the plight of everyone.
Saul: And David?

Jobina: He will be king. He must be king.
Saul: I know.
Jobina: And you will never conquer the land.
Saul: And so there is no way to conquer myself? Except . . .
Jobina: Yes.
Saul: And then the questioning, the tormenting fire and all supplications will end.
Jobina: (weeping) Yes.
Saul: And there will be shade, peaceful, quiet shade after one explosion?
Jobina: Yes.
(Amasa enters.)
Amasa: The Philistines are mobilizing. It is time to fight.
Saul: (smiling) . . . and conquer.
Amasa: If God wills.
Saul: (laughing) If I will.
Amasa: That is blasphemy.
Saul: (turning to him) We all blaspheme. We blaspheme when we depend on any power that is not our own. We blaspheme in our waiting and in our wretched prayers. (viciously) Would you have me say that God wills our conquering? What can God will without us?
(begins to recite as if he were given a chant to read)
Who is God without our
"Yes" or "No"?
Damn the powers
High and Low.
God is our pain, our torment,
(Saul now rages for an insane instant.) and -- OUR DISGUST!
(Saul after a few seconds speaks calmly and deliberately.)
All is quieting and cooling. . . .
Let us fight the Philistines.

Scene 3

(Mount Gilboa. Amasa and Saul are both wounded. Amasa has blood on his forehead, and Saul has an arrow through his shoulder.)

Amasa: We have lost. We have lost. My king . . . my king.

Saul: No we have not lost, but conquered all. Look they come upon us. (He begins laughing.) They come upon us but they are nothing. (He hands Amasa his sword) Amasa, hold the sword steady . . . steady . . . (Amasa's hand is shaking too much.)

Amasa: (weeping) I cannot, my king.

Saul: (grabs the sword) You do not understand
but wait --
The Philistines have surrounded us.

And hear these words before I die.

From mules to the town
To a kingdom.

The king had owned the
sun with thorns and a crown of
raving madness.

But the truth. Yes . . .
the truth (laughing)

Watch my friend
I'll conquer the
Sun (Glares at the audience and rages.)

AND SPLIT THE SKY!

(Immediately he drives the sword through his stomach. He falls. Amasa kneels by him, weeping.)

(Darkness)

Judas Iscariot—Or Who Judges Whom?

CAST OF CHARACTERS

First Pharisee

Second Pharisee

High Priest

Judas Iscariot

ACT I

(The entire play takes place in a closed room in the Temple. In the center of the stage is a long-legged brazier where coals are burning. This should be visible in the dark as the play begins. As the lights illuminate the stage three chairs are seen in a semicircle directly behind the brazier. The three chairs face the audience. The 1st. Pharisee is seen seated in the right chair. He is adjusting his headdress and holding a towel on his ear. He is mumbling to himself as the 2nd. Pharisee enters.)

1st. Pharisee: Hello, Benjamin, have you seen the High Priest?

2nd. Pharisee: I saw him as I was coming here. He said he had some unfinished business.

1st Pharisee: Well, I can't wait here all night.

2nd. Pharisee: What's the hurry?

1st. Pharisee: I'm supposed to be paid this evening.

2nd. Pharisee: Why should you be paid? You know we only get paid after the sacrifices.

1st. Pharisee: But there's a particular clause stating that after a zealot attack we're to be fully compensated for physical or emotional damages.

2nd. Pharisee: What attack?

1st. Pharisee: That's right, you weren't there.

2nd. Pharisee: I wasn't where?

1st. Pharisee: I was attacked in the garden of Gethsemane by a zealot with a sword.

2nd. Pharisee: Was anyone hurt?

1st. Pharisee: Yes, I was.

2nd. Pharisee: (goes over to him) You look all right to me. Remove the towel.
(1st. Pharisee removes the towel.) There's nothing wrong with your ear.

1st. Pharisee: It hurts like the devil.

2nd. Pharisee: (shrugging his shoulders) Well, what happened in the garden?

1st. Pharisee: Do you remember the maniac who grabbed the whip and cleared out the temple?

2nd. Pharisee: You mean the rather unkempt one who seemed to have a rather sufficient grasp of scripture?

1st. Pharisee: Yes, that one.

2nd. Pharisee: He was rather unusual. Something about his father and his father's house. Something of an antiquarian, I would say.

1st. Pharisee: Well, tonight we caught him in the garden.

2nd. Pharisee: That's right, section 264528 of the parks and garden law went into effect today. "No olive stealing under penalty of death." Technicalities always get the job done.

1st. Pharisee: But he was kneeling, he seemed to be praying, and there wasn't an olive on him.

2nd. Pharisee: Maybe he was sick. You know that an unripe olive can cause retching.

1st. Pharisee: No, he had this look on his face as if every generation was whispering in his ear. I have never seen such an expression.

2nd. Pharisee: It is only your imagination. No doubt he was under some strain. But please continue.

1st. Pharisee: Then one of his followers, I should say one of his ex-followers, a thin one who looked like death itself kissed him on the cheek in order to point him out to us.

2nd. Pharisee: You don't say. Why that's extraordinary. I thought zealots had something of a rather clannish brotherhood.

1st. Pharisee: They certainly do. Another one grabbed a sword and cut my ear off.

2nd. Pharisee: Oh really. Look at yourself. You look fine to me.

1st. Pharisee: But the one who had been kneeling, the one they called Jesus, replaced the ear on my head.

2nd. Pharisee: You don't expect the High Priest to believe that?

1st. Pharisee: But he was there. But let me continue. Jesus admonished the violent zealot. I couldn't quite make out the phrase. It was something about living by the sword and dying by the sword.

2nd. Pharisee: Well, you know progressive thinking is rampant these days. However there is some inconsistency his being a zealot and all.

1st. Pharisee: And especially the ear.

2nd. Pharisee: Look, the commotion probably got the best of you. No one will believe the bit about the ear.

1st. Pharisee: But I tell you it happened.

(The High Priest enters.)

High Priest: Well, we got rid of that one. Imagine, he called himself the son of God. I'm getting tired of this nonsense. It's causing nothing but disorder and insurrection. Everyday another one. Why, if God had so many sons there would be no room for him to breathe.

1st. Pharisee: What happened to him?

High Priest: We're making a deal with Pilate. Pilate's been stealing from the Roman treasury again. We'll get what we want, or there'll be a new governor.

2nd. Pharisee: Excellent. Nice and clean. No shouting or trouble.

High Priest: (pleased) Yes, nice and clean.

(There is a brief pause.)

1st. Pharisee: Say, I wanted to ask you about my accident compensation.

High Priest: Your what?

1st. Pharisee: You know about the ear.

High Priest: (yelling) I thought I told you to be quiet about that.

2nd. Pharisee: About what?

High Priest: (quickly) It seems our friend has been having hallucinations. I asked him to be quiet about his condition.

2nd. Pharisee: Oh.

High Priest: It doesn't look good when the authorities appear unbalanced.

1st. Pharisee: But you were there.

High Priest: Yes, and I remember you practically bungled the whole thing with your shouting, "We caught the bastard! We caught the bastard!" You're overwrought and need a vacation.

1st. Pharisee: But that takes money.

High Priest: Given your condition, it will be given to you. You'd better leave Jerusaleum tomorrow and stay away until we've seen him crucified.

1st Pharisee: Crucified? I thought we were only going to get him out of the way until he settled down.

High Priest: Don't be so naive. He can't be controlled by us. You saw what happened to the populace when he rode into Jerusaleum on a donkey. They went wild over him. Do you want that to happen again?

1st. Pharisee: No.

High Priest: Do you want all our authority destroyed?

1st. Pharisee: No.

High Priest: You'd better realize right now that you can't get accident compensation from him and his tribe.

1st. Pharisee: I never thought of that.

High Priest: (wearily) Fine. Where are you going on your vacation?

1st. Pharisee: I hadn't really thought about it.

High Priest: But when are you going?

1st. Pharisee: Tomorrow. But I still don't understand about the ear.

High Priest: (furiously) Forget about your damn ear.

2nd. Pharisee: Moderation, gentleman, moderation. There's no reason to get excited. It's only another trial and another death. Things will improve as soon as this Jesus is out of the way.

(Footsteps are heard outside followed by banging on the door.)

High Priest: Who is that at this hour of night?

Voice: It is I, Judas, the betrayer.

High Priest: Can't it wait until the morning? Come back then.

2nd Pharisee: (whispering to the High Priest) Wait, don't turn him away.

High Priest: Why not?

2nd. Pharisee: If he betrayed the leader, perhaps he will betray the rest of them.

High Priest: Yes, of course. (He goes to the door and opens it. Judas enters. He is extremely emaciated and is shaking slightly as he enters. In his hand he holds a leather sack.)

1st. Pharisee: (uncomfortably) We meet again.

Judas: (His head is down as he speaks.) Yes.
High Priest: Well, what is it? Hey, there, stand up straight. Act like a man.
(Judas attempts to straighten up but fails to look directly at any of them.)
Judas: I . . . I have betrayed innocent blood.
High Priest: Preposterous, you've done your civic duty.
Judas: (does not look at him) I have betrayed innocent blood.
2nd. Pharisee: No man was ever innocent.
Judas: I have betrayed innocent blood.
1st. Pharisee: What do you mean?
Judas: (For the first time, he looks up.) You know for you were there. I have betrayed the man who was more than man.
(Judas looks intently into the coals in the brazier.)

(Darkness)

ACT II

(The priest and the two Pharisees are now seated. Judas is still gazing at the coals. There is a brief silence of about three seconds.)

High Priest: (authoritatively) Here, here, what are you staring at?

(Judas does not acknowledge his question.)

High Priest: Come off it. We haven't time for you and your pouting. What's wrong with you?

Judas: (looking up slowly) Come near me and I will tell you.

High Priest: (coming over to him) Well?

Judas: Look into the coals. (The High Priest looks.)

High Priest: I see nothing. (Judas let's out with an hysterically wild laugh and plunges his free hand into the brazier. He pulls out two coals and places them under the High Priest's nose. The High Priest jumps back.)

Judas: Now do you see? (He continues to laugh, almost shrieking. In his other hand he still holds the money bag. He now holds up both hands with their respective objects to the High Priest.)

High Priest: You're mad.

Judas: No, not mad, merely logical. You have just seen two exact equivalents. (Judas throws the coals back into the brazier. He hands the sack to the High Priest, and Judas then takes the High Priest's seat. The High Priest is confused.)

High Priest: Why, the sack is hot.

Judas: (smiling) I know.

High Priest: (Becoming frightened, goes to the second Pharisee.) Here, take it.

2nd. Pharisee: Why it is warm. However I believe the two of you are making too much out of this whole thing. (He waits for a few seconds.) The sack seems to be getting hotter. (He goes to the 1st Pharisee.) Here, take it.

1st. Pharisee: (As he touches it, immediately he grabs his ear and drops the bag.) I cannot touch it.

Judas: (Standing up, he then picks up the bag.) To me the heat and I have become one. (He laughs demonically. He then throws the money at the High Priest, yelling:) Release him! (He jumps at the High Priest while he screams.) Release him!

High Priest: (backing away) Grab him! (The two Pharisees grab him and hold him. Judas resigns himself passively.)

2nd. Pharisee: (to Judas) I don't think all this is really necessary.

1st. Pharisee: Yes, you'll have to get a grip on yourself.

High Priest: (finally in control of himself again) What is the meaning of this? How dare you break in here and cause this commotion. I have a good mind to . . .

Judas: (laughing demonically) To what?

High Priest: To have you sentenced with him.

(Judas begins laughing again. He then stops laughing, sneers at the High Priest, and lowers his head.)

High Priest: This cannot be tolerated! It cannot be tolerated, do you hear?

Judas: (meekly) Yes, I know . . . it cannot be tolerated.

2nd. Pharisee: Of course it cannot be tolerated. Why, do you realize what you've done? You've forced us to discontinue the conversation we were having about you before you entered.

Judas: Oh, I'm sorry.

1st. Pharisee: Yes, how could you?

(Judas is now totally repentant. His arms relax.)

Judas: (meekly) I said I was sorry.

High Priest: The idea!

1st. Pharisee: The idea!

2nd. Pharisee: The idea!

High Priest: What would your mother say if she saw you acting like that after you disturbed a sensible conversation?

Judas: I don't know.

2nd. Pharisee: Yes this is quite unmannerly. You know what your mother would have said.

1st. Pharisee: Yes, you know what she would have said.
High Priest: (He draws near to Judas, the others also come in closer and begin to surround him.) The idea!
2nd. Pharisee: (indignantly) The idea!
1st. Pharisee: (indignantly) The idea!
High Priest: After you betrayed your friend!
2nd. Pharisee: (whispering in his ear) Betrayed . . . betrayed!
1st. Pharisee (whispering in his ear.) A friend -- your friend.
High Priest: (in a higher pitch) The shame!
2nd. Pharisee: (almost yelling in his ear) The shame!
High Priest: (yelling) Betrayer!
1st. Pharisee: (yelling in his ear) Betrayer!
2nd. Pharisee: (yelling in his ear) Betrayer!
(Judas immediately places his hands over his ears. He begins to weep. They push him on the floor. For a few seconds he remains in a prone position. He then kneels with his back to the audience. He holds his head in his hands. The High Priest and the two Pharisees continue as if nothing had happened.)
High Priest: Now, where were we?
1st. Pharisee: My vacation.
2nd. Pharisee: Yes, of course. I recommend Damascus in the Spring. They have excellent courtesans and the April wine is incomparable.
High Priest: Yes, Damascus is fine only it is a little too expensive for my tastes.
1st. Pharisee: But you're not going.
High Priest: But I am paying.
1st. Pharisee: Of course.
2nd. Pharisee: Of course.
High Priest: Have you thought about the Palestine Plaza? They have excellent accommodations, a swimming hole, and topless maids to take out the slop buckets.
1st. Pharisee: No I hadn't thought of the Palestine Plaza.
High Priest: It's just the place for you.
2nd. Pharisee: Of course then there's Jacob's Joint, nice atmosphere, good food, and a tolerable oasis.
High Priest: But it's too close to Jerusaleum.
2nd. Pharisee: You're right.
High Priest: (to 1st Pharisee) And I do want you far away from Jerusaleum.
1st. Pharisee: I understand.

(Judas now raises his head and looks at them.)
Judas: I have betrayed innocent blood.
2nd. Pharisee: Oh God, not this again.
High Priest: We can't really have much more of this.
1st. Pharisee: We certainly can't.
2nd. Pharisee: We're busy men with a million concerns.
High Priest: And with important decisions to make.
1st. Pharisee: And our own problems.
Judas: I have betrayed . . .
2nd. Pharisee: Oh nonsense. (turning to High Priest) I guess we'll have to talk to him.
High Priest: (wearily) Yes, I suppose we must.
1st. Pharisee: Let's not let it last too long. I have an important trip to take.

(Darkness)

ACT III

2nd. Pharisee: All right let's have it. What did you do?
Judas: I betrayed the Son of God.
High Priest: (cynically) Sure, and I picked the devil's nose.
Judas: He is the Son of God.
1st. Pharisee: Maybe that explains it.
Judas: Explains what?
1st. Pharisee: Explains how he fixed my ear.
High Priest: (becoming furious) I told you . . .
1st. Pharisee: I know . . . I know.
Judas: He had worked miracles.
High Priest: (seriously) Sure he had. (to second Pharisee) Humor him, we can't stay here all night.
2nd. Pharisee (to Judas) Of course he had.
Judas: Then how could you arrest him?
High Priest: (Forgetting his advice to the 2nd. Pharisee, he again becomes cynical.) I guess he just ran out of miracles when he really needed one.
Judas: That isn't what I meant. How could you arrest him when you knew he had the power to perform miracles.
High Priest: The devil and rebels also perform miracles. But that isn't the question. How could you betray him?
Judas: I could not understand Him, and I feared Him.
High Priest: You need fear no longer, we shall protect you.
2nd Pharisee: Yes, we shall.
Judas: You cannot protect me.
1st Pharisee: We can if you will tell us the names of the other zealots.
Judas: They have scattered.
High Priest: Are you afraid of them?
Judas: No, they were believers in Him. They would not harm me.

High Priest: I suppose you think that he and they love you now.
Judas: I believe he still does. But I cannot bear such a thought.
2nd. Pharisee: (irritated) Look this is getting too complicated. Say what you have to say and leave.
Judas: (realizing the impossibility of expressing anything to these men) I only say that Jesus of Nazareth is innocent, has harmed no one, and has never intended to harm anyone.
High Priest: Okay we've heard you now, take your money and go.
Judas: No!
2nd. Pharisee: (irritated and pointing to the money) Take it.
Judas: No... no! (He backs off the stage.) No, I don't want it. Take it... take it and bury the wretched with it. (He runs out. The High Priest and Pharisees look at each other.)
High Priest: A rather incoherent person. I hope he doesn't start any trouble.
2nd. Pharisee: For some reason he's too rattled to trouble anyone.
1st. Pharisee: Besides himself. Now, about Jacob's Joint . . .

(Darkness)

PAUL SANCTUS

A Tragic Satire

CHRIST AND FREEDOM

CAST OF CHARACTERS

Paul Sanctus, or the Old Man, a wirey fellow of great energy and great control

Young boy

Dr. Touchy Feely, a therapist

Honnanda Oshamushni, a former dope peddler who discovered he could make more money as a cultic "wise" man. His former name was Bill "The Fist" MacIntyre.

Arthur, a modern minister recently graduated from a modern "progressive" theological finishing school

George, the modern and quite common "involved" and "ecumenical" priest

Housewife I
Housewife II

Husband I, a businessman
Husband II, a businessman

Jane

Stage Directions:
The teller's window should be removed during the intermission and replaced with the statue.

CHRIST AND FREEDOM

EPISODE I

(The Institute By The Sea known for its idols of involvement, commitment, sensitivity, community, and a variety of false gods. A lonely man is seen seeking a ride at the entrance. With thumb out, he attempts to catch the attention of those driving past him. None stop but the motors roar on. He sticks his thumb into his mouth to wet it. Again he sticks his thumb out and smiles into the wind. As he is smiling off stage motors are again heard. A group of men passes by him. He barely notices them. After they have left he begins speaking to himself.)

Old Man:
Care I
that they pass me by?
Wisdom is my friend.
Often times We
have passed the evenings.
Often times We rise above
my ignorance.

Reason -- long lost
blessing in this age.
Together we contemplate
for more than reason.

Will -- once broken
and once renewed --
the strong blessing
bound in steel.

Emotion -- once a screaming
demon, and now a lively
truth . . .

Reason, will, emotion
bound, made definite, made exact
by a Higher Reason, Will, and Emotion.

Alone in the human and natural wastes
I have walked. I have learned that
we need only not to need. But . . .
afar off one can see what the modern
world is bringing. The only Guide is
Freedom from and Freedom to.

But first illusion's flickering shadow
should be observed . . . and then one should
help if help he can. (Lights begin to fade, the Old Man is barely outlined. A young boy is seen crying disconsolately.)
Young Boy: (to himself)
I do not understand . . .
How could it be?
What does one do?

        (Engines are heard off stage. Men walk past the little boy who is weeping.)

George: Well, Arthur, I'm glad you could get out of the house.
Arthur: Yes, the congregation gave me five-hundred dollars for the next three days. Let's get involved. Let's make our commitments. We must find the new compromise with the world on any terms or what will happen to my church, my future pension, and my split-level home?
Young Boy: (going up to Arthur) Sir . . . Sir . . . Something is not right. Something is wrong . . . I . . . (stuttering) I—I . . . I . . .
Arthur: (coldly turning to the boy) Make it fast and speak clearly. I have to get involved. I have to commit to the world.
Young Boy: My father has just . . . (begins stuttering again) . . . j-just-t . . .
George: (impatiently) Make it fast we're in a hurry. We have our "ecumenical" (George sighs rapturously.) commitments to make relevant anything, at any time,

anywhere, for any reason (becoming confused), well, anyway, say what you have to say and leave. We are about the Lord's business. (Pompously he kisses his own ring.)

Young Boy: Excuse me, I'm s-sorry I-I-I bot-bothered you.

(Darkness)

EPISODE II

(Arthur and George are standing before a bank teller's window. Through the bars the face of Dr. Touchy Feely can be seen. Arthur and George are both handing Dr. Feely huge wads of money. The Old Man remains unseen by the other actors.)

Arthur: Let's commit. We'll find those damn answers. I need to grow, to feel, to be alive.

George: Me too . . . but we must be ecumenical.

Dr. Feely: (Dr. Touchy Feely is a big-bellied, dyed-haired therapist with all the intelligence of a "sensitive" bookie.) Welcome . . . welcome, let's commit, grow, be ecumenical (to himself) I wonder if I missed anything (with outward pomp) Yes let us be AWARE of our true selves.

(Jane, a rather unkempt, chunky, long-haired girl enters.)

Jane: Oh Touchy -- OM!

Oh Touchy -- OM!

(She begins pawing Touchy.)

Oh Touchy -- we're committed. Oh, Touchy! Oh, Touchy! Oh, Touchy! Were soooo sensitive. Oh, Touchy, OH, TOUCHY! OH, TOUCHY!

Dr. Feely: And we'll grow into one later, my dear.

Jane: But Touchy, I'm on the pill.

Dr. Feely: That isn't what I meant.

Jane: Oh, I see. Yes, Touchy I understand. Touchy are we really sensitive?

Dr. Feely: (pontifically) It's all one, Jane.

Jane: (adoringly) I know, Touchy.

Dr. Feely: (solemnly) It's all love, Jane.

Jane: (in rapture) I know, Touchy.

Dr. Feely: (with authority) Do your own thing.

Jane: We do, Touchy. At least we did last night.

Dr. Feely: (wearily) I know, Jane.

Arthur: Ahem, Dr. Feely, we've come to find the new involvement, you see our communities are not sufficiently committed; our sensitivity groups are insensitive and . . .

Dr. Feely: (pontifically) I know, Gentlemen, I know. The problem is communication, CoMuniCation, CoMUNicatIon, COMMUNICATION. We must communicate, feel, get with it, do your own thing.

(George and Arthur begin dancing with each other.)

George: Oh Arthur, it's wonderful.

Arthur: Oh George, it's wonderful.

George: Oh, Arthur.

Arthur: Oh, George.

George: (to Arthur) I love you. We're sensitive.

Arthur: I know, George.

George: We're committed.

Arthur: I know, George.

George: But Arthur, are we really communicating?

Arthur: (blushing) Not in public, George.

George: (whimpering) But we are sensitive, aren't we, Arthur?

Arthur: (mothering him) I know, George.

George: We feel, Arthur.

Arthur: I know, George.

George: Oh, it's wonderful. It really is.

(Darkness)

CHRIST AND FREEDOM

EPISODE III

(The Old Man who has been listening and has not been seen by the other characters now goes up to Dr. Touchy Feely.)
Old Man: Say, could you loan me a dollar?
Dr. Touchy Feely: Sir, you've come to commit.
Old Man: My stomach needs to commit itself.
Dr. Feely: That's not important. We must heighten your awareness. Clear up the blockage in your head. Treat that psychosis (He begins chanting.)
Treat that psychosis
Work out that neurosis.
Say <u>OM</u>. say <u>OM</u>,
Dance, we'll give you room.

Tell us all your secrets
Oral, anal, what's the difference?
Pay the fee
for therapeutic riddance.

We'll make you get involved.
Five-hundred bucks and all your problems solved.
On the left there's nudists.
On the right -- the Buddhists.

Say <u>OM</u>, say <u>OM</u> . . .
and for the fee (Dr. Feely raises his eyebrows.) we'll give you room.
Old Man: How much for three days?
Dr. Feely: (smiling) Five-hundred <u>OM</u>'s . . . ah, dollars.
Old Man: (smiling at the audience) Do you have a blank check?
Dr. Feely: (Dr. Feely steps behind the teller's window and hands the Old Man a book of checks.)
    Here you are. (The Old Man begins writing. Dr. Feely takes out an application and begins filling it in.) Your name?
Old Man: Paul.
Dr. Feely: And your last name?
Old Man: Sanctus.
Dr. Feely: Greek?

Old Man: No.
Dr. Feely: Jew?
Old Man: No.
Dr. Feely: Irish?
Old Man: It's not important.
Dr. Feely: (confused) Address?
Old Man: The Los Angeles County Library.
Dr. Feely: (effeminately) Really?
Old Man: (glaring at him) Forget it.
Dr. Feely: Well . . . (clears his throat) . . . to begin, in the morning we have oriental dancing lessons for self-expression. In the afternoon we creatively come to grips with death and negative thinking. In the evening we overflow with joy. At all times we communicate, ComMunicaTe, COMMUNICATE.
Old Man: I've said enough.
Dr. Feely: (conciliatorily) You don't understand. It's not verbal communication. It is communication with the physical.
Old Man: With the what?
Dr. Feely: The total man.
Old Man: Who is physical?
Dr. Feely: (perplexed) I didn't say that.
Old Man: To whom are we communicating?
Dr. Feely: We just communicate to ourselves and among ourselves.
Old Man: That sounds like hell.
Dr. Feely: You're very sick. Stop thinking.
Old Man: What do you offer in its place?
Dr. Feely: Communication, involvement, and commitment.
Old Man: (wearily) When do I eat?

(Darkness)

EPISODE IV

(The Old Man is speaking. The Young Boy is silent and is sitting near him. There is no light on the bank-teller's window.)
Old Man: Man must make his
gods,

in his own image.
And now animal and cosmic gush
is at fault --
another falsity among
the many.

Wholeness
is not found with men alone.
Man dies,
and man is left alone.
Death, Death --
terror to the therapist,
terror to the theorist,
mocker of involvement,
first butcher of all
man's golden calves.

Oh therapist,
answer your own riddle.
Tell us not that man
must come to
"grips" with his only
certainty.
Who shall grip
what he can only know
by dying to false gods?

Emote your say.
You -- the new gods.
Emote, feel, and
forget.

But let us observe.
For now
that is enough.
(Darkness. When the lights come up there is a circle formed of people who have locked arms with one another. Jane is trying to break through the circle. The circle is formed by Housewives I & II and Husbands I & II. Dr. Touchy Feely and Honnanda Oshamushni are conducting this experiment in "sensitivity." Honnanda has a whistle around his neck and

appears to be a synthesis of a football coach and a starter at a racetrack for horses.)

Honnanda: All right, gang, let's see if Jane can break through the circle. (to Jane) Get in there! (Honnanda blows his whistle. Honnanda bellows at Jane as if she had one round to go for the heavyweight boxing title.) GET IN THERE! (Jane bounces around the circle like a clumsy yet frisky walrus.)

Jane: Oh, let me in -- <u>OM</u>.
    I want to participate -- <u>OM</u>.
    I want to communicate -- <u>OM</u>.

Husband I: (i.e., Jim) Oh let her in. She said <u>OM</u> three times.

Housewife I: (i.e., Sally) Yes, the magic and astrologically correct number.

Husband II: (i.e., Mike) Oh . . . oh it's really all love and it's so much FUN to be HAPPY and COMMUNICATE.

Housewife II: (i.e., Doris) Oh, Mike it's so great to be <u>avant garde</u>.

Husband II: (i.e., Mike) Oh, Doris, I love you. Despite the other three hundred women you're still the best I can remember . . . I mean . . . I ever had.

Housewife II: (i.e., Doris) A slip . . . but who gives a damn? (She looks brazenly at the audience.) Oh, Mike I don't care. It's all feeling, love, and wonder.

Husband II: (i.e., Mike) Oh, Doris.

Housewife II: (i.e., Doris) Oh, Mike.

Husband II: (eagerly) Now, Doris?

Housewife II (i.e., Doris) Later, Mike.

Husband I: (i.e., Jim) Doris, don't forget.

Housewife II: (i.e., Doris) Quiet, Jim.

Housewife I: (i.e., Sally) Mike, let's do it now.

Husband II: (i.e., Mike) Later, Sally. First we must let Jane into our circle.

Husband I, Housewife I & II: Why of course.

Husbands, Wives, and Jane: It's all love, feeling, and "god." (Husbands I & II, Housewives I & II, and Jane leave the stage.)

Dr. Feely: (to Honnanda) Well, we've done it.

Honnanda: We certainly have. Thirty-five hundred bucks for five days of nonsense. I couldn't make that kind of money selling heroin. Not only that, this is legal.

Dr. Feely: Yes, and we've done everyone a favor. We've dispensed with all the pessimistic and destructive tendencies in life.
Honnanda: (humoring Dr. Feely) I know, Touchy.
Dr. Feely: I love you, Honnanda.
Honnanda: (somewhat disgusted) Do your own thing, Touchy.
Dr. Feely: (effeminately) We do, Honnanda.
Honnanda: (disgusted) Later, Touchy.

(Darkness)

(INTERMISSION)

EPISODE V

Old Man: (The stage is dark and empty. Only the Old Man is outlined with light.)
Now they proclaim
emotion and instinct
at the cost of will and
reason.

Now they proclaim
the age of the cow and the rabbit,
and cheap sex
the godlike habit.
And God --
God is the small "g"ed
"god" -- the imaginary
"blurp"
of whim and fancy.
(There are three seconds of complete darkness. The teller's window has been removed. When the stage is again lighted a contorted mess of garbage, scrap metal, unfurled rolls of toilet paper, and everything and anything which strikes the director's "fancy" is seen on the stage. Housewife I, Housewife II, Jane, Husband I, Husband II, Arthur, George, Honnanda Oshamushni, and Dr. Touchy Feely are tossing flowers on the heap.)
Old Man: (looking at the conglomerated mess) What is this?
Dr. Feely: The real answer.

Old Man: The real answer to what?
Dr. Feely: (smiling and looking at the Old Man as an "unaware" outcast) "To whom," my poor friend, "to whom".
Honnanda: (taking the cue from Dr. Feely) Yes, "to whom".
Old Man: All right, "to whom" is this the answer?
Dr. Feely: Why, it's the answer for all of us.
Honnanda: Yes, all of us. Actually, it's a monument to the joy which is us.
Old Man: (doubling over with laughter) Ha . . . Ha. You mean it answers death?
Honnanda: We only think of that after our organically-grown lunch. Such a topic cannot be discussed until we feel at one with the universe.
Dr. Feely: For the most part we speak of life and wholeness.
Old Man: Even though man is divided through the middle because of the reality of death.
Dr. Feely: Not after he comes to us and receives our message.
Old Man: Which is?
Dr. Feely: To be whole.
Honnanda: (as if reciting from memory) And be happy and with joy.
Old Man: (inquiring) How can that be? Man dies.
Honnanda: (flippantly) But we've come to terms with death.
Old Man: Even though you haven't died to your false gods.
Honnanda: (nervous and then with authority) What difference does it make? We communicate with joy. We feel.
Old Man: Feel whom?
Dr. Feely: Ourselves, we're alive.
Old Man: For how long?
Honnanda and Dr. Feely: (as if reciting from a textbook) But we approach the infinite in our awareness, sensitivity, communication, and involvement.
Old Man: Then why do the young die?
Dr. Feely: (presumptuously) They're insensitive.
Old Man: What?
Dr. Feely: You're too dialectical.
(The young boy enters.)
My father has died and . . .
Honnanda: Leave the dead to bury their dead.
Old Man: (annoyed to the point of wrath) That's quite a quote.

Dr. Feely: Very good, Honnanda.
Honnanda: (surprised himself) Why, thank you.
Dr. Feely: I love you, Honnanda.
Honnanda: That's enough, Touchy.
Dr. Feely: But it's all one, Honnanda.
Honnanda: Later, Touchy.
Old Man: (He is ignoring both Honnanda and Dr. Feely. All except the Young Boy and the Old Man resume throwing flowers on the monument to "blurp" or "joy." The Old Man attempts to listen to the Young Boy.) What has happened?
Young Boy: My father died and my mother has no one and . . .
Dr. Feely: It's not important.
Honnanda: You have to communicate and feel; that's all.
Old Man: (He speaks to Dr. Feely, Honnanda, and the others, as he leaves with the Young Boy.) I'll be back later.
Dr. Feely: (nervously) Where are you going.
Old Man: I am going to console someone.
Honnanda: How quaint; it's all joy.
Old Man: Sure it is. (He exits with the Young Boy.)
Honnanda: (anxiously) Will he come back? Does he know my real name? Will he report me to the police? . . .
Dr. Feely: Don't worry, Honnanda, I'll take care of you.
Honnanda: (acting like a scared baby) Oh, I hope so, Touchy.
Dr. Feely: Isn't it wonderful, Honnanda?
Honnanda: (somewhat depressed) I suppose it is, Touchy.
Dr. Feely: I love you, Honnanda.
Honnanda: I know, Touchy, I know.
Dr. Feely: And it's all love, light, joy, dancing, and wonder, Honnanda.
Honnanda: Are you sure it is, Touchy?
Dr. Feely: Of course, and I love you, Honnanda.
Honnanda: (disgusted) Later, Touchy.

(Darkness)

EPISODE VI

(The Old Man is spotlighted in the darkness of the stage. The Young Boy is not far from him and is partially illuminated by the same light.)
Old Man: (addressing the darkness, the Young Boy, and the audience)
Sorrow -- the private breaking
untainted.

Sorrow -- joy's foundation.

Sorrow -- man has left you and
must always turn
back to you.

The leaves are falling to
blind deceit.
The moon is crying before
the judgment seat.
The winds make havoc
of our souls
the moment we vie
with Real Strength.

Man -- withered, weeping,
bowing
is all that <u>nature</u> portends.
Man so proud and vigorous
will find, will find
that sorrow will not be left behind.
(Old Man to boy): I hope I helped to comfort your mother, but no one alone ever does. Faith alone gives comfort. The hell of loss has but One Answer, but most people believe that two thousand years and modern gush have proven Him wrong.
Young Boy: You mean Jesus?
Old Man: Don't say His name too loudly in these regions.
Young Boy: Why?
Old Man (frowning): We would only be laughed at.

CHRIST AND FREEDOM

(Darkness)

EPISODE VII

(The lights illuminate the entire stage. The statue to "blurp" or "joy" is again seen. The Old Man and the Young Boy are again the only two on the stage. The Old Man is found speaking to himself.)
Old Man:
Man has made his gods.
He turns to them for
help.
Tragedy happens when the
gods are not gods
but men
flying downwards --
seething in the vanity
of imagination,
seething in reason,
seething in will,
seething in emotion.

It is better to be
Nothing
before one activates
his capacities.
It is better to
descend
into the inward
sickness and doubt
than to
ride a wind of thought
which before death comes to nought.
Optimism and false community
when death's scythe is raised . . .
mean inward disunity.

All the gods are dead
save One
Who brings us back
to where we have begun.

CHRIST AND FREEDOM

(two second silence)
(Enter Dr. Touchy Feely and Honnanda Oshamushni.)
Dr. Feely: Well, does comfort do any good?
Old Man: (grimacing) Some.
Honnanda: Was it joyful?
Old Man: You ass.
Honnanda and Dr. Feely: (as if reciting from a textbook) Good. An honest, authentic, emotive, committed, involved and real response. (Dr. Feely and Honnanda look at each other with surprise.)
Old Man: Let me ask the both of you a question.
Honnanda: Go ahead, you will receive a joyous answer.
Old Man: Can you dance?
Dr. Feely and Honnanda: OH, YES!
Old Man: Can you dance as if it were life or death?
Dr. Feely: But it's all life, love, joy and . . .
Old Man: Shut up! Bring out your friends and let's dance.
(Honnanda in lackey fashion goes to call the others.)
Dr. Feely: So you've decided to join us.
Old Man: Perhaps.
Dr. Feely: Well, live dangerous and sin boldly.
Old Man: Precisely.
(By now the entire cast is on the stage as Honnanda returns. The pounding surf is heard in the background.)
Old Man: Can you, I mean any one of you distinguish the true, immanent Spirit from false and demonic joy?
George: Well, I don't know but we've sure learned a lot in our immanent and ecumenical involvement class.
Old Man: (ignoring him) Can you even distinguish between terror and sorrow?
Jane: It's all one, cutie.
Old Man: (ignoring her) Do you know that what is real is hell except when the abyss is filled?
Honnanda: (as one reciting from memory) But the abyss is filled with emotive joy.
Old Man: (ignoring him) Do you understand what the depths really are?
Dr. Feely: If it's whole, it's good.
Old Man: (ignoring him) Do you know that One Person alone destroys our disunity?

Husbands I & II, Housewives I & II, George, Arthur, and Jane: But Touchy and Honnanda have made us see that we're happy, whole, and joyful.
(The Young Boy sits down and begins crying.)
Old Man: (The Old Man looks at the boy, then he glares at the audience, finally he speaks caustically) Then it's time to dance.
(The dialogue goes extremely quickly now. The Old Man and Young Boy stand still. Immediately all the others begin dancing with the grace of wounded oxen. The surging surf becomes louder. Everyone but the Old Man and the Young Boy begin shrieking, crying, and finding themselves more and more out of control.)
Dr. Feely: (in terror) I can't stop.
Honnanda: It's all hell.
George: Arthur, help me!
Arthur: I can't help you.
Jane: Touchy!
Dr. Feely: Go to hell!
Husband I: My god!
Old Man: Which one?
Husband II: Where am I?
Housewife II: Darling, help me.
Husband II: Help yourself, bitch.
Housewife II: The rocks! The cliff!
Husband I: Touchy, stop us or I'll demand repayment. . . . I'll sue you!
Dr. Feely: I can't . . . I can't stop dancing.
Husband II: Somebody do something.
Honnanda: Help yourself. I . . . I can't stop. (The lights begin to fade. Everyone except the Young Boy and the Old Man begin screeching.)
Dr. Feely: Save us!
Honnanda: Help! Someone help!
George: (yelling as loudly as possible) Someone do something.
Arthur: Oh, God!
Jane: Oh no!
Everyone (except the Old Man and the Young Boy): OH GOD!
(Spasmodic screaming. Sound effects bring in the pounding surf as it blends with the screams. Gradually the lights aim on those dancing and screaming. The Old Man is left in the

half-light. The boy is seen weeping in the same half-light. Gradually the Old Man speaks.)
Old Man:
The devils into the swine
and over the cliff.
Thus so man without
the <u>answer</u> to death.
Thus so man without
perspective.
Thus so the smug and
"joyous."
Before joy -- sorrow
and never learn to borrow
from false gods.
At the edge stands man
No buffer-nonsense to contend
with life apart from Christ.

        (Darkness)

John Sanctus

CAST OF CHARACTERS

Mr. Charles Arlington, a retired American businessman

Luigi, a bartender

Giovanna, a prostitute

John Sanctus, a young writer

Harry, an insurance salesman

A police officer

Five beggar children and a priest

An old man

Pietro

A blind man

A well-trained chimpanzee

Four Children of the Apocalypse

ACT I

(All five acts take place in an open Neopolitan tavern near the docks which berth the sight-seeing boats taking passengers to Capri and Ischia. A sidewalk is in front of the cafe. At the back of the stage is a counter with wine bottles, espresso coffee apparatus, glasses, Italian pasties, etc. Behind the counter an old shotgun is hanging on the wall. Directly in front of the counter are several movable stools. To the right of the counter is the entrance door. Between the counter and the sidewalk there are two tables each with four chairs. There is much color in the decor of the tavern; souvenirs, small flags, mementos, etc. Seated in a wheelchair at the left table is Charles Arlington, a retired American businessman. His briefcase is on the table. He is seventy-nine years old. Giovanna, a young prostitute of about twenty-three, is seated at the same table. Luigi, the tavern-keeper, is clearing the counter.)

Charles: Has he arrived yet?
Giovanna: What does it look like?
Charles: He's late.
Giovanna: (sarcastically) Apparently.
Charles: I wish he would hurry.
Giovanna: What's the rush?
Charles: He promised me everything.
Giovanna: Oh, God!
Charles: But, he said he had full coverage.
Giovanna: I suppose you've brought your retinue of children.
Charles: I have.
Giovanna: Are you sure you haven't forgotten one.
Charles: (looks anxious and begins fumbling in his chair. He pulls out of his briefcase a large bundle of papers. He begins dividing the papers.)
　　Let's see; fire, theft, health, accident . . .

(Giovanna laughs viciously.)
Charles: (annoyed) What's so funny?
Giovanna: Oh, I don't know.
Charles: You've made me lose count.
Giovanna: The last one was "accident."
Charles: Oh. Okay accident, car, foreign travel, house, life. Yes, they're all there.
Giovanna: Except the last.
Charles: (fumbling with the last policy) What do you mean?
Giovanna: Never mind.
Charles: You certainly are annoying.
Giovanna: And expensive. How come you haven't insured me?
Charles: Well, I do take penicillin tablets.
Giovanna: You what?
Charles: One can never be sure.
Giovanna: Why in God's name didn't you stay in your own country?
Charles: Because of a possible nuclear explosion.
Giovanna: (with mockery) You certainly are fearless.
Charles: I wish he would hurry.
(The door opens and in enters John, a young American with a writing tablet and a book under his arm. He is wearing a vested suit, is over six feet tall, and seems a little too sophisticated. He sits down at the other table.)
Charles: (over-excitedly addressing the young man) Did you bring it?
John: I beg your pardon.
Charles: Did you bring it?
John: Ah . . . did I bring what?
Charles: Why, the policy.
John: (looking at the man and then the woman) I'm against all policies except of course policies of the heart.
(Giovanna smiles and begins her tacit implication towards flirtation.)
Charles: Aren't you from the Universal Insurance Company?
John: I didn't know the universe could be insured.
(Giovanna begins laughing.)
Charles: (embarrassed) Oh, excuse me. I was waiting for another person.
John: (wanting to keep the conversation going) Maybe I could be of some service.

Charles: (defensively) Oh no, that's quite all right. (He begins fumbling with his many insurance policies. Luigi comes over from behind the counter.)
Luigi: What will you have?
John: Red wine, please.
(Luigi nods. John opens one of his books and begins reading. Giovanna stares blankly for a moment and watches Charles. Luigi returns with the wine.)
John: Thank you. (He takes a sip and continues to read. There is silence for a few seconds.)
Charles: I wish he would hurry.
Giovanna: Oh, shut up.
Charles: What's wrong?
Giovanna: Never mind.
Charles: Tell me.
Giovanna: Everything's just fine.
(Silence. The door opens. Another man enters with a briefcase. He is about forty and overweight. He is dressed in a business suit. He advances cautiously watching both John and Charles. Charles becomes excited and begins to move his wheelchair backwards and forwards.)
Harry: Is there a Mr. Charles Arlington here? I'm from the Universal Insurance Company.
Charles: Yes, yes, right here.
Harry: Oh.
Charles: Have you brought it?
Harry: Yes, I have.
Charles: Well, let me see it.
Harry: First let me sit and think for a few minutes.
(Instead of sitting down at Charles' table he sits down with John who has stopped reading.)
Charles: But . . .
Harry: You can wait.
Charles: But, I . . .
Harry: (fiercely) I said you can wait.
   (to John) What's your name?
John: John Sanctus.
Harry: What are you reading?
John: Machiavelli's The Prince.
Harry: Why?
John: Because it describes human nature.

Harry: Then that's a good book.
John: Do you read a great deal?
Harry: All the time.
John: And you sell insurance?
Harry: Yes. Both tell me what human nature is.
John: Which is?
Harry: It can be seen quite easily.
John: You're sure?
Harry: I will prove it.
Charles: Please come over here.
Harry: Why?
Charles: (furiously) Because that's what you're paid to do.
Giovanna: Please, get this over with.
Harry: Let me understand something. Mr. Arlington, you have asked for an insurance policy to insure your other policies, is that correct?
Charles: That is correct.
Harry: And you expect me to sell you that policy?
Charles: (yelling) That's your job. I have the money. Lots of money. And you WILL sell it to me!
Harry: And if I refuse?
Charles: Why should you refuse?
Harry: Because your terrible uncleanliness all of a sudden nauseates me.
Charles: (incensed) You can't say that to me.
Harry: It's been said.
Charles: But . . .
Harry: But what?
Charles: (crying in frustration) But, I must have the policy.
Harry: (Placing the policy on John's table, Harry goes behind the wheelchair. He grabs the handles of the wheelchair.) Go get it.
Charles: But . . .
Harry: Get it!
Charles: (to Giovanna) Please help me.
Giovanna: But it's your policy. I think you should get it.
Charles: But I can't get it.
Harry: Oh sure you can.
Charles: (very nervous) But I can't . . .
Harry: Oh. (Charles strains to get up. His face turns red. He starts gasping, and falls back in his chair. A look of

horror covers his face. He then closes his eyes and his head falls to one side.)
John: (gets up to help him) He's had a stroke. (Alarmed, he holds his wrist.) My God. I think he's dead.
(Giovanna stands up and Luigi rushes forward. Harry watches for a few moments and leaves during the commotion.)

(Darkness)

ACT II

(A police officer is present. John, Luigi, and Giovanna are speaking with him. They have recounted the incident.)

John: No, I don't know where the insurance man lives. He said he was from the Universal Insurance Company.

Police Officer: We'll look into this. (to Giovanna) Could we see you at the station tomorrow morning?

Giovanna: Yes, of course.

Police Officer: Fine. That's all for now.

(They nod and the police officer leaves. Giovanna sits down at John's table.)

John: I didn't get your name.

Giovanna: It's Giovanna.

John: And you live near here?

Giovanna: I used to.

John: How well did you know Mr. Arlington?

Giovanna: I knew him for about two months but then I didn't really know him at all.

John: Oh. (a brief pause) Do your parents live near here?

Giovanna: Yes. They live just south of those buildings you Americans bombed and failed to repair after World War II.

John: (embarrassed) What does your father do?

Giovanna: He used to be a fisherman. I don't know what he does now.

(a brief silence)

John: You don't see him very often?

Giovanna: I haven't seen him in five years.

(pause)

John: You know you're a rather difficult person to speak with.

Giovanna: (condescendingly): Rather.

John: Would you prefer that I said nothing?

Giovanna: No. I would prefer that you said something.

John: (perplexed) All right. How much?

Giovanna: For how long?
John: For one hour.
Giovanna: (carefully) One hundred dollars for an hour.
(John pulls out his wallet and gives her the money.)
Giovanna: (indifferently) Where shall we go?
John: We'll do it here.
Giovanna: Are you crazy? My God, we can get a room for twenty dollars.
John: Near the bombed-out buildings.
Giovanna: Not far away from them. Let's go.
John: No, let's stay here for awhile.
Giovanna: (indifferently) It's your time.
John: It's also yours. (They sit and stare at each other for a few seconds.)
Giovanna: Look, let's go.
John: Okay, in a little while.
(pause)
Giovanna: I'm going to miss Charles.
John: Why?
Giovanna: Because he was helpless.
John: And wealthy.
Giovanna: (She stands up and throws the money down on the table.) Here, take your damn money!
(She starts to gather her things together and to leave. She is almost ready to go when a group of five ragged and dirty children enter on stage left. A short man of about fifty is among them. The children are laughing and talking as they point at John. Giovanna stops and looks at them. She then sits down.)
John: (to Giovanna) What are they saying?
Giovanna: They want to sell black market cigarettes to you tourists. That's how they live.
John: That's terrible.
Giovanna: (bitterly) That's life.
(A little boy comes up to John.)
Boy: Cigaretti? Five dollari.
John: What is your name?
Boy: Si. Si. Cigaretti, five dollari.
Giovanna: Give him the money, you bastard.

John: Shut up. (All the other children and the old man come up to him. The old man stands a distance away from them.)

Children: (Together they are waving packs of cigarettes in John's face.) Cigaretti—five dollari--cigaretti.

Giovanna: (mockingly) Do you want to know all their names?

John: Be quiet. I . . . I. Here. (He gives them all some money. The children attempt to give him the cigarettes. John gestures that he does not want the cigarettes.)

Children: Thankee you . . . thankee you.

(They move away laughing.)

(The old man does not leave with the rest of the children. He comes up to John.)

Old Man: Thank you, sir. Thank you.

John: You speak English.

Giovanna: (mockingly) You have fifty minutes left.

John: (annoyed) Be quiet. (to old man) Why are you selling cigarettes?

Old Man: To be with them. (quietly) I am a priest who wishes to give them a place to live. They are wild street children. They are starting to come to my shelter, but it takes time.

John: But . . .

Old Man: Do not try to understand. It is the way things are. I have to be one with them or they will never come to the shelter. They must see that I am their friend. Otherwise they will not trust me but only run from me. It is better that they sell cigarettes instead of selling themselves.

John: There must be an easier way.

Old Man: There is no other way. I pray and offer Mass in the morning, and I am with them in the evening. It is the way. Thank you, my friend, thank you. (He walks away.)

John: (He looks at Giovanna. They both watch him go. A few seconds pass.) I had better go.

Giovanna: Why?

John: (He stands up and starts to collect his things.) It's best that I go.

Giovanna: Do you want part of your money back?

John: No.

Giovanna: Then stay. (John stops and looks at her. She smiles. He sits down.)

CHRIST AND FREEDOM

(Lights fall slowly)

ACT III

Giovanna: Then you really don't care?
John: No, let's just stay and talk.
Giovanna: You can have your money back.
John: No . . . no.
Giovanna: But I don't feel right.
John: Here, I'll make you feel better. (He turns to Luigi) A bottle of wine . . . champagne.
Giovanna: Champagne?!
John: Champagne. (Luigi brings the bottle and opens it.)
Giovanna: Now I like you.
John: Oh.
(They look at each other and laugh. There is a great commotion outside the door and in enters Pietro. He is dressed in a dark suit, however the sleeve is torn. His tie is to the side, and he is entirely in disarray. He has about five books with him. As he enters he hurls all five volumes at once at the table where Charles and Giovanni were sitting. He then sits down at this table and says nothing. He begins scratching his head and then starts crying. Luigi, who knows him, comes over and tries to console him.)
Luigi: Pietro . . . Pietro, what's wrong?
Pietro: For fifteen years I've wanted an education and . . . and . . . now . . . and . . .
Luigi: And . . .
Pietro: And today I had my first day at the university, and . . .
Luigi: And . . .
Pietro: And . . . no . . . I can't say it. On the tomb of my mother I can't say it.
Luigi: Say what?
Pietro: Say . . . oh, no. (He continues sobbing for a few seconds.)
Luigi: Say what?

Pietro: Say that . . . that my father and our ancestors came from apes.

(John begins laughing. Giovanna is rather perplexed.)

Luigi: But they can't say that. Why, your father and I were great friends. We fought in the Second World War together. We read aloud the poetry of D'Annunzio. Your father was a man of spirit! (He goes behind the counter and takes a shotgun off the wall.) We'll kill them! No one says this . . . no one.

John: Wait a minute. Wait a minute. You don't understand.

Luigi: (furious) Damn understanding. The dead have been insulted. I'll . . .

Pietro: (grabbing at the gun) I'll do it.

John: Listen . . . listen.

Luigi: To what?

John: Why to . . . to . . .

(Nearby a melody is heard. The melody is from the Neapolitan song "Santa Lucia.")

"Now beneath the silver moon,
The ocean is glowing."

(A Blind Man appears with an accordion. He continues to sing. Attached to his belt is a chimpanzee on a chain, trained to beg with a cup.)

"Over the calm sea,
Happy winds are blowing."

(Luigi and Pietro look at each other and stop. Pietro is exasperated not knowing what to do. The blind man continues singing. In the meantime the chimp with the cup pulls the blind man over to Pietro.)

"Here balmy breezes blow,
And pure joys invite us.
And as we gently row,
All things delight us.
Hear how the sailor's cry
Joyously echoes nigh!
Santa Lucia! Santa Lucia!"

(The chimp begins taunting Pietro with the cup. Pietro turns away. The chimp begins poking Pietro on the leg with the cup. Giovanna, John and Luigi applaud the Blind Man's singing. Pietro looks at the chimp with horror.)

Blind Man: (bowing to all) Thank you, thank you.

(Luigi goes and gets him a glass of wine. The blind man pulls the chimp away with the chain. John takes the blind man by the shoulders and shows him a place to sit down. John also puts some money in the chimp's cup. Luigi hands the Blind Man a glass of wine.)
Thank you . . . thank you.
Pietro: (Furiously speaking to the Blind Man) Did you know that this ape of yours is your grandfather?
Blind Man: What?
Pietro: I had my first day at the university today and that's what they told me.
Blind Man: Well, don't believe them.
Pietro: Why not?
Blind Man: Because the ape can't sing. (The Blind Man begins humming to himself.) A man is what he sings. The ape tugs on the chain but even when he tugs, he lacks melody. An ape's a good thing, mind you, but the poor devil just can't sing. Maybe he'd like to sing, but he just can't. Besides, why were you stupid enough to go to school? I can't see, but I know.
Pietro: Know what?
Blind Man: Know that God is a song sung in the evening breeze, and that He would rather have us listen to our own song . . . and His singing within us than do anything else.
Pietro: But . . .
Blind Man: It's not easy to listen for most. They see a lot but then they don't see much. I'd rather be blind and know God, and hear His melody than see both the sun and the moon collide. Sometimes I think it is better to only see inwardly. That is where God is.
Pietro: Where are you going next?
Blind Man: Why, to the evening breeze. It blows free and is always there. It's like the Spirit of God . . . it blows where it will.
Pietro: Do you care if I join you?
Blind Man: Not at all, just don't annoy the ape. He feeds me, and he is my friend.
(The Blind Man and Pietro stand.)
   "Home of fair poetry.
   World of pure harmony . . ."

(The two of them leave. As they leave the final words of the Blind Man are heard.) "Santa Lucia, Santa Lucia."

(The lights begin to fade into darkness. Luigi watches them leave. He stops for a moment and then decides to follow them.)

ACT IV

John: That was a great thing.
Giovanna: You mean the blind man's song?
John: Yes, and Pietro's concern for his father's memory.
Giovanna: Pietro's stupid.
John: Why stupid?
Giovanna: He just is.
John: But why?
Giovanna: Oh, I don't know. Leave me alone. (silence. They look at other).
John: You have something against men, don't you?
Giovanna: No, just against fathers.
John: For any reason?
Giovanna: You and your damn reasons!
(silence)
   Look, I'm sorry. I had better go.
John: But you can't go.
Giovanna: (standing up) Why the hell not?
John: All right, go.
Giovanna: (hesitates) But I don't want to go.
John: Oh.
(silence)
Giovanna: (She sits down. quietly) No, I don't want to go.
John: Something is pressing in upon you, isn't it?
Giovanna: (becoming upset) Yes.
John: And you want to get rid of it?
Giovanna: Yes, but I can't.
John: There is a way.
Giovanna: Yes, there is a way.
John: But it takes time.
Giovanna: No, it would only take a few seconds and all would be over, and I wouldn't see my heavy ape of a father after me in the night. . . . Oh, I can't stand it. (She begins sobbing.)

(silence)
John: (softly) It takes time.
Giovanna: (in a rage) Time to what?
John: Time to be healed.
Giovanna: (She looks at him and then begins digging into her purse. She takes out a small bottle and a handkerchief. She begins wiping her eyes.) Some of us have no time.
John: We all have some.
Giovanna: Yes, and a little time is too much. (She begins unscrewing the bottle cap.)
John: What are you doing?
Giovanna: I'm going to beat time. It's all too much anyway. I'm tired. Very, very tired. . . . And there is no peace.
John: Wait! It takes time.
Giovanna: You've already said that. (John grabs at the bottle, spilling the pills on the floor. They stop for a moment and look at each other.)
John: If you want to kill yourself bad enough you'll have to pick up the pills.
Giovanna: (sadly) It doesn't matter. I'll buy some more tomorrow.
John: But . . . but you can't do that.
Giovanna: What can I do? Go back to the plaster falling from the ceiling and fight off my father? Is that what I can do?
John: No.
Giovanna: I won't find another Charles.
John: (vehemently) You don't need another Charles.
Giovanna: Then what do I need?
2ohn: You need your own evening breeze.
Giovanna: But I see too well.
John: Or not well enough.
Giovanna: But I grope and stumble now. I see the black market of selling myself and nothing more.
John: And do you listen to yourself?
Giovanna: I cannot. I want to escape myself.
John: The blind man is not far away.
Giovanna: Should I go and find him?
John: He is not far. He can listen to the God within. Maybe he can teach you to do the same.
Giovanna: And can I come back, if I do not find him?
John: If you wish.

Giovanna: (standing up and taking her purse) I will look, but I doubt if he can be found.

John: Then return. (She leaves as the lights fall. John sits for a minute thinking. He then opens his book and begins reading. The lights fall slowly.)

ACT V

(John is reading as the lights come up. A few seconds pass and he stands up. He comes out to the sidewalk and looks at the audience. He then turns at a 45° angle facing the cafe. He returns and pulls out a chair to sit nearer to the evening breeze. He sits down, looks at the book, and closes it and put his head on the table. A few seconds pass and the stage darkens. Only an outline of his sleeping face can be seen. A few more seconds pass. The lights come up slowly. Surrounding John are four boys on horses. The first three are rocking horses. The fourth is stationary. The first horse is white, its rider is also arrayed in white. He wears a crown and holds a bow and an arrow. The second horseman is dressed in red, his horse is red, and he holds a red sword. The third horseman is dressed in black and rides a black horse. He is holding the scales. All three horsemen are rocking slowly and quietly.

The last horseman is upon a stationary pale, dull, off-white horse. He holds a skull in his hand. All wear gold and silver medals. The medals are attached to ribbons corresponding to the colors of their respective horses.)
Four Horsemen Together:
We serve the Lamb
not of this world
but who offered Himself
for this world.
Constant obedience
is our rank.
Our medals were
wrought in blinding heat.
Our ribbons stream as tears.
Speak we must to
those who hear.
When we move

it is His design.
When He moves
it is within man's time.
First Horseman: (The First Horseman personifies faith in Christ versus faith in money and human security.)
He who would be secure
Has many worlds to bear.
No one can stop the
mortal arrow.
Yet many seek a
monied hope.
I shall conquer all
who answer but the earthly call.
(Lights fade upon First Horseman. He is engulfed in darkness.)
Second Horseman: (The Second Horseman personifies The Divine Justice.)
Blessings to him
who has helped the child . . .
for he has helped
Our Master.
Blessings to him
who served the child . . .
for the Kingdom comes now
faster.
And woe to him
who mocked the child and
made him beg
for pennies.
And woe to him
who broke the child
and made him beg
for pennies.
This sword is a rich red now. . . .
It will only become the richer.
(Lights fade on the second horseman. Now only two horsemen can be seen.)
Third Horseman: (The Third Horseman personifies Abundant Life in Christ as a balance to "The Divine Justice.")
The Love of God
for the singer.

And His smile
for human laughter.
My brothers
speak of woe and
terror.
Listen to them
and obey their Truth.
But in the Truth
remember
a laugh and a song. (Lights fade on third horseman. Now only
  the fourth horseman is seen.)
Fourth Horseman: (The Fourth Horseman personifies natural
  death protesting suicidal behavior.)
I cannot move
and I need not move.
To me many are
now running.
To me the multitude
is coming.
Oh, unnatural world,
seeking harmony upon
my back.
Oh, inward terror,
your demons set
my bridle
and tighten
too fast my reins.
Give me air
I pray you,
And let me run my course.
(Lights fade on final horseman. There is a lengthy silence. Footsteps are heard. Giovanna returns. She sees John sleeping and goes up to him. She gently touches him upon the shoulder.)
Giovanna: I could not find the blind man.
John (He awakes slowly. He then speaks thoughtfully.) But, you have come back.
Giovanna: Yes.
John: Then let us leave together.

(John picks up his book and writing tablet. He places his arm around her. They walk off the stage together. The lights slowly fade.)

Luke Sanctus

CAST OF CHARACTERS

Luke Sanctus -- age 45, a pediatrician with graying hair

Jim -- age 25, a young ex-student addicted to the modern drug culture

An old Italian woman -- age sixty-five

CHRIST AND FREEDOM

(It is a sunny Christmas day in San Francisco's Golden Gate Park. Two benches are arranged as to present a wide "V" opening to the audience. Trees, flowers, etc., make up the background. An old woman of Italian descent sits in the center of the left bench. An umbrella is propped up next to her. She is knitting and humming gently to herself. Luke Sanctus, a middle-aged man carrying a doctor's bag, enters with a newspaper under his arm. He sits down on a bench next to the old woman and watches her for a few moments.)
Luke Sanctus: Nice day, isn't it?
Old Woman: (not wishing to be disturbed) Yes, it is.
Luke Sanctus: (wishing to continue the conversation) Ah . . .
Old Woman: (explaining by her glance that she does not wish to be disturbed) Yes?
Luke Sanctus: Yes, it is a nice day.
(The old woman shrugs her shoulders and continues knitting. However, she discontinues her gentle humming. Luke opens his paper and begins reading. This continues for a few moments and Jim enters. He has long hair, a beard, a mustache, and is wearing beads, buttons, and other sundry paraphernalia. He is pushing a perambulator with a built-in sun visor. After he pushes the perambulator into the center of the stage he sits down on the same bench with Luke Sanctus and begins reading a book.)
Jim: (after a few moments) Oh, no. (He reads a little further.)
   Oh, no. Oh, God. Oh, no.
(Jim takes out an envelope and begins examining the papers
   inside.) Disgusting. Absolutely disgusting. (He puts the
   papers back into the envelope and places the envelope
   into the book. He then looks up at the sun.)
Luke Sanctus: (to Jim) Hello.
Jim: (turning to him) Oh, hello.
Luke Sanctus: Quite a day isn't it?
Jim: It was.
Luke Sanctus: What's the trouble?

Jim: (handing Luke the book) Just look at that.

Luke Sanctus: (taking the book and reading the title) THE MYSTICAL PATH TO ULTIMATE REALITY AS TRACED THROUGH VEDANTA, BUDDHIST, CHRISTIAN AND WESTERN PHILOSOPHICAL SYSTEMS WITH SPECIAL REFERENCE TO GERMAN IDEALISM AND DISCOVERIES AND DISCLOSURES SEEN IN THE LIGHT OF THE MODERN AND POST MODERN PERIOD by the Yogi Yatamushni. (examining the book) All that in one hundred and fifty pages?

Jim: (groaning) I know. Look at the price.

Luke Sanctus: Fifty dollars!

Jim: (groaning) I know.

Luke Sanctus: (scanning a few pages) Why this doesn't make any sense.

Jim: (looking at the sky) I know.

Luke Sanctus: (smiling) May I ask you a personal question?

Jim: You might as well.

Luke: (trying to hold back his laughter) Who is the Yogi Yatamushni?

Jim: (slightly irritated) Do you have today's paper?

Luke: Yes. The Chronicle.

Jim: Turn to page seven, column three.

Luke: (opening the paper) You mean the article entitled, "The Yogi Yatamushni Unmasked."

Jim: (wearily) That's it.

Luke: (reading) The personal history of the popular Indian Guru, Yogi Yatamushni, has recently been discovered.

Jim: (impatiently) That's enough. I'll tell you the rest. (Luke folds the paper and turns to him.) It seems that the Yogi Yatamushni is in reality a Maltese ex-soldier of fortune named Benito Bandito. For seedy and political reasons Benito Bandito was forced to flee to India in order to maintain a very earthly continuity between his head and his body. There he became a guru and is now making more money than he ever did as a mercenary.

Luke: (laughing) And you bought his book?

Jim: My wife wrote to India three months ago to get the book for me as a Christmas present. Fifty dollars. It's unbelievable!

Luke: (still laughing) It certainly is.

Jim: Oh that's not the half of it. Benito also makes his own Christmas seals. (Jim pulls a page of stamps out of the envelope.) Just look at that.
Luke: (laughing) That's terrible. (still laughing) Why that's the height of blasphemy. Jesus Christ in a turtle neck sweater driving an Alfa Romeo with a blonde and a dog in the front seat.
Jim: I know. It's amazing that he got it all on a Christmas seal.
Luke: (laughter subsiding) Highly creative.
Jim: (beginning to laugh) Not only that, he really is a great teacher.
Luke: What do you mean?
Jim: Along with the book came a few pamphlets to explain the Christmas seals and a prospectus of his non-American forthcoming publications.
Luke: (amused) Oh, really.
Jim: No, I'm serious. He can get you a deal on the Alfa-Romeo at the port of Gibraltar. If you go through him, he can save you the Italian government's taxes and cut down the import and export taxes. Not only that. He remarks somewhere that the dog in the front seat is a Vizsla, a purebred race of Hungarian canine that is quickly becoming extinct. Benito can get you a Vizsla with all the papers for only five-hundred dollars if you can get a ship to meet one of his men beyond the three mile limit in any ocean.
Luke: He must be amazing.
Jim: That's not all. The book he's working on now: WHITE SLAVERY AND THE SUBJUGATION OF WOMEN AS JUSTIFIED IN THE BIBLE AND THE KORAN AND ITS IMPLEMENTATION FOR THE CAUSE OF YAHWEH AND/OR ALLAH, promises to be a best seller in the Near East.
Luke: That takes care of the blonde.
Jim: He can even get you a deal on the turtleneck sweater.
Luke: (becoming weary) I can well imagine.
Jim: It makes me sick.
Luke: Of course then (looking at the book) the Yogi Yatamushni or Benito Bandito is not alone.

Jim: You're telling me. Just walk through the city. Two weeks ago someone tried to sell me a Christmas tree on which the branches alternated from black to white. He was trying to promote an "integrated" Christmas. What man will do.

Luke: Yes, what man will do.

Jim: (after a few seconds) By the way, what do you do?

Luke: (looking at him and smiling) Why, I steal children from the poor and sell them to the rich.

Jim: (embarrassed) No, I mean, excuse me, I didn't mean it that way.

Luke: I was just kidding. Actually I'm a pediatrician.

Jim: That must be a wonderful occupation.

Luke: Yes, it is . . . most of the time.

Jim: What about the rest of the time?

Luke: Well, I do a lot of volunteer work in the Hunter's Point area. Being a pediatrician there is the most horrible of occupations. Ill-fed children, rat-bites, mothers who have to work so hard that they have no time to be with their children; and nobody seems to give a damn except the people blocked off from help.

Jim: Hunter's Point is aptly named. I've been out there and it seems everyone had to be chased into that district in order to stay there. The people remind me of rabbits guarded by dogs with no chance of escape.

Luke: That's very true. But there is an even worse form of being hunted. My brother is a psychiatrist in the General Hospital's suicide ward. He told me of a young patient who slit her stomach with a razor, sprayed hairspray on the cut and then lit the bleeding gore on fire. Then the patient said she felt good and that she had gotten herself together and no one was after her.

Jim: (looking down) Horrible.

Luke: It can wear you out thinking about it.

Jim: Yes, how do you stop thinking about it? I was hoping to find a way out to perfect peace and harmony. Nirvana, anything, anything but this.

Luke: Did it work?

Jim: Well, let's say it hasn't.

Luke: When I was younger I used to rebel and attempt to fight my brooding on such matters. But the rebellion increased so much that I exploded. I could accept no abstraction nor ideology that spoke of better worlds. Too much had already gone on that could never be remedied by the future or by man. Unfortunately I stayed with each individual's plight and inner hell and rat-bitten life.

Jim: Unfortunately?

Luke: Yes, unfortunately I couldn't deceive myself with human projections of overmen and new societies and other worlds.

Jim: What did you do when you were not working?

Luke: (A hardening overtakes his face. The glare of rage overtakes his voice.) Once or twice a week I went out to the riptides and the waves below the Cliff House. I would go swimming there. It is a good thing to strike against the surf as though it were the face of a god. It is also a good thing to be caught in a riptide and then to bide your time until it carries you back to shore. It seems that in a terrible and ferocious ocean one can, alone, use will and reason to overcome great odds. But you walk away from the fight and another wave breaks inside and that wave, the cries of the children, the insane laughter of the suicides, and the people who drown because they are not strong enough to swim against the torrent . . . yes, that wave -- that inward wave, that scarring wave (now his rage reaches its peak) -- that wave CRUSHES, SPLITS, AND DIVIDES!

Jim: (after a few moments) Then you see no unity, no realm beyond the realm of scars and suffering?

Luke: (after a few moments) Does it not seem to you that there are the two of us here in this park? We know that in forty or sixty years we will be dead. Yet in the center of our time and questions there is such a place of solace. Look around you: to the east there is the suicide ward; to the south, Hunter's Point; to the west, the ocean; and to the north (Luke begins laughing.) yes to the north, I almost forgot.

Jim: Why? What's to the north?

Luke: (sarcastically) why you must know. The universities of "higher learning."

Jim: I quit a long time ago.

Luke: You're wise. Yes, the universities which so isolate and burden young people that they are forced to explode in the name of anything. Yes, the universities who make students wish they had a gun in their mouths, or were simply normal people without hope, or were fighting the surf in the hope of dying. Yes, the universities!

Jim: But wait a minute. What about the park?

Luke: I was going to say that you and I in the center of this colossal jail could at least speak to one another. I was also going to say that no doubt tomorrow a bird will sing near something green and that the water buffalo in the zoo on the other side of the park will at least, out of spite, ram his head against the steel pole which holds up the fence that imprisons him. I was going to say that in this center of time there seemed to be such a hope held out to us, and this hope was itself vibrant and nasty enough to be admirable.

Jim: Sort of a last stand.

Luke: (smiling) True, but like an ass I also started thinking about the day after tomorrow when they build a parking lot here, poison the bird and shoot the water buffalo . . . and, well, you know.

Jim: (after a brief pause, he also smiles) Maybe I'm not as old as you are but, well . . . well don't laugh.

Luke: Sure, go ahead.

Jim: Well what about the media and Moses?

Luke: (roaring with laughter) What about what?

Jim: (excited) You know, there's still some hope for the transformation of things. Perhaps by making people aware of these problems there can be more of an alleviation of pain and hell. You know, like when Moses led the people out of Egypt and God gave them a new land and . . .

Luke: True, but many of these new Moseses either become insane with their power and step on everyone; or they drown in their own red sea of committees, presuppositions and redundancies. There's an entire lack of focus.

Jim: Yes, you're right.

(There is a silence for a few seconds. Jim looks at Luke. Luke looks at his paper. Both look around for a few seconds. Then at once their eyes rest on the perambulator.)
Luke: You know it is Christmas.
Jim: I know.
Luke: (magnanimously) After all.
Jim: (smiling) After all.
Luke: I mean it is troubling -- Christ being a baby and saving the world and all of that.
Jim: It certainly is troubling.
(They both pause for a few moments and think. Luke looks again at his newspaper. He jumps up, ripping the paper in half.)
Luke: To hell with Moses and the media!
Jim: To hell with Benito Bandito!
(They rush to the perambulator. Luke is so exited he breaks the sun-shield off the perambulator.)
Luke: I'm sorry.
Jim: (laughing) Don't worry about it.
(Luke picks up the child.)
Luke: What a forehead! You've got a genius here!
Jim: I know.
Luke: (exuberant) What arms. They'll bear the world!
Jim: I know.
Luke: (ecstatic) What a child!
Jim: (exuberant) I'll say.
Luke: (kissing the child) What a doll! I've never seen such an attractive child.
Jim: (taking the child) Me either.
(The child awakens and begins screaming. For the first time in the play the old woman looks up from her knitting.)
Luke: Don't worry, I'll get him a sucker (runs to his bag) I always keep a few for emergencies. (As he opens his doctor's bag, the old woman picks up her umbrella and cracks him over the head.)
Old Woman: (in an irate tone to Luke) You call yourself a man, and you wake up a poor child with your talk and nonsense! (Flourishing her umbrella as he cowers.) Stupido . . . stupido! (Authoritatively she waddles over to Jim and says,) Here, give him to me, you young fool. (She all but forcibly takes the baby from Jim. She begins

humming again and rocking the child gently. The baby's screams subside.)

Jim: (meekly) But . . .

Luke: (moving close to Jim and putting his finger to his own lips for Jim to remain silent) Shhh . . .

Jim: But . . .

Luke: Shhh.

(The old woman's humming is all that is heard as the lights fall.)

Constantino V. Riccardi is an instructor in philosophy, critical thinking, and world religions at various colleges and universities in Southern California. His produced and videoed drama, THE BURDEN OF CHRISTMAS, has received acclaim from Off-Broadway directors, psychiatrists, theologians, and suicide prevention centers. He is also the author of <u>Light in the Labyrinth</u> and <u>The Agony of Shopping</u>.

H. Travers Newton, Jr. is an accomplished artist and lecturer on art restoration. Mr. Newton has worked for numerous museums in the actual process of restoring masterpieces. In addition, his illustration which appears on the cover of this book was awarded the gold medal at the Concorso Internazionale Grafico di Roma in 1972.

www.ingramcontent.com/pod-product-compliance
Lightning Source LLC
Chambersburg PA
CBHW050433240426
43661CB00055B/2374